D0706314

FACULTY
DIVERSITY

FACULTY DIVERSITY

Problems and Solutions

JoAnn Moody

ROUTLEDGEFALMER
NEW YORK AND LONDON

Published in 2004 by
RoutledgeFalmer
29 West 35th Street
New York, NY 10001
www.routledge-ny.com

Published in Great Britain by
RoutledgeFalmer
11 New Fetter Lane
London EC4P 4EE
www.routledgefalmer.com

Copyright © 2004 by Taylor and Francis Books, Inc.
RoutledgeFalmer is an imprint of the Taylor and Francis Group.

Printed in the United States of America on acid-free paper.

All rights reserved. No part of this book may be printed or utilized in any form or by
any electronic, mechanical or other means, now known or hereafter invented, including
photocopying and recording, or any other information storage or retrieval system,
without permission in writing from the publisher.

10 9 8 7 6 5 4 3 2

Cataloging-in-Publication Data is available from the Library of Congress.
ISBN 0-415-94866-5 (hb: alk. paper)
ISBN 0-415-94867-3 (pb: alk. paper)

To B.B., Justin, and Joan

CONTENTS

Acknowledgments — xi

Introduction and Organization of the Book — 1

PART ONE: PROBLEMS

Chapter 1 Succeeding as a Professor on a Majority Campus — 11
Disadvantages versus Advantages
A. Extra Taxes and Burdens versus Hidden Profits
B. Unfair Evaluations versus Overly Generous
Evaluations

Chapter 2 Succeeding Outside the Ivy Walls — 39
Disadvantages versus Advantages
A. Maintaining Professional Standing and Generating
Wealth
B. Securing Educational Credentials

Chapter 3 Extra Disadvantages for Colonized Minorities — 65
A. Not All Minority Groups Share the Same Cultural
Status and Context: Differences between Colonized
and Immigrant Minorities
B. Asian Americans: Immigrant Minorities
C. Women as a Colonized Group?

PART TWO: SOLUTIONS

Chapter 4   Good Practices in Recruitment   89
            A-1 through A-19: Good Practices for Campus
            Presidents, Provosts, Deans, and Academic Departments
            A-20 through A-27: Good Practices for Search Committees
            with Emphasis on Cognitive Mistakes to Avoid

Chapter 5   Good Practices in Retention   113
            B-1 through B-13: Good Practices for Campus Presidents,
            Provosts, Deans, Trustees, and Mentoring Programs
            B-14 through B-21: Good Practices for Departments

Chapter 6   Good Practices in Mentoring   129
            C-1 through C-11: Good Practices for Senior Mentors
            D-1 through D-20: Pointers and Strategies for Pre-tenure
            Faculty Mentees

Chapter 7   Other Remedies: Macrocosmic and Microcosmic   159
            A. Structural and Institutional Changes: Dismantle
               Castelike Elements; Continue to Act Affirmatively; and
               Pay Reparations
            B. Create More Diverse Student Bodies and Faculties
            C. Educate Students about Unearned Advantages and
               Disadvantages
            D. Create Learning Communities in Colleges and Universities
            E. Create K–12 Learning Communities

PART THREE: ITEMS FOR DISCUSSION, ANALYSIS,
AND PRACTICE

Chapter 8   Minority and Majority Faculty Speak   173
            A. Why Diversify the Faculty? (quotations 1–5)
            B. Stresses and Vulnerabilities (quotations 6–16)
            C. Different Views of Affirmative Action in Academia
               (quotations 17–21)
            D. Bad Practices That Must Be Replaced (quotations 22–26)
            E. New Practices and New Visions (quotations 27–34)

Chapter 9   Bad Practices   185
            *Scenarios for Discussion and Application (with Discussion
            Guides)*

Scenario 1: Deliberations of an Academic Search Committee
Scenario 2: An Academic Search Committee Narrows the
Field
Scenario 3: Second Week as a New Assistant Professor of
Mechanical Engineering
Scenario 4: Preparing for the Tenure Review
Scenario 5: Conversation between a Mentor and Mentee
Scenario 6: Deliberations of a Tenure and Promotion
Committee

Conclusion   215

Bibliography   217

Appendix: Checklist of Chapter Contents   231

Index   237

Biography   249

ACKNOWLEDGMENTS

I wish to express my appreciation to the minority and majority faculty and administrators from across the country I have had the honor to know and work with. Over the past several years, a number of department chairs, mentoring groups, entire academic departments, and student organizations have reacted to early elements of this book that I have used in my consulting and program work. Such field-testing has been invaluable. Others have graciously allowed me to interview them and to hone in on their expertise and experience related to minorities on majority campuses.

Yet others, with red pencil in hand, have reviewed parts or all of the book and suggested changes—with gratitude I single out Sharon Hogan, Patricia Aron, Ricardo Stanton-Salazar, Joseph White, David Schuldberg, Stacy Blake-Beard, Daryl Smith, Christopher Jones, Sheila Ewing Browne, and above all, Joan Tonn. Being stubborn, I have not followed all of these reviewers' suggestions—so the mistakes remaining belong only to me.

Special thanks to the very competent staff at RoutledgeFalmer for their help: Sara Folks, Assistant Editor; Catherine Bernard, Education Editor; Nicole Ellis, Production Editor; and Andrew Schwartz, Copy-editor.

INTRODUCTION AND ORGANIZATION
OF THE BOOK

ALTHOUGH U.S. COLLEGES AND UNIVERSITIES are enrolling far more minority *students* than ever before, they are failing to diversify their *faculty*. During the 1990s and into the early part of this new century, the percentage of underrepresented minority faculty in the academic workplace has not budged. African-American, Puerto Rican-American, Mexican-American, and Native American faculty remain clustered in minority-serving institutions and two-year colleges. At most U.S. campuses, where European-American students and, in particular, European-American faculty predominate, minority faculty are rare (taking up barely five percent of the total in the faculty ranks), and they are astonishingly rarer still at the tenured- and full-professor ranks. The only progress to be found is in the increasing number of Asian-American professors (now five percent of the total), especially in science fields.

Why such disappointing overall results? The cause stems not from an undersupply of job candidates with doctorates (a popular but inaccurate assumption), but rather from unconscionably high barriers to minorities' entry into and success in the professoriate (Harvey, 1994, 1999; Harleston and Knowles, 1997; Mervis, 2001; Smith, 1996, 2000; Cooper and Stevens, 2002; Trower and Chait, 2002). What exactly is wrong, and how can it be fixed? In this book, I set forth in concrete detail how the academic field is uneven and how that unevenness makes it difficult for majority faculty and their departments to appreciate the talents and strengths of non-majority faculty candidates. I then turn to what can be done to level the field. Because majority faculty and administrators, I argue, are often unwittingly *causing the problem*, it should not be surprising that they must *become a large part of the solution*. This book focuses on how majority campuses, departments, and individual faculty members and administrators can improve their

1

evaluating, recruiting, mentoring, and retaining of underrepresented minority faculty.

I started my academic career as the first and only woman faculty member in a department composed of thirty-three male European-American faculty (I, too, have European-American ancestry). Being a pioneer and a token in such a setting brought me a variety of eye-opening experiences, which continue to inform my thinking. The insights and practices set forth in this book arise partly from my early years as a professor on two majority campuses but primarily from my later work as co-founder of and adviser to the national Compact for Faculty Diversity; as founding director of the regional Excellence through Diversity Initiative at the New England Board of Higher Education; and as founding director of the Northeast Consortium for Faculty Diversity. In these roles, I have worked since 1990 with hundreds of minority and majority graduate students and faculty at predominantly majority campuses throughout the country. As a national consultant since 1994, I have had the additional opportunity to coach majority faculty, department chairs, deans, and provosts—at a range of public and private colleges and universities—on how to diversify their faculty ranks.

Doing this coaching, I have found it heartening that many majority leaders genuinely want their campuses and departments to be more diverse. And while they sincerely want to become more effective and empowering with their minority faculty colleagues, they simply do not know *how* to locate roadblocks and remove them. These power-holders often lack sufficient time—to dig into national studies on departmental climate and change; conduct or read ethnographic interviews with minority faculty; find out how other institutions and departments are pursuing faculty diversity; and distill the wisdom offered by effective cross-cultural mentors and other seasoned practitioners—in order to piece together what *they themselves* should be doing differently. This book answers that need.

ORGANIZATION OF THE BOOK

The book is divided into three parts. Part One shows how U.S. educational, political, and economic institutions favor some groups and disfavor others. Despite our cherished political belief that we live in a democracy promising equal opportunity for all, the playing fields within these institutions have been constructed unevenly, through the intervention of sexism and racism. This unevenness promotes the success of those in the dominant majority group while it hampers, to different degrees, the success of those in non-majority groups.

Yet in my consulting and program work, I have found it insufficient to maintain to majority faculty and administrators, the prime movers in educational institutions, that the problem—the paucity of minority faculty on their campuses—is caused by sexism and racism. Because most of the leaders understandably do not regard themselves as bigots, they tend to dismiss or belittle the problem when it is stated so superficially. To counter this dismissal and *reframe* the problem—in conceptual, structural, and personal ways as well as with hard-to-deny examples—is my purpose in Part One. After such reframing, I have found many majority leaders more motivated to assume new obligations, welcome coaching on new cognitive habits, and consider new practices that their academic departments can adopt or adapt to improve faculty diversity.

To accomplish the reframing of the problem, I set forth sixteen pairs of disadvantages/advantages that help majority power-holders understand, often for the first time, how *they* unconsciously benefit from privileges and hidden profits accruing and accumulating to the favored group. These benefits, they often are surprised to learn, occur outside as well as inside the ivy walls. Further, I make sure that majority administrators and faculty grasp another key principle: Minority faculty from colonized groups (that is, African Americans, Native Americans, Puerto Rican Americans, Mexican Americans, and Native Hawaiians, all of whose roots are deep in this country and whose ancestors were enslaved, conquered, dispossessed, colonized, or almost decimated by European Americans) usually face the highest barriers not only to entering academia but also to succeeding there. By contrast, immigrant minority faculty who have voluntarily come to this country usually discover a far more favorable cultural and political context to inhabit and are more highly regarded by the European-American majority. Unless these different contexts and different historical relationships to the majority group are grasped, gatekeepers and power-holders in academe will continue to overvalue international minority faculty and undervalue domestic minority faculty. I see this sad pattern all the time in my consulting and program work with majority campuses.

Turning now to specifics, I aim in chapter 1 to demonstrate how cumulative unearned *disadvantages* (a total of twelve, I suggest) hamper minority professors' advancement in academia. Moreover, cumulative unearned *advantages* (the obverse side of the same twelve) enhance the advancement of majorities. By examining, one by one, each disadvantage/advantage pairing within the cluster of twelve, I try to make clear in this first chapter how the academic system is structured and how and why some are favored and others disfavored. Most faculty are woefully unaware of this pervasive system and its daily workings.

Chapter 2 spotlights key domains outside academia—the housing market, the political arena, and social networks and organizations— where another cluster of four advantages/disadvantages operates, again with impact on daily life. Cumulative unearned advantages enable majority professors operating in these outside domains to reap greater monetary and political power as well as more enduring social status from their professional achievements. Cumulative unearned disadvantages are found on the obverse side of this cluster and translate into fewer rewards and more risks for minority professors, a fact that majority power-holders such as deans, chairs, and provosts must grasp as they move to diversify their faculty. If such understanding does not develop, these power-holders are likely to be cavalier with and unsupportive of their new minority colleagues as well as ineffective as champions for diversity on their campuses.

Chapter 3 reminds us that the United States is a land of *immigrants* but also *non-immigrants* and demonstrates that non-immigrant minority faculty usually have the greatest taxes and burdens to carry. It is important to realize that non-immigrants, incorporated into the nation "by force and not by choice" (political scientist Jennifer Hochschild's phrase, 1995), possess a unique context and must constantly struggle against social stigma. Those non-immigrant groups named above— American Indians, Mexican Americans, Puerto Rican Americans, Native Hawaiians, and African Americans—are likely to face, over many generations, castelike stigmatizing and both explicit and implicit discrimination from majority members and the powerful institutions they control. Chapter 3 maintains that faculty with membership in such groups often face exceptional challenges. Again, this lesson is important for deans, provosts, department chairs, and senior faculty to comprehend—so they can rise above the tendency to unwittingly overvalue the competence of their international colleagues and students and, at the same time, to undervalue the competence of their U.S. minority colleagues and students.

Part Two, composed of chapters 4 through 7, recommends ways to systematically undo the pairings of advantages/disadvantages and hidden profits/hidden taxes that I highlighted in the first three chapters. These pairings, routinely delivering gains for many of those in the favored group and losses for many in the disfavored groups, delineate just how uneven the academic playing field actually is. To provide a blueprint for a more equitable plain is the purpose of Part Two, with its array of Good Practices that have been compiled from my own consulting and program work and from interviews and site visits at campuses and departments already proving effective in their faculty diversity efforts. Successful applications of these Good Practices and innovative approaches appear throughout the second part of the book.

Chapter 4—Good Practices in Recruitment—sets forth twenty-seven guidelines for campus presidents, provosts, deans, and especially academic departments to follow. A separate and crucial section for academic search committees is provided, in light of the notorious mistakes that are made again and again during the search process. This chapter uncovers a number of traditional procedures, myths, and mind-sets operating during the faculty search process that, unwittingly, block the diversifying of the faculty ranks. Adopting more effective procedures, dispelling myths and easy excuses, and learning to recognize and rise above sloppy, biased thinking and decision-making—all are concerns of chapter 4. It will be the responsibility of provosts, deans, chairs, and other leaders to foster the activation of these new procedures and new ways of processing information and evaluating job candidates by their colleagues and departments. The provosts and other leaders should wisely seek guidance and problem-solving assistance from outside consultants, successful practitioners from other campuses, and diversity advocates found among the faculty in various departments across their campuses. Problems and backlashes will occur, as most deans and other leaders already realize. Promoting change of any kind is not for the faint of heart or mind.

Chapter 5 sets forth twenty-one Good Practices for *retaining* non-majority faculty. Some of these practices must be the responsibility of senior administrators, while others are the responsibility of departmental units and their faculty. This chapter answers such questions as: What do effective orientation and mentoring programs—serving all pre-tenure faculty, majority and minority—look like? Who should direct and fund such programs? Who should train senior faculty in cross-cultural mentoring skills? Who should be involved in the welcoming and monitoring of new faculty hires?

Chapter 6 highlights both Good Practices for mentoring as well as caveats about what to avoid in the mentoring relationship. The approaches and practices here are addressed to majority faculty and administrators in their roles as mentors to pre-tenure faculty, especially those from stigmatized domestic minority groups. In addition, I include for pre-tenure faculty *mentees* a number of self-help strategies they should activate, often with the support of their allies and mentors. Senior mentors, department chairs, faculty colleagues, and mentoring programs, I believe, should discuss both parts of this chapter—the good practices and the self-help steps—*with* their mentees. Such an exercise often moves the mentoring relationship to a deeper level. And invariably, minority faculty express relief not only when I name and demystify the crosscurrents they are contending with, but also when I outline specific actions that they, as agents, can take to enhance their success and satisfaction. [This chapter extends some of the points made in my earlier monograph, *Demystifying the Profession: Helping Junior Faculty Succeed* (2001), now in its second printing.]

Chapter 7 offers additional remedies for ensuring equal opportunity inside and outside academia. Some of these remedies are global and macrocosmic, others local and microcosmic. I offer chapter 7 because I recognize that the Good Practices laid out for mentors, departments, and campuses are necessary but, unfortunately, not sufficient by themselves. Broader efforts in the larger society are also required.

Part Three, comprising chapters 8 and 9, is the practicum section of the book. Here, readers are invited to wrestle with thorny issues and problems centering on recruitment, screening and evaluation, retention, and mentoring and to think through how to apply relevant principles and Good Practices set forth in the preceding chapters. The scenarios and critical incidents in chapter 9—as well as the pithy quotations from minority and majority faculty in chapter 8—can be used to animate thought, discussion, and action. I recommend that senior administrators and faculty leaders use parts of this practicum section not only in their coaching sessions for search and tenure-review committees, but also in their informal and formal meetings with departments, colleagues, and trustees.

The almost three dozen thought-provoking (and sometimes lengthy) observations appearing in chapter 8 are drawn from my conversations with majority and minority faculty and administrators and from their publications. These quotations can serve as catalysts in faculty meetings and in orientation and mentoring programs for new hires. In addition, classroom teachers might ask their students to discuss relevant principles and Good Practices set forth in chapters 1 through 7 as they apply to one or more quotations in chapter 8. The quotations are assembled into five categories: Why Diversify the Faculty?; Stresses and Vulnerabilities; Different Views of Affirmative Action in Academia; Bad Practices That Must Be Replaced; and New Practices and New Visions.

Chapter 9 sets forth six scenarios (some would call them mini–case studies) that I have developed and use in my consulting sessions with administrators, faculty, departments, and their search committees. Accompanying each scenario is a discussion guide that suggests how to resolve or lessen the problems and dysfunction I have dramatized by applying guidelines and principles from previous chapters. Each scenario can serve as the centerpiece of a faculty or administrators' meeting, to elicit creative problem-solving and sharing of insights. The first two scenarios in the chapter illustrate bad practices—in fact, *terrible* practices—being followed by search committees. The last scenario depicts a tenure-review committee and its own dysfunctional process. The other three scenarios in chapter 9 illustrate bad practices related to the mentorship and monitoring of pre-tenure faculty that are thwarting the juniors' professional development as teachers, scholars, and colleagues.

To widen the appeal and applicability of this book, I draw on insights generated by a wide range of leaders: philosophers, psychologists, engineers, scientists, anthropologists, novelists, journalists, medical doctors, political scientists, lawyers, and educators from various levels and specializations. Too often, faculty-diversity books written from an exclusively social science perspective prove difficult to use for readers outside the field. Furthermore, I make it a point to use testimonials from both majority and minority professors whom I have interviewed or whose work I have studied; most faculty-diversity books include only minority faculty's viewpoints or frustrations. Because most U.S. campuses are dominated by majority faculty and administrators, I believe their viewpoints, confusions, and hopes must be included.

By separating out and numbering the major points found in Parts One and Two of the book (regarding disadvantages/advantages; Good Practices for provosts, departments, and academic hiring committees; pointers for mentors and self-help strategies for their pre-tenure faculty mentees), I aim to make these sections of the book patently easy to discuss, *point by point*, in meetings of faculty, administrators, college trustees, mentoring programs, and so on. (Note that for the convenience of users, the appendix provides a checklist of contents for all nine chapters.) Various parts of the practicum section, Part Three, can also serve as catalysts in meetings large and small. Compelling quotations as well as discussion scenarios call for analysis of bad practices and then thoughtful application of good practices.

By reframing the problem and then recommending short-term and long-term solutions, I trust this book will move faculty diversity closer to becoming a reality on majority colleges and universities.

A note about terminology. I use *majority* and *minority* to indicate stratified differences in political power and advantage. (Only infrequently do I use *people of color* and *white* in this book because these words do not seem to me to underscore differentials in political power as I believe *minority* and *majority* do.) However, in no way do I wish to imply that those in the majority possess superior morals, intellect, spirituality, and so on, and those in the minority inferior capacities. Political power is the critical difference. The dominant majority group in an organization or society determines what customs, laws, language usage, and norms will be observed, saluted, and maintained. With its superior power and prestige, the dominant group can enforce these parameters and advance its particular interests and needs. The dominant and privileged group determines the overall outlook of a society: "Its philosophy, morality, social theory, and even its science" (Goodman, 2001, p. 14). By contrast, a minority group possesses far less political power and finds not only that its interests are not sufficiently nurtured by the society's political, economic, and educational institutions, but also that its social status is kept relatively low by the majority group. Political power then is the key distinction, as Norman Yetman shows so clearly in his edited collection of essays, *Majority and Minority: The Dynamics of Race and Ethnicity in American Life* (1999, pp. 1–9).

1
Problems

CHAPTER 1

SUCCEEDING AS A PROFESSOR ON A MAJORITY CAMPUS
Disadvantages versus Advantages

IN THIS CHAPTER, I ISOLATE and discuss significant disadvantages and (on the flip side) significant advantages that often face professors working on majority campuses. To assist the reader, I have categorized these interrelated disadvantages and advantages into two main groupings:

- Extra taxes and burdens in academia *versus* hidden profits (nos. 1–7)
- Unfair evaluations *versus* overly generous evaluations (nos. 8–12).

European Americans, as members of the majority group, often enjoy unearned advantages and "concealed profits" (a phrase brilliantly used by Professor Frances Rains, 1998a & b, 1999). Those in other groups do not reap such profits. According to Professor Ron Howard, himself of European-American ancestry, majority males enjoy "having our voices heard, of not having to explain or defend our legitimate citizenship or identity, of seeing our images projected in a positive light, of remaining insulated from other people's realities, of being represented in positions of power, and of being able to tell our own stories" (1999, p. 62). Such privileges are taken for granted by those who hold them; those who do not have such political, legal, and social legitimacy have to continually reestablish (if they can) their voices, stories, citizenship, and rights to be included and heard.

Those in the majority often do not think of themselves as possessing a cultural context, by reason of their ethnic and racial backgrounds and identities. In fact, they don't think that they themselves have an ethnicity and race. Instead, they view themselves as Americans who represent the *norm*—while everyone not in the majority is outside that norm and un-American, in a sense (Doane, 1999). The fundamental privilege of being in the majority, according to Wellesley College researcher Peggy McIntosh, is that you "take for granted" the legitimacy and power that such social status automatically bestows on members of the majority group. In fact, those with such status are taught to be *oblivious* to their social privilege (McIntosh, 1989, p. 13). "To be white in America is not to have to think about it" (quoted in Doane, 1999, p. 75). Law professor Patricia Williams expands on this point: "Those who privilege themselves as Un-raced—usually but not always those who are white—are always anxiously maintaining that it doesn't matter." Nevertheless, they feel pity toward those who are raced because they view race as a "social infirmity" (p. 8) or "some sort of genetic leprosy or a biological train wreck" (p. 9). With such an attitude, those in the majority often feel a vast distance between "us" (other majorities like themselves) and "them" (non-majorities). Professor Williams, as an African American, sees no choice but to deal incessantly with that divide: "[I] have little room but to negotiate most of my daily lived encounters as one of 'them.' How alien this sounds. This split without, this split within" (1997, p. 13).

Discussed below are some typical daily encounters that majority and minority faculty often have on predominantly European-American colleges and universities. These encounters will shed light on a cluster of interrelated taxes and cumulative disadvantages and, on the other side, a cluster of interrelated hidden profits and cumulative advantages. (The notion of accumulating advantages and disadvantages is derived from Cole and Cole, 1973; Cole, 1979; and Corcoran and Clark, 1984.) For instance, if one is unfairly evaluated at early stages of schooling or professional development, then a door of opportunity can firmly shut and one's own confidence and momentum can be shaken. If a positive evaluation is received, it is likely that this one success will lead to another door of opportunity being opened and even more self-esteem being generated. Successes and failures tend to build on one another, particularly in formal educational settings.

A. EXTRA TAXES AND BURDENS VERSUS HIDDEN PROFITS

1. Disadvantage: Minority professors in majority academic settings often must struggle against the presumption that they are incompetent.

Advantage: Majority professors (especially males) in majority academic settings usually enjoy the presumption of competence.

Early on, University of Massachusetts–Amherst Professor Sonia Nieto recognized the stereotypical reactions that she knew she would have to overcome regularly. While she proudly speaks Spanish and proudly claims her Puerto Rican heritage, she nonetheless has "strived to make it very clear that I was intelligent" *in spite of* these cultural markers that distinguish her from mainstream scholars (2000, p. xxiv). Princeton historian Nell Painter agrees: "Intellectually, any woman and any black person must prove that she or he is not dumb. . . . The phrase 'qualified white man' simply does not exist." Painter, of African-American heritage, understandably pronounces it "tiresome in the extreme" to be made to feel as if you are always being evaluated and that your qualifications and achievements are always suspect. Even attending social gatherings—where one is "always on show, always standing for *The Negro*—saps one's energy" (quoted in Reiss, 1997, pp. 6–7). As one minority professor on a majority campus puts it, "Man, from the day we're hired until the day we're retired, we are on probation!" (quoted in Moore and Wagstaff, 1974, p. 9). Can it be any wonder that non-majority faculty whom I work with often lament that they are never given the benefit of the doubt, that they are always "on stage" and feel they are being judged? Hampton University sociologist Lois Benjamin found that almost all of the one hundred African-American professionals she interviewed for her book *The Black Elite* felt they were on "perennial probation" and had to prove themselves twice as accomplished as majority colleagues in academe, law, and medicine (Benjamin, 1998, p. 28; also see Cooper and Stevens, 2002).

By contrast, minority professionals see that their majority colleagues can relax and at times fade into the woodwork without anyone noticing. They can be irritable or aggressive at times without worrying that such atypical behavior will be used against them in the future. Their majority colleagues can win professional society or book awards and not have to endure whispers behind their back that their work is actually overrated. As one majority professor anonymously disclosed to me, "Even getting a Pulitzer Prize would not count as much for a recipient of color as for a white male. I'm certain of that." In other words, the presumption of inferiority lingers and endures. A 1999 internal survey of University of Michigan faculty revealed that women and minority professors at this Big Ten university frequently felt they were discriminated against, scrutinized far more than majority professors, and undervalued as intellectuals. By contrast, the majority faculty surveyed frequently expressed satisfaction with the psychological climate in their academic departments and with the collaborative interactions they had with peers (*University of Michigan Faculty Work-Life Study Report*, 1999). Unless professors in the majority group become aware of and then work to overcome the stereotypical presumptions they often hold, their minority colleagues will be shortchanged and, in a way, inhumanely harassed. Such treatment violates the principles of collegiality and fair evaluation that should operate in academia.

A stunning example of disadvantage/advantage is spotlighted by M.I.T. management professor Thomas Allen, himself European American. As both a faculty member and administrator he has observed that "racism is so ingrained in this society that people don't see it in themselves." Repeatedly he has seen the following scenario play out: "Without even thinking, two people will walk in—one's white, one's black—and they [his colleagues] assume the black isn't capable. Yet they don't know a thing about either one of them, nothing." As a dean, he was repeatedly frustrated and angered: When he would bring in an African-American job candidate, his European-American colleagues, in subtle but unmistakable ways, "would discount that person right away" and assume that this candidate was "not as capable" as the majority candidate. While Allen didn't see this behavior in everyone, he saw it "in so many people who you wouldn't expect it from, people who espouse liberal values." He strenuously underscores, "These aren't rednecks I'm talking about." Rather, these are educated colleagues who "make wonderful talk" about equal opportunity and democratic values but unconsciously make simplistic and damaging assumptions about who can be competent and who cannot (Allen's intriguing oral history interview appears in C. Williams, 2001, pp. 314–19).

Philosopher Laurence Thomas speaks of the "profound sense of vulnerability" that comes with being a member of a "diminished social category." Persons in this category are victims of the assumption "that they lack the wherewithal to measure up in an important social dimension." Part of the vulnerability arises, first, from "being weary of always feeling the need to prove that this [negative] social claim is a lie." The need to prove they do measure up, over and over again, is "tiresome in the extreme," as Painter vividly phrases it. Second, Thomas posits that the vulnerability is linked to the fact that "almost nothing" can be done to decisively and once and for all establish the falsity of the belittling stereotype. Third, more weariness derives from the feeling that one will have to speak out and protest "because no one else will, although one is concerned that continually speaking up will diminish one's effectiveness." And finally, memories of numerous past encounters and vulnerable moments usually mount up and intensify the feeling of powerlessness for the victim (Thomas, 1992–93, p. 241).

By contrast, those not found in the stereotyped group do not have these stresses and memories. Those in the favored group are anointed, in a way, with the presumption of competence and deserved authority. The phrase "well-qualified white man" is simply *not* in the lexicon. With the presumption of worthiness in operation, the favored group can easily come to feel entitled to success and assume an air of unearned "elitism," according to Robert Boice, emeritus professor of psychology at the State University of New York–Stony Brook. Such elitism, unfortunately, is rampant in academia (Boice, 1992a, p. 265; also see Smith, 1996, 2000). In his decades of faculty-development work on campuses throughout the country, Boice has found that minority faculty often have to constantly deal with insinuations that they are unworthy. They must brace themselves for almost daily snubs and put-downs, both large and small. Boice's finding is compellingly reinforced by two nationally distributed videotapes that feature more than twenty minority professors in various academic disciplines: *Through My Lens* (Women of Color in the Academy Project at the University of Michigan, 1999) and *Shattering the Silences* (produced by the Public Broadcasting Company and now distributed by several outlets). These two eye-opening videotapes make painfully clear the costs exacted from minority faculty as they undertake their daily struggles for professional recognition and dignity.

2. Disadvantage: Minority professors in majority academic settings are often viewed as "outsiders" and, because of this, have to endure extra psychological stresses and the general feeling of not belonging. This uneasy psychological context can undermine their success.

Advantage: Majority faculty in majority academic settings are often viewed as "insiders" who belong and thus feel comfortable and accepted. This psychological context can boost their success.

For many years, ethnic studies professor and department chair Evelyn Hu-DeHart was one of only three women faculty of color (full professors) at the University of Colorado, where there are more than one thousand faculty (she is now at Brown University, as professor of history and director of the Center for the Study of Race and Ethnicity). Hu-DeHart observes that new faculty hires who are European-American males are the most easily accepted by departments already dominated by European-American males. This is because "a common language and other shared codes of communication already exist between them . . . the risks of miscommunication, mistrust and missteps are minimal on both sides of this evolving relationship" (Hu-DeHart, 2000, p. 29). But for minority faculty (and especially minority women faculty who enter majority departments), a much longer and more daunting cultural distance must be bridged, with great potential for mishaps, slights, and misunderstandings. To put it starkly, minority faculty are frequently treated as "aliens." This disheartening finding, from a 1974 survey of more than three thousand African-American faculty and administrators on majority campuses (Moore and Wagstaff), still unfortunately has validity (Vargas, 2002; Neimann 1999).

Poignant descriptions of such alienation abound in national studies and in my own program work. A senior non-majority faculty member at a midwestern university tells this story: "People ask me *'Why do I speak English so well?* . . . They've already superimposed on me that I don't belong here. . . . I used to think it was a harmless little question but now I feel that the message that I've received is that I don't belong. I don't look like I belong" (quoted in Turner and Myers, 2000, p. 120). An African-American scientist reflects on his stressful experience in a majority setting: "Regarding racial prejudice in science, you should know that although people I work with are pretty open-minded and we have a lot in common (family, professional interests, politics, kids, etc.) . . . as a black person you are never over the hump." Feeling that he must always be on guard, he tries to head off tensions and to stay on common ground with his colleagues—because "a split can always develop" (quoted in Smith, 1996, p. 103). Assistant professor of education Ana Martinez-Alemán has written: "To be a professor is to be an anglo; to be a latina is not to be an anglo. So how can I be both a Latina and a professor? To be a Latina professor, I conclude, means to be unlike and like me. *Que locura!* What madness!" (1995, p. 75). Dr. Alemán, formerly at Grinnell College, is now at Boston College.

Even majority women students in male-dominated academic settings often experience psychological isolation as outsiders. According to national studies undertaken by University of Colorado researcher Elaine Seymour and underwritten by the Sloan Foundation, a chilly climate often motivates college women to leave science, math, and engineering majors. The women pick up signals, both blatant and subtle, that they are outsiders and do not fit into the male, majority culture of their declared field of study. Seymour and other scholars have documented that what drives women away is psychological isolation—*not* the women's grades and inability to do the intellectual work. (In fact, the women's grades are usually as high as those of the men who persist.) If the female students could count on a supportive community and feel they belonged in the science departments, they would feel renewal of energy and commitment. But they usually do not and so they leave these majors (Seymour and Hewitt, 1997).

Exhaustive research on minority faculty at universities in eight midwestern states underscores that majority faculty do *not* make it a habit to reach out to befriend and coach new minority faculty hires. In *Faculty of Color in Academe: Bittersweet Success*, Professors Caroline Votello Turner (now at Arizona State University) and Samuel Myers Jr. (University of Minnesota) document the lack of mentoring and the "personal and professional effects of a decidedly chilly work environment" for minority faculty. In these work settings, minority faculty frequently "experience exclusion, isolation, alienation, and racism" (Turner and Myers, 2000, p. 54; also see C. Williams, 2001). A similar finding repeatedly shows up in nationwide surveys of thousands of majority and minority college faculty, conducted by University of California–Los Angeles professors Helen and Alexander Astin and associates (Astin et al., 1997). Such substantial extra taxes and stresses must be understood by everyone in academia: At any moment, they are capable of impeding one's progress and sapping one's energy and drive.

Majority insiders, by contrast, usually do not have these extra burdens to carry—they feel they already belong and are a member of the club. A majority person can spend most of his/her time with majority people and not have to allocate extra energy to learning the language and customs of non-majorities. Being a member of the majority club also brings instant acceptance and validation, according to McIntosh. The fundamental privilege of being white, she observes, is that we can ignore that fact. An extreme example of this occurs when majority people claim that they are simply "Americans" who have no racial or ethnic background. They feel that only "other" people (dissimilar to them) possess atypical and out-of-the-norm backgrounds requiring them to use hyphenations like "Mexican-American." This sense of privilege makes majorities feel confident and comfortable, while at the same time making non-majorities feel uneasy, marginalized, and unduly taxed (McIntosh, 1988, 1989).

As a member of the club, a majority person is likely to be included in several informal social and intellectual networks made up mostly or exclusively of majority scholars and educators. Being so situated in such networks is a distinct advantage at several different stages of an academic career. Take hiring, for instance. As University of Colorado law professor Richard Delgado has noted, when an academic search committee, after several months of work, has not found "its mythic figure who is black or Hispanic or gay or lesbian," they then turn to non-mythic insiders whom they already know and trust. "Persons hired in this fashion are almost always white, male, and straight," because most members of the hiring committee are likely to have those characteristics and know others similar to themselves. Because majority faculty "rarely" have incorporated minorities into their networks and circles of acquaintances, their default candidate is almost always a clone of themselves (Delgado, 1998b, pp. 265–266).

Reflecting on this state of affairs, a European-American professor confesses that "for all of us white guys who are honest enough to admit it, we know in our heart that we have been blessed by birth to have had options not available to those who are not white and not male" (Frank, 1999, p. 75). In a similar vein, President John F. Kennedy once archly observed that majorities who touted the astounding progress being made by minorities in this society nevertheless would not *for a moment* consider exchanging places with them. Being a majority insider has its incontestable privileges and hidden profits.

3. Disadvantage: An outsider in academia usually receives little or no mentoring, inside information, or introductions to valuable connections and networks. Such deprivation will hamper professional growth and satisfaction.

Advantage: An insider in an accepting academic climate will receive benefits that speed along professional achievement and satisfaction.

Minorities often find "uninviting territory" as they begin their academic careers in some majority settings. This is the conclusion of Harvard education professor Richard Chait and Harvard educational researcher Cathy Trower. Their studies confirm what many others have found: Social isolation, a dearth of mentors, and even explicit discrimination are common experiences for non-majority faculty in academe (Trower and Chait, 2002, p. 35; also see Gregory, 1995, and Moore and Wagstaff, 1974).

There is indisputable evidence that minority and women faculty do not receive their proportionate share of sponsorship from majority senior faculty—nor inside information nor links to influential leaders in their field (see the study of midwestern universities by Turner and Myers, 2000; also Gainen and Boice, 1993). The lack of mentoring and sponsorship from senior faculty was a theme sounded repeatedly and anecdotally by pre-tenure minority faculty at the national "Keeping Our Faculty of Color" Conference held in April 2002 in Minneapolis. Additionally, in a national study of one hundred African-American professionals, Hampton sociologist Benjamin found that only a small handful of the thirty-one academics she interviewed ever had a majority mentor to bolster their career advancement in their majority institutions (1998). Further, the twelve essays by Latino and Latina professors in *The Leaning Ivory Tower* (Padilla and Chavez, 1995) underscore the marginalization they deal with, including their exclusion from important academic networks and the absence of majority mentors to coach them.

In the American Indian Faculty Survey, only fifty percent of respondents, according to survey director Wayne Stein, reported that they had found mentors in their departments or campuses. As graduate students, they had indeed counted on the support of mentors, "but once the Indian person has secured a position with a four-year institution, gaining the friendship and guidance of a mentor has proven much more difficult." Stein, professor of education and director of the Center for Native American Studies at Montana State University, points out that "those American Indian faculty without mentors express frustration and worry that they may not be making the right career choices" (1994, p. 104; also personal correspondence with Stein, 2000). Instrumental career-enhancing actions by senior faculty—such as taking time to critique the junior members' scholarly work or grant proposals, nominate the juniors for national awards, and arrange for them to chair forums and submit invited manuscripts to journals or multiauthor books—are unlikely to flow evenly to all new faculty. Due to the operation of a "buddy system" composed of majority power-holders, pre-tenure faculty from the same majority group (that is, insiders) find inviting avenues leading them to publications and professional development (Moore and Wagstaff, 1974, p. 13). Interventions—such as assigned mentors and department chairs' proactive guidance—are usually necessary in order to guarantee that minority students and faculty (outsiders) receive the extra benefits that most majorities routinely receive. These conclusions are reinforced by University of Southern California professors William Tierney and Estela Bensimon, who interviewed forty-five minority professors as part of their study for *Promotion and Tenure* (1996), as well as by University of California–Riverside professor Adalberto Aguirre, who exhaustively reviewed the research literature in his *Women and Minority Faculty in the Academic Workplace* (2000).

Likewise, minority and women students do not always receive the faculty support that is available to majority students. In his national sociological studies, University of Massachusetts–Boston professor James Blackwell found that "those who teach are often guilty of subconscious (though sometimes conscious and deliberate) efforts to reproduce themselves through students they come to respect, admire, and hope to mentor." Majority male faculty, quite naturally, can more easily "see themselves" in their majority male students. As a result, such faculty tend to provide majority students with inside information (about how things in academia and the academic discipline really work) as well as introductions to important professional contacts. Minority students and women, by contrast, seldom receive this sort of mentoring and advice from majority male faculty. Blackwell's research findings, reported in *Academe* and elsewhere, have since been confirmed by a number of other comprehensive studies (Blackwell, 1989, p. 11; also see Willie, Garibaldi, and Reed, 1991; Turner and Thompson, 1993; Turner and Myers, 2000).

Preferring to mentor those who are *clones* of themselves may be one reason that majority faculty often neglect to reach out to minority faculty. Another reason may be "aversive racism," which University of Delaware psychologist Samuel Gaertner and Colgate University provost and psychologist John Dovidio see at work when members of the majority group, in liberal fashion, sympathize with victims of past injustice and claim they support egalitarian policies but nonetheless still hold negative feelings about these victims and their identity groups. Rather than expressing frontal hostility and hatred (as ugly bigots would do), aversive racists feel ambivalence, superiority, discomfort, unease, and even fear. These complex feelings prompt them to avoid association with members of these identity groups (Gaertner and Dovidio, 1986). In academia, this aversion translates into little or no mentoring, inside information, and coaching for certain faculty members.

To repeat, as they begin their careers, new hires from the majority group are far more likely to have a strong start, thanks to the mentoring they received in graduate school. Once in the professoriate, these new hires are more likely than their minority colleagues to enter inviting territory where they will receive personal encouragement and professional coaching—as a result of their cordial association with senior gatekeepers.

4. Disadvantage: A minority is often thought to represent his/her whole tribe or group and, as such, has to worry that his/her behavior or performance can open or close doors of opportunity for an entire generation.

Advantage: A majority person has more latitude and tends to worry only about him/herself.

So many times, undergraduate and graduate students of color are embarrassed when their majority professors naively call on them in class to provide the "African-American viewpoint" or the "Puerto Rican" or "Hispanic" or "American Indian" perspective on an issue or a class assignment. The professors mistakenly assume that all members of a minority group think and behave similarly—but they, of course, do not assume the same about members of the majority group. As one New England doctoral scholar complained to me, "I feel like I am standing for my *entire* tribe. Is this goofy or what?" He explained that when this happens, he feels trapped in a no-win situation: If he scoffs at the professor's question, he can trigger hostility from some of his classmates and the instructor. If he responds as complexly as he can to the question, he wonders if "his people" will be honored or dishonored by his answer.

Several minority faculty whom I have interviewed report they, too, have been put in the same awkward position of being expected to speak for all Mexican Americans or all Native Americans or whatever (see also Tippeconnic, 2002). Moreover, women and minority faculty often feel that any performance problems they might have as individuals will have important negative consequences for *all* minorities or *all* women. As one anonymously observed to me: "If a minority person does something magnificent, then it's an exceptional event. But if a minority person does something awful, then it's a typical event for 'those people.'" In other words, it is much easier to accrue lasting impressions of inferiority or incompetence for people in marginalized groups.

5. Disadvantage: Because minority faculty members are likely to be treated as both super-visible and invisible, depending on the circumstances, they will have to cope with psychological dissonance. When deemed super-visible, they will be overloaded with student advising and academic committee work. When deemed invisible, their opinions will be ignored.

Advantage: Majority faculty escape this psychological dissonance, the work overload, and the demeaning associated with being voiceless.

Being "both super-visible and invisible," according to Simmons College professor Sarah Nieves-Squires, is a jarring experience. "On the one hand," Nieves-Squires discloses, "a Hispanic's comments in classrooms or at staff and faculty meetings may be ignored; on the other, she or he constantly may be called upon to present the 'minority view' or the 'Hispanic woman's view' rather than her own views" (1991, p. 12). Such a crazy-making situation is also routinely experienced by several minority professors interviewed by Pennsylvania State University professor Frances Rains and reported in her article

"Dancing on the Sharp Edge of the Sword: Women Faculty of Color in White Academe" (1999). Being ignored and being regarded as inconsequential can be characterized as "imposed" invisibility, according to Rains. One of her interviewees explains, "I am on several committees and—and I can go to a meeting and if they're talking—if they're talking about anything other than minority issues, I'm invisible EVEN WHEN I'M VERBAL."

But dissonance can be just around the corner. If the conversation in the same committee meeting "turns to minority issues, then the talking stops, and the eyes drift to wherever I am, and I am supposed to expound on 'what it is to be a minority' or 'what Hispanics think'" (quoted in Rains, 1999, p. 160). The shift has clearly been made at this point so that the minority colleague now possesses, according to Rains, "designated" visibility (p. 161). Business expert Rosabeth Kanter, in her superb book *Men and Women of the Corporation,* elaborates on several aspects of this heightened visibility that tokens—the numerically rare—have to cope with in "skewed" organizations where they compose fifteen percent or less of the total population. Kanter explains that tokens suffer from high *visibility* because they are a very few "Os" greatly outnumbered by "Xs"; from artificial *contrast* because the dominant group members tend to exaggerate, in their minds and their perceptions, the differences between themselves and the tokens; and from rampant *stereotyping* because the dominant group tends to deny the token any individuality and uniqueness and instead fits the token to the group stereotype (Kanter, 1997, pp. 206–42).

Majorities in the corporation or academic department should be thankful they do not have to struggle with high visibility, artificial contrast, or stereotyping—all of which their minority peers are likely to face. Their minority colleagues, moreover, are very likely to be regarded by high-ranking administrators on a majority campus as embodiments of "diversity"—another form of designated super-visibility. Carrying such symbolic weight, the minorities are asked or appointed to serve on an excessive number of departmental and campus committees so that each committee will have at least one diverse member in its composition. National studies (by Turner and Myers, 2000; Tierney and Bensimon, 1996; Astin et al., 1997; and several others) have documented how frequently minority professors are overloaded with service and committee requirements that most certainly impede their scholarship and publishing. This is a most significant cultural tax that majority faculty escape, along with the excessive advising of students that usually falls to minority faculty. In fact, department chairs often direct all minority students to the very few or the one token minority faculty in the department. Preventing both these overloads is the responsibility of the minority faculty member but *especially* the department chair and mentoring programs. Another strategy (rarely followed, unfortunately) is to give minority faculty, during the review for tenure and promotion, credit for the exceptional advising load they may have carried and the exceptional service contributions they may have made to various committees and the campus overall.

6. Disadvantage: Because minority professors must constantly prove they are qualified and worthy, they can begin to suspect that they are imposters.

Advantage: Majorities can enjoy more confidence and entitlement.

Women and people of color often enter higher education "consumed with self-doubt," according to Arizona State University professor Laura Rendon, as a result of the negative stereotypes they have repeatedly encountered. The belittling stereotypes hold that they are intellectually inferior and will make poor material for college, graduate school, and the professions; they lack innate abilities for science, math, and rigorous analysis; and their mere presence "diminishes" the academic quality of the institution (Rendon, 1992, p. 61; also Bronstein, Rothblum, and Solomon, 1993).

Minority students, especially those in stigmatized groups, often are actively discouraged as early as middle school and high school by teachers and guidance counselors who steer them away from higher education toward vocations like hairdressing. At least three-fourths of the future-faculty candidates I have coached over the past decade have disclosed that they were proactively *discouraged* from visualizing themselves as future professionals. How can one *not* internalize some of this negativity—especially when it comes from supposedly informed authority figures? The result is often an overriding fear of failure and a sense that even when succeeding, one will soon be defrocked and shown to be an "imposter" (Clance, 1985; also see Bronstein, Rothblum, and Solomon, 1993). By contrast, majority faculty I have worked with often report that as youths they received a "green light" from authority figures who expressed unqualified confidence in their innate abilities and potential.

James Bonilla captures the feeling of not belonging and feeling like an imposter when he repeatedly asked himself, while in graduate school, "What is a working-class, New York Puerto Rican trying to do entering the ivory tower?" Only with the bolstering and encouragement of the other two members of his writing support group was he able to overcome his "internalized fear and racial vulnerability" (quoted in Moody, 1996, p. 8). Bonilla now works as an assistant professor at Hamline University.

7. Disadvantage: Minority professors in majority academic settings often have to spend precious time and energy deciphering the complex psychological dynamics unfolding between them and majority students or colleagues.

Advantage: Majorities tend to save time and energy by not being overly concerned about these dynamics.

Psychiatrists who have studied disfavored populations find that "microaggressions" and put-downs by some in the majority clan can be incessant. These microaggressions function to reassert the supremacy of the dominant group over subordinate groups. Higher education administrator Mary Rowe often speaks of the "microinequities" that women students and faculty regularly face at male-driven campuses (personal conversation, 1998). To manage these slights consumes precious psychic energy. "In addition to maintaining an internal balance, the [slighted] individual must continue to maintain a social facade and some kind of adaptation to the offending stimuli so that he can preserve some social effectiveness," according to New York University law professor Peggy Davis. "All of this requires a constant preoccupation" (1993, p. 145). In addition, many women and minorities feel they must make another adaptation: perform "smile work." That is, they must spend extra energy in being congenial and easygoing so that their majority colleagues do not view them as aggressive or threatening or overly sensitive about possessing minority status (Tierney and Bensimon, 1996, p. 83).

Yet more energy must be expended as one ponders and tries to determine whether the perceived microaggression was in fact deliberate or accidental. Sorting through the dynamics surrounding the microaggression takes thought and care. Questions like the following race through one's head:

- *Did the dean just insult me, or was that merely a canned joke she trots out for every new assistant professor?*
- *How in the world could the computer for my office not be up and running when I arrive the week before I start teaching? Is this just a typical technical snafu, or is this a sign that they don't really want me here?*
- *Why was I not consulted before that report was sent off—doesn't my opinion count around here?*

Faculty of color must activate their emotional radar in order to think through, on a daily and at times an hourly basis, "Is this (event, person, demand, slight, racist remark, incident of exclusion, lack of professional opportunity, etc.) important enough to give it my energy?" (Turner, 2000, p. 122; also see P. Williams, 1991). Following the sorting through, minorities have to decide what they should do: perhaps confront the person or slight head-on; perhaps express their hurt or rage; or perhaps assume the role of "cultural worker" and try to process the incident with the majority person (Alemán, 1995, p. 70; the term *cultural worker* was coined, I believe, by Giroux, 1992). Of course, *any one* of these responses has the potential to boomerang and bring on even more stress. Yet another option is to swallow the pain and internalize the perceived slight.

A compelling explanation of how slights and disparagement mount is presented in *Inequality by Design*, written by several sociologists at the University of California–Berkeley. While the authors concede that "white Americans are definitely less prejudiced than they used to be," nevertheless African Americans and other minorities can still have to cope with frequent put-downs, oblique or frontal. Think about it this way: "Were only one in eight whites bigoted, that would still leave one hostile white for each black in America." The authors continue: "Numbers like that would leave whites with the reasonable impression that bigotry was rare and yet leave blacks with frequent experiences of bigotry—one way that racial groups can experience the same reality so differently" (Fischer et al., 1996, p. 183).

Majority students and faculty are more or less oblivious to the put-downs and complex dynamics that confront their minority peers. Moreover, the majorities typically *resist* learning about their own protection from put-downs, and about other similarly unearned advantages they inherit, as a result of their position in the society. A psychology professor and now president of Spelman College, Beverly Daniel Tatum has taught in a variety of predominantly European-American colleges (she herself is African American). Tatum has observed three predictable lines of resistance in students and faculty who prefer to remain oblivious and willfully innocent:

- They deem it impolite to publicly talk about power and race relations because these are considered taboo and too politically volatile to bring up in racially diverse settings (Tatum, 1992, 1997a & b). Nobel laureate Toni Morrison makes a similar point: People regard talking about race as "impolite," whereas "ignoring race is understood to be a graceful, even generous, liberal gesture. To notice is to recognize an already discredited difference" (Morrison, 1992, pp. 10–11). Recall that Professor Williams believes most members of the majority group regard race as a social infirmity or biological train wreck that one should not mention!

- Many students and faculty (no matter what their background) categorically deny and try to gloss over systemic injustice based on race and social position, according to Tatum, because they have been taught that the United States is a fair, free, and equal-opportunity society. They do admit, however, that there are some blatant and ugly white supremacists sprinkled about in the society, especially in the *southern* states.

- Many students and faculty, particularly belonging to the majority group, initially deny that they possess any prejudice against others. Furthermore, they do not interpret racism, according to Tatum, as a "system of advantage" but rather as isolated discrimination and bad behavior by obnoxious white-supremacist individuals. While majority students and faculty do recognize some of the negative effects of widespread racism and discrimination on non-majority people, they often do not recognize how they themselves *benefit* positively from racism and enjoy unearned privileges and advantages as a result of this *system* of advantage.

It is Tatum's belief that "we cannot have successful multiracial campuses without talking about race and learning about racism" and without surfacing and understanding the complex power dynamics at work (1997a, p. 16). I concur, but would add that campuses could make these discussions more concrete by methodically discussing the cumulative *disadvantages* that accrue to many in minority groups as well as the cumulative *advantages* that accrue to many in the majority group.

B. UNFAIR EVALUATIONS VERSUS OVERLY GENEROUS EVALUATIONS

8. Disadvantage: Minority professors are often vulnerable to unfair evaluations of their worthiness and their work, because of negative stereotypes associated with their gender and racial/ethnic backgrounds.

Advantage: Majorities often benefit from positive stereotypes and mind-sets holding that majority males, in particular, are "natural" professors, scientists, medical doctors, and business and political leaders.

Evaluations on the Job If you are a minority in a majority department, "you spend a lot of time proving you that you are competent," observes an African-American professor. But even if you are competent, other faculty members often "feel that you are not as competent as other people they could have hired" (quoted in Smith, 1996, p. 119). Minorities, in particular *stigmatized* minorities, labor under the presumption of incompetence, while majorities enjoy the presumption of competence. As a European-American professor candidly admitted, "I think you're a couple of steps ahead [in my department] if you are a white male around here, but that's probably stating what people already know or stating the obvious" (quoted in Tierney and Bensimon, 1996, p. 83). To beat back the negative presumption, usually on a daily basis, calls for exceptional endurance. As Professor Herman Garcia at New Mexico State University has quipped, progress will be reached when minorities throughout academia can save energy and feel as relaxed "about being mediocre" as majorities now seem to feel (1995, p. 156). A similar point is made by Joan Steitz, professor of molecular biophysics and biochemistry at Yale University. Women "superstars" in predominantly male departments, she observes, seem to have an easier time than do "sort of average" women who are bunched in the middle with "most of their male colleagues." Steitz believes that women, unlike men, seem to have a difficult time in the middle (quoted in Reis's Listserv, 2001). Only "super-duper women rise to the top," according to a female vice provost for faculty affairs, "because the mediocre ones are beaten out by the mediocre men. They [the women] have to prove themselves, to have published 26 articles, look the part, be assertive, tough-minded." A female presidential candidate, the vice provost adds, would be assumed by college trustees to possess less business sense than a male candidate, even if their backgrounds were almost identical (quoted in Glazer-Raymo, 1999, p. 161).

A mid-1990s study of more than 300 letters of recommendation used in hiring and promotion processes at a large medical school likewise underscores that competent women faculty are professionally underestimated and stereotypically described as caring, refreshing, and diligent. By contrast, competent men faculty are praised in specific ways for their research brilliance and for their concrete career achievements. Following a medical school convention, the letters were written by heads of departments; eighty-five percent of the heads were male (another convention). The two anthropologists who conducted the study issue three warnings to academics involved in the gatekeeping processes of screening, hiring, making awards, and reviewing candidates for tenure and promotion: double-check and eradicate from their own verbal and written evaluations "unwarranted signs of gender schema and omissions of essential topics"; make sure that their colleagues understand how the evaluations of applicants may be typically biased toward males and prejudiced against females; and coach female colleagues on how they can ensure that department chairs evaluate their individual accomplishments and promise rather than rely on negative stereotypes about their gender (Trix and Psenka, 2003, p. 217).

For the past several years, M.I.T. has been publicly acknowledging the presence of positive and negative stereotypes on campus. A groundbreaking book from M.I.T. Press, *Technology and the Dream: Reflections of the Black Experience at MIT, 1941–1999*, by Clarence Williams, presents more than seventy-five oral-history interviews with former and current African-American and European-American professors, students, administrators, and staff. In his superb introduction, Williams underscores the stereotypes that often hamper the fair evaluation and steady advancement of African-American students and faculty. Having been a high-level administrator at M.I.T. for decades, Williams has no doubt that on campus there remains "ongoing distrust and suspicion about blacks as potential intellectual leaders in science and engineering fields." African-American students and faculty are often thought to be deficient in "quantitative and analytical skills (an idea reiterated recently in *The Bell Curve* and other studies)," Williams points out. Even though such a negative mind-set is unlikely to be publicly expressed, some authority figures in the majority group continue to behave in the old patterns: "as when a non-black professor expresses amazement when a black undergraduate earns top marks in his mathematics class, or when a black graduate student finds herself on the outer edges of a lab's research program." Asked why M.I.T. still has so few African-American faculty, Williams, also an adjunct professor in urban planning, says the depressing answer "has less to do with the often cited pipeline problem than with cultural and racial attitudes that die hard" (C. Williams, 2001, pp. 45–47).

Seconding Williams's sobering answer is Cornell University environmental studies/biology professor Eloy Rodriguez (the first U.S.-born Mexican-American to hold an endowed science chair in the nation). Throughout his academic career, based first on the West Coast and now on the East Coast, Rodriguez has seen sexism and racism operating in a host of recruitment committees and tenure and promotion committees at various campuses. Based on these experiences, he warns that women and minorities still face formidable obstacles to succeeding at majority campuses. To level the playing field, he urges departments and campuses to reduce the enormous subjectivity that academic decision-makers can indulge in as they make personnel decisions: "The measurements being used for the tenure decision must be clearly set forth, and campuses and departments must be mindful and vigilant against exclusionary patterns in their evaluations and their granting of tenure" (quoted in Moody, 2000, p. 33).

Students, too, are likely to hold and act out stereotypical views about who is worthy and who is not. Professor Painter observes that in academia "students of all races and genders seem extremely judgmental toward non-white, non-male faculty. . . . Time and time again I've seen white women and people of color harassed, questioned, and rebuked by students who accept just about any behavior from white male faculty" (quoted in Moody, 2000, p. 30). When the minority doctoral scholars I coach begin their teaching-assistant duties, they often experience aggressive questioning from some of their undergraduate students about the validity of their credentials or their organization of the course—in other words, about their right to be the teacher. Even *established, tenured* professors of color also have to deal with this continuous jousting and testing, as several of them disclosed at an eye-opening discussion I attended at the University of Massachusetts–Boston. In fact, some minority students may participate in this testing and jousting because they, too, have internalized the norm that only majority males (not minorities and not women) are automatically entitled to legitimacy and authority. Because of the internalization of the norm, some students in their written evaluations of courses taught by non-majorities may be disproportionately harsh.

Conversely, majority males are granted not only more authority and acceptance, but also more leeway to make mistakes in the classroom. Penn State Professor Frances Rains describes such authority and leeway as "concealed profits" that the favored group enjoys. Members of this group reap these profits because students view them as the norm and as automatically entitled to intellectual authority and deference inside and outside the classroom (Rains, 1998a & b). Arizona State University professor Caroline Turner (formerly at the University of Minnesota) agrees with the metaphor of concealed profits: Because "professors of the dominant group are assured of addressing (in classroom lectures or other settings) individuals and groups of their own racial and ethnic composition," they do not have to expend extra energy and are likely to receive the benefit of the doubt (Turner, 2000, p. 122).

The concept of concealed profits is a helpful way to look at the corporate world as well. A study of 3,200 engineers in twenty-four U.S. corporations demonstrates how bias prominently threads through job evaluations (DiTomaso, Farris, and Cordero, 1993). The study demonstrated that not only access to constructive work experiences but also positive evaluations of job performance were secured most often by majority U.S.-born males. They were followed, in invariable order, by European-born majority males; then U.S.-born majority women; then East Asian men; Hispanic men; African-American men. African-American and other minority women were the most disadvantaged in their access to constructive work experiences and positive evaluations of job performance. In short, the thinking processes of corporate power-holders (usually majority males) together with conventions and customs in the workplace clearly influence who gets ahead in the corporation and who does not. This conclusion is reinforced by a 2001 Harvard Business School Press book, *Our Separate Ways: Black and White Women and the Struggle for Professional Identity,* by Ella Bell, visiting professor of business at Dartmouth College and Stella Nkomo, professor of business at the University of South Africa. In their study of 120 black and white women in business careers, the authors found that women in business continue, as a matter of course, to have their authority and judgment questioned and their ideas undervalued. And this is especially true for minority women (Bell and Nkomo, 2001). Likewise, University of Pennsylvania sociologist Jerry Jacobs finds that being a woman in an overwhelmingly male setting "can create a host of problems for women, including systematic misperception [of job performance] by the majority, a lack of political allies, and difficulties in winning acceptance from peers and subordinates" (Jacobs, 1989, p. 201).

Exactly How Do Misperception and Bias Unfold in Job Evaluations? Helpful details can be found in an organizational behavior textbook written by Professors Afsaneh Nahavandi (Arizona State University–West) and Ali Malekzadeh (St. Cloud State University). One extremely common form of bias occurs through a psychological process called channeling—this is "the process of limiting our interaction with another so that we avoid receiving information that contradicts our judgment." In other words, we set up a situation so as to gather the data needed to confirm our notion about the other person. Research has shown, for example, "that women are generally perceived by both male and female managers to be less competent, less capable of leading, and more likely to quit because of family pressures." The negative perception quickly leads to action that confirms these perceptions: Managers "provide women with fewer training opportunities, limited exposure to diverse experiences, and more routine, less challenging assignments. In many professions, women are bypassed for key promotions because the position requires that they supervise men." Can it be surprising, the textbook authors ask, that many women leave less challenging jobs or feel stymied with their underemployment? The clear caveat is this: "Organizations that channel women's behavior because of gender stereotypes assure that the stereotypes become reality" (Nahavandi and Malekzadeh, 1999, p. 167).

Getting a Job It is simply not true that the labor market will match up workers of equal qualifications with jobs paying equal rewards. In particular, minorities and women are less able to secure the jobs, promotions, awards, leadership posts, and economic power commensurate with their credentials and talent. This holds for Mexican Americans, Native Americans, Puerto Ricans, and African Americans in this country as well as stigmatized minorities in other nations, such as Koreans living in Japan. Numerous reports have shown that there are glass borders, glass ceilings, Keep Out signs, and jealously guarded stations of inside information at every turn for women seeking to enter male occupations and for minorities seeking high-paying and prestigious occupations and professions (Federal Glass Ceiling Commission, 1995; Catalyst report, discussed in Fitzgerald, 2001).

In seeking desirable jobs, majority males will be aided by the phenomenon that *like people hire like people.* Employers tend to hire those who look, think, and speak like themselves, unless they become conscious of this evaluative bias and concentrate to overcome it. Without a doubt, majority employers faced with equally qualified applicants "prefer white to black or Latino job applicants three to one" (Fischer et al., 1996, p. 182). A wry story captures the *reproduction* principle of hiring: An elderly, European-American manager is preparing to meet job candidates. Leaning into the intercom on his desk, he instructs his secretary to "Send in someone who reminds me of myself as a young buck." In other words, this employer is putting up a Welcome sign for those who are clones of himself.

In his national research studies, sociology professor Ronald Breiger at the University of Arizona has found that professional, managerial, and even technical workers are almost three times as likely to have secured their jobs through personal contacts than through direct application or responding to newspaper advertisements. The jobs with "the highest pay and prestige and affording the greatest satisfaction to their incumbents were most likely" to be filled through personal contacts (Breiger, 1988, p. 78). Because they are usually outsiders, minorities and women have to work extremely hard to secure academic posts. In recognition of this, I make it a point in my program work to help them build very wide professional networks, to compensate for being outside the usual circles of academic tradition and influence.

It is also simply not true, argues Claremont Graduate University professor Daryl Smith in a 2000 *Academe* article, that minorities find it easy to land attractive academic posts. She found in her comprehensive study of Ford, Spencer, and Mellow doctoral fellows that campuses are *not* beating down the doors of these minority candidates. Nor are the well-endowed campuses in the nation engaging in bidding wars for these new minority hires. These are myths. Nor is it true that European-American men are being passed over and suffering disadvantage in the job market. What *is* true, Smith found, is that institutions must fine-tune their hiring processes if they ever hope to diversify their faculty. In both the hiring and the promotion processes, minorities usually find it harder to secure academic and other professional posts and then to receive fair evaluations of their performance. In other words, their educational credentials and performance will bring them fewer job offers, slower promotions, and less recognition. Comparable credentials and performance will bring majorities more rewards, faster. A senior professor, of European-American heritage, confided anonymously, "I have no doubt whatsoever that discrimination is 'alive and well' in the academy and that, at whatever level of conscious or unconscious behavior, it serves to thwart minority hires and, all the more insidiously I believe, their retention" (quoted in Turner, 2000, p. 115).

9. Disadvantage: Because minorities are typically underrated, they need formal affirmative action programs in order to have the chance to prove themselves.

Advantage: Majorities are typically overrated and thus enjoy de facto and *invisible* affirmative action.

Though invisible affirmative action, majority women and especially majority men have accrued enormous unearned benefits. One European-American male professor admits that "while I worked like a Trojan to earn my way in this life, I, nevertheless, assert that a good measure of my success as an educator is the result of a constant, deep, and abiding affirmation action for white males." He knows that he has received breaks and positive evaluations "just by showing up. I try to be grateful" (Frank, 1999, p. 148). A similar sentiment is expressed by management professor Peter Couch, who describes himself as "a White, middle-class male in my early sixties. . . . [With this status] I have always found myself in a world of opportunities—opportunities that I thought were available to anyone energetic and capable." While Couch admits that he "knew that those outside the White male category didn't always have access to all opportunities," he found that fact easy to ignore because of the way his world functioned (quoted in Gallos and Ramsey, 1997, p. 21).

Likewise, doors of opportunity automatically open for offspring of college alumni: They enjoy reserved "legacy" admission slots at a parent's alma mater. These legacy reservations operate as a kind of invisible and unquestioned affirmative action program for European Americans (Takaki, 1989, p. 479). Needless to say, the reserved legacy slots usually go to those already holding high status and power. What is stunning is that critics of affirmative action make no move to criticize these legacy set-asides. One is reminded of the sardonic quip, "It isn't that white males don't believe in affirmative action, it's that they don't believe it should be for blacks and other minorities."

Because women and minorities, in the past, were categorically blocked from attending certain schools, using certain libraries, and entering certain professions and managerial positions, majority men in fact were enjoying a *monopoly*, that is, a lack of competition for these places. Today, women and minorities can indeed attend the University of Virginia, Harvard, and other institutions once closed to them, and they can go on to pursue medicine, law, and other professions once forbidden to them. But a lack of fairness still exists if their promise and performance in these settings are undervalued and unfairly evaluated because of negative stereotypes surrounding them. In other words, majority men will *retain* the unearned competitive advantage in evaluations if they retain the positive stereotype. This remains true at the Swedish Medical Research Council, where studies have shown its peer-review process for grants to be clearly tilted toward men: "women [applicants] had to produce twice as many scientific papers of equivalent quality to those written by men to be considered equally competent," according to articles in *Nature* and other science publications. At the U.S. National Cancer Institute, the same pernicious tilt is clear. An analysis of women and men researchers with equal rank and seniority uncovered a glaring disparity in the composition of grants awarded: Women on average "receive less than two-thirds of the budget and 63% of the research staff" that their male peers receive (Wenneras and Wold, 2000, p. 647; also see the Wenneras and Wold study on nepotism and sexism in peer reviews, 1997).

To counter the belittling of women and minorities and the overvaluing of white males are the motivations behind affirmative action policies, in both education and the workplace (Graham, 1995; Valian, 1998b; Powell, 1995; Patterson, 1998a). Affirmative action is needed exactly because white men are surrounded by such a positive bias. In the presence of this bias, people who are unlike white men often get short shrift. To reduce or eliminate that short shrift will require sustained work and policies by leaders at many levels.

Today, of course, some majority men complain that with the advent of affirmative action, they are unfairly disadvantaged when seeking academic posts while minorities, on the other hand, are unfairly advantaged. "A lot of people in my demographic group," writes one classics professor, "talk about the lost-white-male syndrome and they say that all the jobs are going to women." But assessing the validity of this claim, he admits that "the [classics] field is still largely dominated by white men" and those who are different from the norm "are not taken as seriously from the interview stage onward" (quoted in Smith, 2000, p. 50). Berkeley professor Ron Takaki insists that "throughout American history, there had always been affirmative action for white men." White men did not have to compete with women or minorities for educational and employment advancement. "Many of them are the beneficiaries of their history of exclusion based on race and gender, and pass their economic and social advantages on to white men in the next generation." Takaki strongly believes that affirmative action for white women and minorities is necessary in order to create equality of opportunity (1987, p. 231).

Bolstering Takaki's judgment is the fact that affirmative action for majority men was, in fact, written into the U.S. Constitution. Recall that *white, male property owners* were the only group granted citizenship and political legitimacy by the constitution of the new democracy. The exclusion and deliberate omission of all others gave the favored group a long-term monopoly on economic and social advantage that it did indeed pass on to its clones: Is it any wonder that this group continues to hold, by far, the greatest power in business, government, finance, and education (Dahl, 2001)? The Founding Fathers themselves "effectively established America's first affirmative action policy." This first policy now needs to be supplanted by a long-term affirmative action policy for those who have been systematically and historically *excluded* for centuries (Howard, 1999, pp. 77–78). Removing preferential treatment for majority males is exactly what affirmative action should do, according to Herbert Hill (1989) and Pat Williams (1991). The playing field must be leveled.

10. Disadvantage: Minority faculty often are unfairly constrained in their choice of scholarly pursuits and face a "brown-on-brown" taboo.

Advantage: Majorities can set themselves up as scholars of almost anything and expect fair evaluation of their scholarship.

Emeritus professor of political science Willard Johnson recalls his lifelong struggle with his own department and several others at M.I.T. to "appreciate the quality and relevance and significance of black scholarship. It is just an overwhelming problem." Why the blinders on many majority colleagues in those departments? Johnson believes it's because scholarship only on *their* group seems worthwhile to them (oral history interview, C. Williams, 2001, p. 191).

A Native American tenured professor at a large four-year southwestern university reports a continuous battle with most of his departmental colleagues over his research projects. They devalue his work for two reasons: because it is on American Indian topics and because he himself is American Indian—so, in their minds, he could not possibly perform "objective scientific research on his own people." Editors of mainstream journals also resist publication of his work because they believe that scholarship on Indian issues should be done by "objective non-Indian" academics! Needless to say, most editors of such journals are European-American males, as shown in the article "Lily-white University Presses" (Shin, 1996).

The irony here, of course, is that majority academics can study and publish to their heart's content on issues related to majorities. Why is their objectivity not suspect (Peterson-Hickey and Stein, 1998)? Hisauro Garza, formerly a professor of Chicano and Latin American studies at California State University–Fresno and now president of Sierra Research and Technical Services in California, analyzed the responses of 238 college faculty throughout the United States who were included in the National Latino Faculty Survey. Almost half of these faculty felt that any kind of social science or humanities scholarship, if undertaken by Mexican Americans and Puerto Ricans, is viewed as intellectually *inferior* by most members of their departments. If the scholarship focuses on minority issues, then the value of that research shrinks *even more*. Yet if European Americans undertake research on minority issues, the value *rises* dramatically (Garza, 1993, pp. 37–38).

Several analysts have graphically named this the taboo against "brown-on-brown" scholarship, a taboo not affecting majority intellectuals, who are granted great latitude to study most anything of interest to them. For example, majority scholars are presumed to be objective and competent when they study majority group members' criminal activity, business activity, musical and cultural contributions, or whatever. No one will say they are "too close" or "too similar" to their subjects. But minorities in humanities and social science commonly face the brown-on-brown taboo and the concomitant underestimation of their work if it focuses on minorities.

11. Disadvantage: Minority job candidates can face a very high barrier to being hired in departments that already have one minority faculty member and subscribe to the "one minority is sufficient" quota system.

Advantage: Majority job candidates are unlikely to face such a quota barrier.

Law professor Derrick Bell has repeatedly called attention to an unspoken and rigid quota in academia: Only one or only a very small handful of minority faculty will be tolerated at mainstream law schools. This can be referred to as a tolerance for only *token* diversity, I suppose. An organizational psychologist would probably theorize that power-holders in the law schools (especially the Harvard Law dean, in Bell's case) sense a dreaded power shift if the number of minorities in their midst continues to climb. When Bell persisted in bringing extraordinarily qualified minority job candidates to the dean's attention, the administrator complained and told Bell that Harvard Law School was not and would not become a Woolworth's lunch counter in the South, destined to become integrated by minority activists. Possessing such an attitude, the dean could not see and genuinely appreciate the strengths of any new job candidates who possess minority status, Bell understandably maintains. That is, once a token number of minority faculty are hired, a "real ceiling" is reached that prevents the hiring of any more "regardless of their qualifications" (Bell, 1992, p. 141). Thus, an unspoken kind of quota system seems to be operative, which blocks minorities from receiving fair evaluation and fair access to entering the professoriate.

Other analysts have also focused on this quota system. In a an article originally appearing in the *Harvard Educational Review,* the authors found that "many colleges and universities operate under an unwritten quota system that manifests itself as reluctance to hire more than one minority faculty member per department." This "one-minority-per-pot" syndrome is best illustrated by the refrain heard from numerous department chairs across the country that "we hired a minority last year" and thus diversity has been satisfied (Reyes and Halcon, 1991, p. 75).

Being the lonely token minority in a majority department can understandably bring disquiet. A tenured professor muses, "I have been at the University for thirteen years; in that period, I remain the only faculty member of color in my department. I listen to the assurances [that the department is open to hiring more minority candidates]. I look at the statistics." Yet the numbers do *not* change. (Turner, 2000). How can a professor in such a situation not come to suspect departmental colleagues of paying merely lip service to equity?

A quota system—that restricts minorities to token representation and marginal power in the organization—serves to privilege majority members and their standing. That is, competition for faculty posts is artificially manipulated so that majority candidates are more likely to be *hired* and then, once hired, more likely to professionally thrive as a result of their majority status. Yet having minorities included in a hiring committee's candidate *pool* is acceptable and indeed very desirable: "Apparently, an applicant pool that includes minorities is considered by White faculty as evidence of a 'good faith effort' in hiring and integrating minorities—even if minorities are not ultimately hired." In fact, it is predictable that minorities will *not* be hired. The one-minority-only rule restricts the "career goals and aspirations of Hispanics and other minority faculty" and is largely to blame for the lack of diversity on America's campuses (Reyes and Halcon, 1991, p. 75).

12. Disadvantage: During the academic search process, minority job candidates are vulnerable to the "raising the bar" syndrome often manifested by search committees.

Advantage: Majority job candidates usually are not subjected to this syndrome.

In my consulting work, I often find that search committees need reminding and coaching so that they do not continue to raise the qualifications for minority candidates. It is unfortunately a common practice for committees to seek from minority candidates (but not majority ones) extra assurances that they are qualified: Additional writing samples, letters of recommendation, and the like are requested (Reyes and Halcon, 1991). Two things seem to be at work. First, committee members do not realize that the stigma of incompetence, discussed earlier in this chapter, makes them suspicious. They fear that a particular minority candidate or indeed any minority hire whatsoever may lower the department's reputation and standards. Their fear leads them to compulsively double-check the minority's credentials and even to read, word by word, his/her peer-reviewed articles to determine their soundness—a precaution never felt necessary for majority candidates.

The stigma-induced fear leads search committees to insist that minority candidates must hold doctorates from the most prestigious graduate schools—a requirement that is not necessarily essential for majority applicants. While majority candidates will probably enjoy the assumption of being competent and well qualified as search committees conduct their work, minority candidates will probably be saddled with the assumption of being incompetent and not sufficiently qualified. Unless search committees become aware of and overcome these assumptions (as I discuss in chapter 4), their evaluations of minorities and majorities will likely continue to be skewed.

Such skewing was uncovered by Robert Haro, who interviewed Latino/a leaders in higher education as well as trustees and other members of hiring committees at twenty-five colleges and universities. On the basis of 120 personal interviews, Haro (a professor at San Francisco State University) found that Latinos/as are often stereotypically treated: Their academic credentials and experience are viewed as suspect, and their styles of personal interaction are regarded as inappropriate. For instance, European-American job candidates for a college presidency were not required to have had previous experience as an academic dean or provost, but Latino/a candidates were. European-American candidates might squeeze by with a doctorate from less than a top research university but not a Latino/a. Latino/a candidates were sometimes regarded as inappropriately dressed and wearing "cheap and distracting" jewelry, in the words of a trustee and member of a search committee (Haro, 2001).

CONCLUSION

This chapter has isolated and examined a dozen important ways in which majority faculty are usually privileged and favored at majority colleges and universities—at the same time that minority faculty are usually disadvantaged and disfavored. In fact, the privilege and favor of the majority group exist and accrue only when the corresponding minority groups are culturally taxed and handicapped. The hidden profits of majority professors must be accounted for and recognized. If they are not, one will naively believe that merit and ability of majority group members cause or significantly contribute to their comparatively rapid and steady advancement whereas the deficiencies of minority group members cause or significantly contribute to their slow advancement in higher education. What must be seen *as a whole* is the elaborate and interlocked *system* of disadvantages/advantages that favor some and disfavor others. Institutional discrimination, as we have seen, "involves patterns of resource allocation, selection, advancement, and expectations" that perpetuate higher status and likely success for the favored group but have just the opposite effect for all others (White and Cones, 1999, p. 81).

CHAPTER 2

SUCCEEDING OUTSIDE THE IVY WALLS
Disadvantages versus Advantages

Chapter 1 highlighted typical disadvantages for minority faculty working on majority campuses as well as typical advantages for majority faculty on those same campuses. It is likewise important to recognize that additional difficulties and stressors often loom for minority professionals and their families as they conduct their lives in realms *away from* their colleges and universities.

Minority faculty and their families often do *not* find the public deference, social standing, and police protection they deserve outside the halls of ivy. In building assets to pass on to later generations, they usually encounter exceptional barriers that slow down not only their securing of wealth (such as real estate) but also their being invited into the powerful social networks so necessary for fueling their and their children's advancement.

Section A of this chapter will focus on these worldly disadvantages that minority faculty face and, on the flip side, the advantages that majority faculty reap. Section B highlights the process of earning educational credentials and the roadblocks that predictably impeded the progress of many minority faculty but not that of their majority colleagues. The educational blocks are poor public schooling at the elementary and high school levels together with invalid standardized tests such as the Scholastic Aptitude Test (SAT) and the Graduate Record Examination (GRE) that severely underestimate minority students' potential and academic worthiness. To shoulder these academic disadvantages in their younger years and rise above them, minority faculty and administrators had to invest enormous energy and will-power. Their accomplishments should be better appreciated by their majority peers.

Moreover, majority power-holders, such as provosts, deans, and department chairs, should be mindful of what experiences their new faculty hires are probably encountering as they make their way outside the campus boundaries. Members of the favored group are likely to need less support and encouragement than members of disfavored minority groups. Not to realize and attend to the different contexts enveloping different faculty colleagues is a shortcoming, especially for those in academic leadership roles.

A. MAINTAINING PROFESSIONAL STANDING AND GENERATING WEALTH

A-1. Disadvantage: In the world outside academe, minority faculty often experience a devaluation of their professional standing as well as an exclusion from networks of influence and power.

Advantage: In the larger world, majority faculty and administrators usually can enjoy steady valuation for their credentials and standing and can count on being included in important networks.

Devaluing by White-Supremacist Systems   Racial and ethnic profiling seems widespread. Police departments across the country are being pressured to stop such profiling, that is, questioning or arresting certain groups of citizens because of the negative stereotypes the police officers associate with them. Such profiling not only affects minority youth milling about on street corners but also well-educated minority professionals carrying on their routine business, as a number of minority faculty have disclosed to me. When distinguished professor of African-American studies and religion Cornel West taught at Princeton University, he was repeatedly stopped by city police who insisted he was driving *too slowly*, according to articles in prominent newspapers and magazines. "Driving while black," Harvard Law School professor Charles Ogletree vigorously complains, is only one danger. There are others, such as "riding while black," "shopping while black," "jogging while black," "walking while black," and indeed "living while black" (quoted in MacQuarrie, 1999, pp. A1, A9).

One educator has disclosed to me his theory that police harassment is a vestige of mob lynching and a clear expression of white supremacy: The harassment terrorizes minorities and keeps them in their fearful place at the bottom of the caste system. The harassment, he continues, is perpetrated mostly by working-class European-Americans whose forbearers were, in fact, the instigators in lynchings. But who benefits the most from such violence and harassment? Property-owning, *wealthy whites* not only have their property protected by poor whites (who typically make up "our militia and our police") but also have the caste system preserved and their top position in that system protected—through the terrorizing efforts of poor whites whom they encourage to scapegoat minorities, especially African-Americans. While poor whites feel an elevation of social status due to white supremacy, they are in fact being cheated of decent wages and blocked from organizing for more political and economic power in solidarity with exploited minorities (Kushnick, 1981, p. 196).

A *Harvard Law Review* article, summarizing numerous local and national studies, maintains European-American police officers "use ethnicity/race as an independently significant, if not determinative, factor in deciding whom to follow, detain, search, or arrest" (quoted in Reiman, 1998, p. 108). This is bad news, of course, for Mexican Americans, Native Americans, African Americans, and other minorities throughout the nation, whether minors or highly educated professionals. It is also bad news for the children of minority faculty, for they can be vulnerable to being followed, detained, and arrested by police. As a minority professor at a southwestern majority university complained, "You have to spend so much time thinking about stuff that most white people just don't even have to think about." While the professor legitimately worries when she is pulled over by a traffic cop, she intensely worries when she thinks about her partner or her son getting pulled over: "I'm very aware of how many black folks accidentally get shot by cops." Although "the freedom to just be yourself," she continues, is something that should be guaranteed to all citizens of the country, this freedom is denied to her and her family, despite their professional status and income. Understandably, she "gets resentful" that she must worry about so many things that "even my very close white friends, whose politics are similar to mine, simply don't have to worry about" (quoted in Feagin and Sikes, 1994, p. 398; also see Feagin and Vera, 1995).

Minority professors repeatedly cite not only police harassment and overreaction but also hostile remarks or behavior from some majority-group members they encounter on public streets and in public accommodations. Restaurant staff, for instance, are notorious for trying to seat minority customers near the kitchen or otherwise trying to hide them away. Interviewing a number of middle-class African Americans in several large cities, Professor Joe Feagin found that almost all underscored how much emotional energy they had to spend daily as they cope with racial discrimination—energy that majority-group members do not have to draw on (Feagin and Sikes, 1994).

In 2001, Ruth Simmons left her presidency of Smith College to become president of Brown University. Neither campus had ever before been headed by an African American woman. In a segment of *60 Minutes*, Simmons described the shock she felt when she was shadowed by a security guard as soon as she walked into Saks Fifth Avenue in New York City to shop. Corporate lawyer and college professor Lawrence Graham, in his book *Member of the Club*, points out that he, like other African Americans of the middle class, "can shop in the same stores, work in the same firms, and live in the same neighborhoods as our white peers," yet they are still routinely vulnerable to slights and insults. Their status and acceptance are undercut when "we are shadowed by store clerks, passed up by cabdrivers, ignored by bosses who are looking for protégés, and rejected by [social and country] clubs that offer networking opportunities" (Graham, 1995, p. xiv). Majorities belonging to the same professional class would not have their social standing undermined in this way, of course. In a more ideal world, according to chemical engineer Paula Hammond, "you won't have to fight just to be who you are. . . . When you go places there [will be] an assumption that you too are interested in, say, the education of your child, or you too are interested in investments . . . [and you possess] the same concerns as upper middle-class white folks" (quoted in C. Williams, 2001, p. 973). But enjoying this ideal and positive assumption is still decidedly the exception. In short, middle-class African-Americans and other stigmatized minorities find themselves denied the "comfort" that education, a prestigious job, and money in the bank should be bringing them (Hochschild, 1995, p. 93).

The stereotypical slights endured by minority professionals mean that their professional and social status is never really secure for them or their families, not in the same way it is for majority professionals. The presumption that they are, in some way, *suspect* can be expressed on any given day in a variety of blatant or subtextual ways. Resilence, one Mexican-American faculty member disclosed to me, "has to be manufactured in your psyche every day. There's no letting up. You never get the brass ring tightly in your hand, ever." In other words, *castelike* not classlike dynamics seem to be at work. To prove that you are worthy, day in and day out, demands extra energy. But this is a necessary defense in the face of the presumption of unworthiness held by many in the society. As one wit has sardonically observed, "Have you ever noticed that white men always enjoy the benefit of the doubt about their professional competency? It's only the usual suspects—minorities and women—who have to constantly show they are 'well qualified' (which is code for exceptional and not like the *others*)."

Political scientist Jennifer Hochschild underscores this very worrisome situation in *Facing Up to the American Dream: Race, Class, and the Soul of the Nation* (1995). If educational credentials, hard work, and a decent salary don't guarantee social stability and something approaching social invulnerability for recipients, then something is dreadfully wrong. The American dream and upward class mobility cannot be reserved for only certain people.

Exclusion from Important Networks   To achieve financial and professional advancement, professionals must (almost always) become networked with a variety of powerful people who can open doors of opportunity, help them solve problems, alert them to impending dangers and reorganizations, and introduce them to yet more power-holders. Personal contacts with powerful people are the most likely avenue to securing prestigious and high-paying jobs (Breiger, 1988; Boissevain, 1974). But these contacts provide inside information, invaluable coaching, and guidance in securing desirable positions and promotions (termed social capital by some scholars) in *exclusive* places "where disadvantaged minorities and women are not to be found"—namely, on corporate boards; at country and golf clubs; and in middle- and top-management positions in professions, businesses, hospitals, publishing houses, learned societies and journals (Shin, 1996), and so on.

Because of the paucity of minorities and women in these strategically significant locations, other minorities and women lower down the ladder cannot reach out to them for intervention and assistance, according to Harvard sociologist Orlando Patterson (1998a, p. 18). This is the reason, Patterson maintains, that vigorous affirmative action policies in education and employment are needed for the next fifteen years for African Americans, Puerto Rican Americans, Mexican Americans, Native Americans, and European-American women, in order "to insert them into network-rich educational institutions of the nation and the self-generating career networks in the workplace—networks that Euro-Americans take for granted" (p. 20). Patterson observes that impressive educational credentials will *never* be sufficient to generate professional and monetary advancement for disadvantaged women and minorities. Inclusion in powerful networks is essential.

Other scholars have pointed out that housing segregation severely limits middle-class minorities' access to influential networks. Minority professors are no exception. A close connection exists between social mobility and spatial mobility. As a family's assets grow, members usually relocate to a better neighborhood where they can "consolidate their own class position and enhance their and their children's prospects for additional social mobility"—through better public schooling, higher value of housing, more desirable living conditions, and intermingling and *networking* with neighbors who possess an attractive social standing. By choosing to move to "successively better neighborhoods," immigrants to this country and their children found a way to consolidate and extend their financial and social gains. Levels of residential segregation "have fallen for each immigrant group as socioeconomic status and generations in the United States have increased." In short, having the freedom and the means to move to a better neighborhood is part of the American dream (Massey and Denton, 1993, p. 150). Yet even in the twenty-first century, there are affluent neighborhoods where minority professionals and professors are not welcome and where they cannot buy houses because of the prejudice against them, as I well know from working with these professors (also see Hochschild, 1995). As we will learn in chapter 3, only Asian-American professionals are thus far treated in most places in this nation as "honorary whites" (to use a colleague's term) who experience few or no barriers to their residential choices and preferences.

A-2. Disadvantage: Minorities, including minority faculty, have a harder time accumulating wealth because of federal, state, and labor union policies.

Advantage: Majorities, including faculty, have an easier time accumulating wealth because of these policies.

Accumulating Wealth or Accumulating Poverty   Much has been made of the fact that the African-American middle class now earns seventy cents for every dollar earned by European-Americans with similar qualifications. This is heralded by some as a strikingly positive development. Sociologist William Julius Wilson, for example, argues that young blacks are close to having life chances equal to those of young whites, but other scholars vehemently disagree (Willie, 1990; Oliver and Shapiro, 1995; Marable, 1995). Income from wages and salaries is, of course, not the whole story. While it is true that their wages are improving in relation to white wages, the African-American middle class possesses only fifteen cents of wealth (in the form of stocks, real estate, and so on) for every dollar possessed by the European-American middle class. A number of economists and sociologists argue convincingly that cumulative advantages and disadvantages over generations have determined who has built up wealth and enjoyed increased life opportunities and who has *not* been able to do so (see, for instance, Oliver and Shapiro, 1995; Marable, 1995; Thurow, 1969).

Clearly, the dream of accumulating wealth and passing it on to future generations is more viable for some groups than for others. Take real estate as one example. The way that most European-Americans have generated capital is through owning their own homes. Older homeowners in white suburbia have been particularly fortunate: Even quite modest homes, especially suburban tract homes that were bought in the 1940s and 1950s, have appreciated beyond their owners' wildest dreams. Oliver and Shapiro calculate that "between 1987 and 2011 the baby boom generation stands to inherit approximately $7 trillion." Much of this wealth has accrued to them through appreciation of their elderly parents' residences (1995, p. 181). But the elderly parents of African Americans, Mexican Americans, and other stigmatized minorities were blocked, sometimes subtly and more often blatantly, from acquiring houses in suburbia where housing appreciation was and still is the greatest. (The places where many stigmatized and poor minorities were and are concentrated—reservations, barrios, ghettos, or migrant worker camps—realize no such buildup of equity, needless to say.) In dollars alone, Oliver and Shapiro maintain, institutional biases in the residential area "are costing the *current* generation of African Americans about $82 billion" (1995, pp. 9, 151). Two other scholars—Kenneth Jackson in *Crabgrass Frontier* (1985) and Bruce Haynes in *Red Lines, Black Spaces* (2001)—make similar points.

It may be surprising to discover that governmental legislation and policies–federal, state, and local–have methodically, over many generations, prevented African Americans and other minorities from acquiring wealth. By contrast, the very same legislation and policies have given unearned advantages to *majority* members of society. For instance, American Indians and Mexican Americans were forced from their lands to make way for European American farmers and ranchers; government policies and law courts paved the way for that dispossession. African Americans, once freed from slavery, did not receive forty acres and a mule for farming, which some political theorists believe would have been the genuine start of the American democracy. Ruthless discrimination—in both the economic and social spheres—continued with Jim Crow laws against minorities. And, of course, minorities were blocked from participating in the huge land giveaways in the Midwest and West under the homesteading acts. Because only European-Americans were allowed to lay claim to new ranches and farms, they were granted a head start on accumulation of land wealth (Ignatiev, 1995; Roediger, 1999; Woodward, 1966; Littlefield and Underhill, 1973).

In modern times, the Federal Housing Administration (FHA) has prevented minorities from enjoying dramatic financial appreciation in the residential real estate market. Beginning in the 1930s, the FHA sought to bolster the weakened construction industry by directing resources away from older housing stock in the cities and toward construction of new single-family housing outside the cities. What was created was the modern mortgage system that enabled 35 million majority families of very modest means between 1933 and 1978 to build or buy single-family homes with small down payments, at reasonable interest rates, and over a long time period. Suburbia was the result. The FHA, as well as the Veterans Administration, was determined to create "exclusively white suburbs" all over the country and to keep out all others, especially African Americans (Massey and Denton, 1993, pp. 52–55). City planner Charles Abrams gives this stunning analysis: "The FHA adopted a racial policy that could well have been culled from the Nuremberg laws. From its inception FHA set itself up as the protector of the all-white neighborhood. It sent its agents into the field to keep Negroes and other minorities from buying homes in white neighborhoods" (quoted in Oliver and Shapiro, 1995, p. 16). The expression "redlining" became code for housing discrimination. The *FHA Underwriting Manual* warned that "if a neighborhood is to retain stability, it is necessary that properties shall continue to be occupied by the same social and racial classes." To accomplish this, the FHA recommended that "subdivision regulations and suitable restrictive covenants" should be used to maintain the lily-white composition of neighborhoods (Massey and Denton, 1993, pp. 52–55; also see Oliver and Shapiro, 1995). The high walls around suburban tract housing, in other words, were built by the FHA. The significant appreciation of tract homes in suburbia has meant that majority folks of modest means have accumulated some wealth that already has been, or soon will be, passed on to their fortunate offspring.

Are redlining practices a thing of the past? No. Newspapers across the country and the Federal Reserve Bank continue to unearth discrimination, not only by realtors but also by commercial banks that reject minority applicants two or three times as often as majority applicants with the same qualifications. Banks in certain cities, such as Boston, Philadelphia, Chicago, and Minneapolis, are especially culpable (Massey and Denton, 1993; Oliver and Shapiro, 1995). Early in the twenty-first century, the *Boston Globe* continues to spotlight several

New England banks' unscrupulous mortgage practices toward minorities. Moreover, segregation in both rental and residential housing most certainly persists in this century. Such segregation translates into diminished opportunities—financial, educational, networking, psychological, political—for those who are systematically excluded from living in mostly majority communities (Massey and Denton, 1993; Fischer et al., 1996; Oliver and Shapiro, 1995; Marable, 1995).

A telling example of very recent discrimination is provided by law professor Patricia Williams. Initiating a home mortgage over the phone, she found that her loan was approved quickly. "With my credit history, with my job as a law professor, and no doubt with my accent, I am not only middle-class but match the cultural stereotype of a good white person." Because of this, the loan officer of the bank mailed her the contract, and he himself checked off her race as "white." She marked through that, wrote in "black," and then mailed back the signed contract. "Suddenly said deal came to a screeching halt," Williams observes. The bank demanded a heftier down payment, more points to be charged for the loan, and a higher rate of interest—because (she was told) the property values in her neighborhood "were suddenly falling" and the bank's risk had thus increased (P. Williams, 1997, pp. 39–40).

Another law professor, Cheryl Harris at Chicago-Kent College of Law, has brilliantly demonstrated that whiteness *is* property—but not pertaining solely to real estate. Although whiteness certainly brings property advantages (such as owning a home, thanks to the FHA), whiteness also brings political privileges, relatively high social status, and personal identity—as well as the right to exclude non-white people from some or all of these privileges and rights. In fact, Harris argues that the concept of whiteness, early in our country's history, came to mean white supremacy and that the courts and legislatures (in the past and in the present) take deliberate steps to protect this supremacy and ensure that it passes on to subsequent generations. Concomitantly, the exclusion and disadvantaging of non-whites is carefully preserved and passed on to new generations (Harris, 1993). Agreeing that white supremacy allows "the spoils of discrimination" to be passed on to subsequent generations, University of California–San Diego professor George Lipsitz concludes that European Americans "are encouraged to invest in whiteness, to remain true to an identity that provides them with resources, power, and opportunity." Whiteness, while not a biological or anthropological fact, is indeed a most powerful "social fact" and identity (Lipsitz, 1998, p. vii).

Labor Unions and Their Roles in the Accumulation of Wealth or Poverty

European Americans have benefited over several generations—and still do—if they belong to labor unions. The unions usually bring them some financial protection and the means to steadily build up wealth. For example, "what especially boosted the Irish as a class was their opportunity to participate in the higher-waged skilled and unionized trades" (Takaki, 1993, p. 163). But these organizations, designed to protect powerless workers, were very *exclusive* in their policies. In the early twentieth century, written clauses in the bylaws, for example, of the Brotherhood of Locomotive Firemen, the Brotherhood of Railway Carmen, and the Clerks, Mates, and Pilots Union permitted only white male members. The bigotry in unions, after the 1960s antidiscrimination laws, became unwritten policy but remained just as effective: "By 1970, Blacks in construction unions made up only 1.7 percent of iron-workers, 0.4 percent of elevator construction workers, and 0.2 percent of plumbers." Even currently, labor unions in this country remain close to ninety percent European American in their membership (White and Cones, 1999, p. 42; also see Thurow, 1969).

As European immigrants struggled to create unions in order to protect and advance their interests, they deliberately excluded all others, including women. For example, in 1870 in New Orleans, there were 3,460 African Americans listed in the city directory as carpenters, cigar makers, painters, clerks, shoemakers, coopers, tailors, bakers, blacksmiths, and foundry hands. Yet by 1904 the number had fallen to 346 although the African American population of the city had increased by more than fifty percent. The new construction unions ensured that the jobs within their jurisdiction became "white men's work"—whereas prior to the Civil War, there had been a "concentration of black workers, both slave and free, in the building trades" (Hill, 1989, p. 214). This conversion to "white men's work" occurred in many cities along the eastern seaboard and throughout the southern states. In New York City between 1890 and 1910, African-American workers were steadily forced out of employment as longshoremen, caterers, tailors, brick makers, wagon drivers, stable hands, house painters, and hotel and restaurant waiters. Organized labor unions and corporate managers and owners—working together as partners—relegated African Americans to a severely exploited class of workers and blocked them from entering all-white skilled occupations. The government did little or nothing to stop this exploitation. Economist Herbert Hill believes that the chronic poverty and social disorganization found in African-American ghettos over generations has been caused and perpetuated, in large measure, by corporate leaders and by European immigrants and their labor union policies that locked African Americans into the lowest caste position (Hill, 1989).

The same pattern—creating a permanent underclass of Mexican-American laborers—occurred in the Southwest. European-American migrants to California and other parts of the Southwest soon learned that by playing up their "whiteness," they could receive the best-paying and more permanent jobs while Mexicans would receive the worst-paying and most erratic (Takaki, 1993). Economists quaintly call this a dual-wage system. In domestic servant jobs, African-American women were also pushed out. In New York City in 1830, they held most cooking and cleaning jobs in affluent households, but by 1850 Irish immigrant women did. In San Francisco, Irish men organized anti-Chinese activities and shouted that the Chinese threatened the employment of Irish women: "Chinese Must Go! Our Women are degraded by coolie labor" (Takaki, 1993, p. 154).

Several leaders, including Frederick Douglass as early as 1853 and W. E. B. DuBois in the early twentieth century, repeatedly complained about this displacement of African-American workers by German, Irish, Jewish, and other immigrants. Douglass noted that "every hour sees the black man elbowed out of employment by some newly arrived immigrant, whose hunger and whose color are thought to give him a better title to place, and so we believe it will continue until the last prop is leveled beneath us" (quoted in Hill, 1989, p. 216). Reflecting on how new immigrants systematically push out minorities already here, Princeton professor and Nobel laureate Toni Morrison has observed that one of the first words learned by immigrants is "nigger." By invoking this word and concept, penniless and desperate immigrants could begin to socially and politically elevate and entitle themselves, at the expense of those *frozen* at the bottom of the caste system (quoted in Roediger, 1998, p. 19). In fact, "it is not just that various white immigrant groups' economic successes came at the expense of nonwhites, but that they they owe their now stabilized and broadly recognized whiteness *itself* in part to these nonwhite groups" (Jacobson, 1998, p. 9). A fascinating study, *How the Irish Became White* (1995) by Noel Ignatiev, details how the Irish Catholic, treated in Ireland as a castelike and oppressed people, reenacted oppression once they arrived in America and saw the pernicious wisdom of adopting anti-black sentiments. Through persistence, violence, political organizing, and other means, immigrant workers like the Irish Catholic struggled to take over the better jobs and reap higher wages. "The greater rate of exploitation of the black worker, locked into an all-black labor classification, subsidized the higher wages of whites, a process repeated in many industries and codified into collective bargaining agreements" (Hill, 1989, p. 233).

European immigrants gained preferential treatment because their unions routinely refused to consider Mexican Americans, African Americans, Native Americans, and Puerto Ricans for membership or to refer them for employment. By guaranteeing these advantages along with higher wages, the unions enabled many European immigrants to escape crushing poverty. By contrast, non-whites were far more likely to be trapped in poverty and locked out of desirable "white" jobs and workplaces. In short, white male workers came to have a monopoly on clean, secure, highly skilled jobs that had the possibility of promotion (Blauner, 1972; Hill, 1989). This pattern of preferential employment remains: While white males make up only forty-one percent of the U.S. population, they make up eighty percent of all tenured professors, ninety-five percent of the senior managers of Fortune 500 and 1,000 companies, and ninety-seven percent of all school superintendents (Marabel, 1995). The dual labor system—that structurally enhances wealth production for the favored group and undermines such production for the disfavored groups—explains why wealth as well as poverty can be predictably inherited by future generations.

In short, minority faculty on U.S. campuses will probably experience several disadvantages as they operate outside the walls of their institutions. Those people holding stereotypical assumptions will devalue their professional standing and even harass them and their families as they undertake ordinary daily tasks. Those with prejudice will exclude them from membership in influential networks and block them from purchase and residence in houses and neighborhoods marked by steady appreciation of monetary value. These disadvantages mean that minority faculty's hard-earned professional attainments count for less than they do for similarly situated majority professors. Nor should we ignore the fact that past and current policies—adopted by federal and state agencies and by labor unions—have hampered minority citizens' accumulation of financial security over many generations. Thus, minority faculty's financial assets are likely to be more modest than their majority faculty peers because of long-term barriers that unfortunately remain as de facto policies in many places.

B. SECURING EDUCATIONAL CREDENTIALS

Even as minorities could not acquire real estate with the generous help of the Federal Housing Administration and Veterans Administration, they could not reap the benefits from the GI Bill following World War II. The GI Bill was "the most massive affirmation action program [for

European-American males] in U.S. history" and enabled European Americans, especially Jews, to move into the middle and upper classes by securing college degrees and moving into the professions. Before the war, college attendance was only for the elite. But after the war, eight million European-American males of modest means enjoyed college tuition and living-expense stipends from the federal government. Veterans who were African-American or women of any background could not participate in this advancement program (Sacks, 1997). While the bill is no longer operative, its effects in the amassing of wealth and social status are still rewarding later generations of participants and, of course, still penalizing later generations of those who were systematically excluded.

Two other substantial and *current* barriers—prior to becoming a college or university professor—need to be spotlighted. In my work with minority faculty and students, I am impressed by the intellectual *catching up* that many of them undertake, to compensate for the poor public schooling they received before college. I am also struck again and again by how much damage is done to women and minorities by standardized tests such as the SAT (Standardized Aptitude Test) and GRE (Graduate Record Examination). Disappointing test scores prompt many of them to *self-screen* and abandon their dreams of being professors. Fortunately, some women and minorities do not abandon their ambitions, yet they carry with them the gnawing suspicion that perhaps the scores have indeed revealed something dreadfully wrong with them. Several faculty friends have joked with me that not until they had published several peer-reviewed articles did they feel that the GRE "demon" was receding in their consciousness. Joking aside, I believe everyone in academia must consider the immediate as well as long-term damage done by such high-stakes, multiple-choice, hurried, and above all, *invalid* tests. Below is an outline of that damage.

B-3. Disadvantage: Due to stereotype threat, stigmatized minorities underperform and are unfairly evaluated by high-stakes, standardized, timed tests (such as the SAT and GRE). To make matters worse, these high-stakes tests can trigger minority students' self-screening and "dis-identification" with school.

Advantage: Majorities are aided in taking these high-stakes tests by the stereotypical expectation that they will do well. Their success on such tests usually builds self-confidence for the long term, instead of triggering self-screening.

Scholastic Aptitude Test "What did *you* make on the SAT?" This question permeates American culture, obsesses families and students, and in a real way holds hostage the entire academic enterprise, from high school on. In fact, perhaps the obsession stretches into the Beyond. A wonderful story makes it clear that one's SAT scores could be everlasting! Here are the setting and punch line, as I remember them: An old (Christian) guy, recently deceased, is stopped at the gates of heaven by Saint Peter. Saint Peter is quickly checking his ledger book to see if the deceased's tally of good deeds will get him admitted to heaven. The recently deceased man happens to glance down at the ledger book and incredulously says to Saint Peter: *"You're kidding! You count SATs?"* SAT scores not only preoccupy gatekeepers such as Saint Peter, but also college admissions and financial aid committees and some employers such as McKinsey Management and Consulting Company (Lemann, 1999). (McKinsey, it should be remembered, was the primary consultant to Enron Corporation, the recent pinnacle of corporate fraud and greed.)

But the fact is that the SAT, according to a score of statisticians, undergraduate and graduate deans, and psychologists including testing specialist Richard Atkinson, president of the University of California system, has virtually *no predictive value*. In his book, Peter Sacks (1999) names more than a dozen key studies showing this failure. Even the mammoth Educational Testing Service—administering the test to two million students in 2000 (almost half of all high school graduates that year)—regularly issues disclaimers, albeit in tiny print, to campuses about the test's predictive limitations and the inadvisability of setting a rigid cutoff score in the admissions process. The sole scientific claim of the SAT makers is that their test will predict a narrow target—*first-year* grades for college students—but in fact it does *not* even do that. "The SAT according to psychologist Claude Steele, measures only about 18 percent, an estimate range from seven percent to twenty-five percent, of the things that it takes to do well" during the first year of college. An analogy would be to choose only those basketball players getting the highest number of *free throws* out of ten throws to make up a team. This would be silly because much more is involved in playing basketball. Likewise, far more is involved in succeeding in the first and all other years of college and, of course, after graduation (Steele, 2001a).

The SAT is especially unreliable in one area: The test consistently *underestimates* the ability of women and stigmatized minorities, who typically succeed in college at higher rates than the tests say they "should," according to testing experts as well as practitioners such as college deans. In other words, the test is not actually a standardized test that is fair to everyone. Far from it. The underestimation of women and minorities causes admission committees to make enormous mistakes and often prompts students themselves to lower their sails: "The evidence [from national studies] strongly suggests that students adjust their college expectations" based on their tests scores and that those receiving disappointing scores "apply to less competitive colleges and universities than their grades [and abilities] would warrant" (Connor and Vargyas, 1992, p. 20). In other words, tragic conclusions and actions flow from the test scores. "The misuse of standardized tests has been the worst enemy of minorities," maintains Rice University applied mathematics professor Richard Tapia. Tapia points out that his university has established broader admissions criteria and finds that undergraduate and graduate minority and women students on his campus, despite their lower standardized test scores, do as well in their grade point averages and retention rates as those with much higher scores (quoted in "Wanted," 1998, p. 1270). (By the way, most women and colonized minorities seem to be spooked by high-stakes testing *situations* because of the stereotypical threats and stigma looming over them, as I will discuss a bit later in this chapter.)

Like hundreds of other colleges, Bates College in Maine since 1969 has chosen the optional-SAT route. Doing so has made its applicant pool far more inclusive: Twice as many women as men choose not to submit their scores to the college; sixty percent of African-American students do not; *economically poor students* in Maine do not. Bates has found that it can now draw in a diverse and highly qualified group of students who do *unquestionably well* during their college careers and thereafter. Recently, hundreds of colleges and universities have made the SAT optional, with many others reexamining whether they should use standardized tests at all. In fact, the University of California system, led by Atkinson, is abandoning the SAT.

The Educational Testing Service, nevertheless, relentlessly promotes the SAT to every kind of college and university as the only "objective" test of a student applicant's academic merit or aptitude. In newspaper articles about the SAT, invariably an ETS spokesperson bemoans the fact that campuses are thinking of giving up their only "objective" measure of students! (Underlying this ETS stock line is the clear implication and inference that a score, because it is a *number*, is objective!) Most colleges and universities, unfortunately and naively, still buy this argument even when confronted with numerous national studies showing the worthlessness of the measuring tool and with dozens of individual departments and schools demonstrating that there is no correlation between the scores of their majority and minority students and those same students' grades, graduation rates, and success after college. Why? Perversely, many institutions still use the SAT because it is a cheap screening device for sorting through thousands of applications and making swift decisions about admission, scholarships, and financial aid.

In various public forums while she was president of Mount Holyoke College, Joanne Creighton characterized SAT scores as unnecessary "affirmative action" for the affluent white students who typically score the highest (1997, p. A15), usually because in their suburban or private high schools they have taken Advanced Placement courses that help them on the test, because they have also enrolled in costly SAT-prep courses offered by private corporations, and because the stereotype of competence surrounds them during the testing situation. Someone else has observed that the "Volvo principle" manifests itself: Every increase of ten thousand dollars in a white applicant's parental income correlates with an additional thirty points in the SAT score. While majority students can expect to do well on the SAT, stigmatized minority students can expect to do poorly.

Graduate Record Examination   Much the same situation exists in graduate admissions. Graduate departments across the country depend on GRE scores to quickly sort applications. It matters little or not at all that the test, like the SAT, is unsound. I work with a doctoral faculty member from a highly regarded university who has disgustedly quipped: "Tell me the student applicant's *height*. That number would be more helpful for admission decisions than the exalted GRE score. We British educators cannot believe how gullible Americans are about the GRE score." Bryn Mawr College's Neal Abraham, Harvard University's Howard Georgi, and other distinguished scientists began in the 1990s to campaign against use of the GRE because of its predictive invalidity. Despite this invalidity, some admissions committees according to Georgi, continue to find the score very convenient and "very seductive" (quoted in "How Not to Choose a Physicist," 1966, p. 710).

When a graduate department chooses to use the GRE score in its decision-making, it is inadvertently choosing to mismeasure and underestimate the intellectual promise of many talented and motivated students, especially white women and U.S. domestic minorities. Thus, departments themselves are responsible for narrowing and segregating their graduate school enrollments and especially in narrowing and segregating the composition of the scientific workforce. So, too, are federal agencies like the National Science Foundation, when they allow review panels to weigh GRE scores in deciding which student applicants will receive doctoral-study fellowships or other funding from federal agencies. (Although I understand anecdotally that some NSF review panels are finally beginning to take a skeptical view of GRE scores.)

Standardized test scores should *not* be used by academic gatekeepers in making decisions about admissions and financial aid. Drawing on his own professional experience in teaching and supervising doctoral graduate students, Brown University physicist Robert Brandenberger observes: "There is little correlation between GRE scores and later success as a scientist. Those being tested by the GRE must race against the clock, decide on pat answers, and do this in isolation." These test conditions differ radically from scholarly and research conditions: "Real research, by contrast, requires imagination, in-depth working and thinking with others, and grappling with questions that have no answers" (personal correspondence, 1998). The GRE is "virtually useless from a prediction standpoint," according to a meta-analysis (in the highly regarded journal, *Educational and Psychological Measurement*) of more than twenty studies covering over five thousand test takers from 1955 through 1992. "When this finding is coupled with studies suggesting that performance on the GRE is age-, gender-, and race-specific . . . the use of this test as a determinant of graduate admission becomes even more questionable," the authors conclude (quoted in P. Sacks, 1999, p. 277). National Academy of Sciences president Bruce Alberts likewise disparages standardized, multiple-choice, timed tests because the tests measure nothing important and because they spoil the enjoyment and thrill of science and critical thinking for countless students, majority and minority (Alberts, 1997).

Tests Serve the Interests of America's Elite Law professors Lani Guinier and Susan Sturm worry that American power-holders continue to confuse a paper-and-pencil "testocracy" with a true meritocracy. They are especially concerned about minorities and low-income majority students who predictably get low scores on standardized tests and then suffer the penalties—in academia, social life, and the workplace—as well as diminishment of their self-esteem and ambitions. The two convincingly argue that these tests function as old-fashioned *poll taxes* because of their chilling and undemocratic purpose and effect: to exclude certain stigmatized groups (Guinier and Sturm, 2001; Sturm and Guinier, 1996). Like poll taxes, standardized tests are used as a very effective—but nonetheless very unfair—screen. As the authors of *Inequality by Design* explain, certain U.S. minority groups, just like low-caste groups *around the world*, predictably score lower because of socioeconomic deprivation, segregation, and most especially, accumulation of *stigma* (Fischer et al., 1996, p. 202; also see chapter 3 of this book).

Guinier and Sturm, psychologist Howard Gardner, and other experts have outlined more complex and reliable "portfolio" measures that should be used instead of timed, paper-and-pencil tests, but having these adopted will be a fierce struggle because of the stranglehold now enjoyed by ETS and other big testing companies. Standardized tests are the foundation on which the pseudo-meritocracy of U.S. schools is built, according to Nicholas Lemann's *The Big Test: The Secret History of the American Meritocracy* (1999) and David Berliner and Bruce Normally's *The Manufactured Crisis: Myths, Fraud and the Attack on America's Public Schools* (1995). The ubiquitous testing in this country serves "the interests of America's elite, further stratifying the society by race and socioeconomic class; second, the companies that produce, administer, score, and coach for standardized tests of all types have gotten rich off the nation's testing habit," argues Peter Sacks in *Standardized Minds: The High Price of American's Testing Culture and What We Can Do to Change It* (1999, pp. 2–3).

Clearly, to evaluate students using a much broader range of characteristics will require engaging more admissions staff and faculty in a more time-consuming process. As one critic has pointed out, if campuses can afford big sports stadiums, they can certainly afford fair admissions processes. In fact, some campuses have begun hiring retired faculty and other educators to lend them a hand in processing more comprehensive and fairer applications from students.

Far more than any other country, the United States relies on a single numerical score to indicate a student's competence, ability, and promise. To my mind, this "bean counter's" worship of one invalid number seems un-American—that is, it runs counter to the ideals we hold about equal opportunity for citizens to develop their talents and have a decent chance to work hard and show their mettle. To be fair, the measures we use will have to be complex and far more comprehensive—we can no longer afford to worship a pseudo-objective number.

Yet foes of affirmative action in education want the opposite. They demand even greater reliance on standardized test scores because they believe test scores are the true measure of "merit." In their view, the academic meritocracy must be built on two objective numbers and two numbers only: a student's grade point average earned from the previous educational institution and, especially, the student's standardized test score. In their view, the student receiving the higher number should win admission. If a student with a lower number, such as a white woman or stigmatized minority, wins admission, then they claim to have evidence of "reverse discrimination" against majority students. Significantly, reliance on numbers undergirds lawsuits brought by the National Center for Individual Rights and other conservative outfits on behalf of several majority students. These anti–affirmative action cases hinge on a flawed assumption: that standardized tests are sound and tell us something important and reliable.

The All-Important Cultural Context of Tests Stanford psychologist Claude Steele has brilliantly identified the "cloud of suspicion" and the "stereotype threat" that make African-Americans and other stigmatized minorities *panic and slow down* as they take timed, standardized, multiple-choice tests. This panic is the very opposite of how they should proceed in order to maximize their test scores, but they typically cannot help clutching and becoming overly careful. Steele theorizes that stigmatized minorities are dealing with a *debilitating cultural context* that majority students do not have to concern themselves with. Stigmatized minorities are all too aware of the widespread belief that they are inferior in intelligence and academic abilities. Thus, as they take the high-stakes, timed tests, they fear that they will *reinforce* the negative stereotype. Laboring under such a psychological overload, they clutch and stumble and do indeed fulfill the prophecy. They do poorly because they are conscientious students determined to do well. "Only those who care about how well they perform ever feel the pressure of stereotype threat," explains *New Yorker* writer Malcolm Gladwell. To admonish these conscientious students to "work harder and take the test more seriously would only make their problems worse." Clearly, standardized tests do not fairly measure students under stereotypical threat. "Sometimes a poor test score is the sign not of a poor student but of a good one," Gladwell asserts (2000, p. 92). In fact, Steele has discovered that stereotype threat *most seriously impairs* stigmatized minority students who are the *most invested* in doing well and are the most accomplished, confident, and ambitious (Steele, 2000, 2001a and b). The SAT's stereotype threat unravels the most promising students! What a waste! There can be no doubt that the *wider cultural context and symbolism* of both the test and the test situation make a great deal of difference about who will do well and who will not.

As a further illustration, University of Connecticut law professor Angel Oquendo recalls how intimidated he felt as he took the SAT as a high school senior in Puerto Rico. In the first place, "a test that measures aptitude can make you feel insecure and challenged" (notice the *common* and tragic misperception that SAT is measuring innate worthiness). But for a Puerto Rican student, the test had another kind of psychological significance: "It symbolized America's continuing dominion and control over Puerto Rico." He realized that he "was being tested by the people who kept us [Puerto Rico] afloat with their massive economic support, who from afar made important decisions for us, and who generally were successful where we had failed" (Oquendo, 1998, p. 61; also see chapter 3 about colonized minority groups). Oquendo's sensitivity about this cultural domination was heightened when he was required to complete a racial profile before the test could officially begin!

Steele has demonstrated that the cultural context of a high-stakes test can indeed be manipulated either to intimidate students or to puff them up. The social psychologist ran a series of experiments and found that he could, in a way, "spook" (this is my word) various groups of math students if he told them they were not expected to do well on an upcoming test. Conversely, he could pump up other groups of students by telling them they were indeed expected to do very well.

Here is what Steele did. He told Asian-American students with above-average grades that for some reason Asian Americans did not usually fare well on the upcoming math test but that European-American students did. The prophecy was fulfilled: Although the Asian Americans had competencies very similar to the European-American students, they did appreciably worse. Switching the experiment, Steele told another group of European-American students that for some reason students from their background did not usually fare well on the next math test but that Asian Americans did. The prophecy was again fulfilled: The European-American students, even with very similar competencies, did poorly.

When Steele told European-American *women* students they were expected to do better on a particular math test than European-American men students, they did indeed score much higher than the similarly situated men. Should the importance of the psychological context surprise us? After all, coaches and athletes understand the importance of mental confidence in individual and team contests—and Steele's work suggests that academic performance on timed, multiple-choice tests can also be dramatically affected by either psychological pumping up or deflating (Steele, 2000, 2001a and b; Steele and Aronson 1995).

Self-Screening Because of Standardized Tests   According to school reformer Deborah Meier, the low SAT scores almost inevitably earned by stigmatized minority students in high school do long-term damage: "The wound to children's confidence and self-respect is enormous. . . .

Attacking the testmakers doesn't relieve the [youths'] burden of self-doubt" (1995, p. 159). In my own work, I have observed that most minority students are predictably frustrated and demoralized because they have done poorly on the GRE and other such tests. (Yet they are highly motivated and gifted students.) Very few have the chutzpah to quickly shrug off the wound. In fact, many dramatically scale back their academic and professional ambitions in the face of poor performance on the tests believed by most in U.S. society to be trustworthy and objective. In Steele's words, these students come to "dis-identify" with the academic domain (Steele and Aronson 1995; Steele 2000 and 2001a and b). Physicist Georgi in several public forums has explained why he, too, believes the GRE does enormous damage. Georgi observes that many of his talented women students shelve the idea of going to graduate school because they both fear and despise the multiple-choice, race-against-time, "macho" character of the GRE. Rather than submit to the GRE, the students choose a career path that does not involve the GRE—this is another example of self-screening. Such self-screening will predictably happen at a much *earlier* age because of a new development on the horizon.

High-Stakes Tests for Younger Students   Throughout the country, states have begun requiring high-stakes, standardized, paper-and-pencil, timed tests for all students in elementary and high school; a number of states hold back the high school diploma until the test is passed. In the face of doing poorly or even *before* they do poorly on the tests, some minority students will predictably drop out of school—a very drastic form of self-screening and self-protection. In fact, this is happening. Author of *Subtractive Schooling: U.S.-Mexican Youth and the Politics of Caring,* University of Texas professor Angela Valenzuela deflates the "Texas miracle." That state's approach to testing (which is serving as a model for the nation) has caused the *dropout rate of minorities to increase.* Valenzuela, in *Hispanic Outlook,* explains that the Houston test scores are improving largely because schools often switch low-performing students to special-education or bilingual-education tracks or use other test-exempting diversions. In the meantime, the city's dropout rate—one of the absolute worst of the nation's one hundred largest school systems—steadily rises (quoted in Alicea, 2001, pp. 7–10).

To use high-stakes, multiple-choice, timed tests is a *bad practice.* Such tests, purporting to measure students' intellectual worth, thicken the cloud of inferiority and stigma over certain students—and will quicken their self-screening and dropping out of high school. Misguided state legislators and school officials should find other ways to hold *schools* accountable and improve all students' learning outcomes.

B-4. Disadvantage: Marginalized minorities usually are relegated to poor schools that have the effect of keeping them in the lowest social strata and chilling their ambitions.

Advantage: Majorities usually attend resource-rich schools that have the effect of keeping them in higher social strata and enhancing their ambitions.

It would be naive to assume that most minority faculty, especially U.S. stigmatized minority faculty, have benefited from the same secondary school preparation that most majority faculty have. And it would be naive to gloss over the fact that many minorities begin their postsecondary education in community colleges. These two facts about prior educational experiences are very relevant.

Two-thirds of minority students *still* attend predominantly minority elementary and high schools in rural areas and central cities that are basically unequal, separate, and impoverished—a startling fact that must be grasped, argues Professor Linda Darling-Hammond (1998, p. 29). Despite court cases such as *Mendez v. Westminster School District* (1945), *Delgado v. Bastrop Independent School District* (1948), and *Brown v. Board of Education* (1954), these schools largely serving minorities are substandard and operate on the assumption that "only a few students will be successful" (Rendon, 1996, p. 12). Disparities in school funding remain dramatic after decades of failed reform, points out Darling-Hammond: "The wealthiest 10 percent of U.S. school districts spend nearly 10 times more than the poorest 10 percent, and spending rations of 3 to 1 are common within states." She underscores the simplistic and cruel implication that is usually drawn: "Despite stark differences in funding, teacher quality, curriculum, and class sizes, the prevailing view is that if students do not achieve, it is their own fault" (Darling-Hammond, 1998, p. 28).

William Ayers uses the example of the Chicago public schools to show that "all the structures of privilege and oppression apparent in the larger society are mirrored in our schools." The State of Illinois, for instance, has created in effect two "parallel" school systems: The one outside the inner cities is "privileged, adequate, successful, and largely white; the other disadvantaged in countless ways, disabled, starving, failing, and African-American." The disabled and failing schools in Chicago and other urban areas are reserved for "children of color and children of the poor" (Ayers, 2000, p. 66). It should be noted that these failing schools for minorities and the poor are almost always huge in size and staffed by underqualified and overwhelmed teachers. Darling-Hammond maintains that decades of research have shown that students' learning and academic achievement can be consistently boosted by small *school* size (three hundred to five hundred students) and small *class* size, which allow students to be known and to have trusting relationships with teachers; by a stimulating curriculum; and by highly qualified teachers. Minority schools usually have none of these (Darling-Hammond, 1998, p. 30). Jonathan Kozol dramatizes this tragic situation in *Savage Inequalities: Children in America's Schools* (1991).

Community colleges, as the lowest rung on the higher education ladder, are also reserved mainly for minorities and the poor. Educational rhetoric holds that community colleges are a wonderful entry point, especially for minorities, in obtaining higher education and social and economic mobility. But a closer look shows that most community colleges have "the overall effect or reproducing existing class and racial differences," according to Berkeley sociologist Jerome Karabel. He has found that attending a community college *discourages* a student from transferring to a four-year campus for a bachelor's degree. His and others' studies have conclusively shown that "otherwise similar students (in terms of educational aspirations, social background, academic ability, and other relevant individual characteristics) are more likely to complete the B.A. if they initially enroll in four-year institutions." In addition, attendance at community college often has a "negative effect" and economic penalty on students' occupational choices and workforce wages. In other words, talented minority and poor students are being segregated and tracked once again—this time, into community colleges, where their already low economic and social status will be reinforced (Karabel, 1986, pp. 13–18).

What should community colleges be doing? Arizona State University professor Laura Rendon believes community colleges should not be producing workers for "low-level, short-term, dead-end jobs" but instead helping students—whether in vocational or academic classes—dream big dreams, broaden the array of careers they are considering, and develop their own critical-thinking skills so they can become empowered learners and workers in a democracy (1999, p. 202). Unfortunately, not many community college classrooms are settings for such transforming education.

There is ample evidence that schools and colleges, for the most part, are *not* the great equalizer between haves and have-nots—most especially if the have-nots are stigmatized minorities caught in a castelike system. Look at the example of Mexican Americans in the Southwest. In the public schools, Mexican-American youth are treated by teachers and officials, consciously or unconsciously, as "conquered" minorities who are expected to fail because they are inferior, according to a College Entrance Examination Board study by Thomas Carter and Roberto Segura. The teachers, counselors, and principals automatically assume that these students are marked for menial jobs after they finish or (more likely) drop out of school. In short, the school personnel devalue the prospects of these students. Clearly absent is a genuine financial incentive for Mexican Americans to gain educational credentials—that is, if the credentials are not likely to bring them desirable jobs, then why should they obtain these credentials?

By contrast, in the same school the European-American offspring of the dominant social group can bank on genuine financial rewards for their educational credentials; they are nurtured by teachers who expect them, after graduation, to assume their rightful roles as leaders, owners of capital, and managers of other workers. Maintaining the current social order—the castelike, low status of Mexican Americans together with the castelike, high status of majority students—is clearly the barely hidden curriculum of these majority schools in the Southwest, according to the study (Carter and Segura, 1979).

The curriculum described by Carter and Segura remains intact, in the view of University of Colorado law professor Richard Delgado, who underscores that Mexican-American youth in 2000 had one of the highest high school dropout rates of any ethnic group, with *close to one-half* leaving school in the Southwest. Unemployment for Mexican Americans is twice that of European Americans; very, very few Mexican Americans manage to secure professional and high-paying trade jobs. Where Mexican Americans are overrepresented is in *prisons*, due to the disproportionately harsh sentences they receive (Delgado, 1998a, p. 284; also see studies of Puerto Rican youth by Weinberg, 1977, and Nieto, 2000).

Despite the familiar mythologizing of schools and colleges as the great equalizers in American society, these institutions in the United States and indeed in any country almost always *reproduce* the existing economic and social pecking order and reaffirm the culture of the dominant group, according to influential scholars (Tierney, 1992; Giroux, 1992, 1997; Stanton-Salazar, 1997, 2000; Bourdieu, 1977). Schools and colleges are usually not agents for widespread change, no matter how painstakingly they are gilded with inspiring rhetoric. They are, in fact, elitist in their history and mostly remain so, despite liberal assumptions to the contrary and in spite of the hard work of school reformers.

A kind of planned deprivation marks most public schools serving stigmatized minorities. A score of analysts—including Jonathan Kozol and Pulitzer prize winner Ron Suskind in *Hope in the Unseen* (1998)—have highlighted how underfunded, understaffed, overcrowded, and inhumane are typical schools for inner-city African-Americans and other minorities. While minority students in these inferior schools sometimes lack even textbooks, that does not stop the state education authorities from expecting the students to answer questions on state-imposed standardized tests related to the subject matter of those non-existent books. What madness is this? Clearly, unfortunate students are being victimized by poor schools and misguided state officials.

Catching Up   For minorities intent on becoming professionals, they must often work doubly hard to catch up if they attended "planned-deprivation" schools and colleges. Many of the minority students and faculty I deal with have indeed caught up, by drawing on incredible stores of willpower, intelligence, and persistence. As Rice University math educator Richard Tapia has said, there is "no magic": The minority doctoral scholars in his highly successful program usually devote two extra years on average to catching up and to filling in gaps in their schooling (personal conversation, 1999). Low-income majority students attending inferior schools must do the same in order to truly progress. What deserves celebrating, of course, is these students' intellectual progress fired by fierce determination.

Psychologist Steele recognizes that sometimes students, in particular minority students from inferior schools, do have to catch up. But he advises faculty and department chairs to frame their "scaffolding" feedback carefully as they talk with students about their gaps. Here are his suggestions: "This department [or this professor] has high standards. So far your work is not meeting these standards but we believe you can and we plan to help you." Or: "You are a talented person but you are somewhat behind at this point. We want to help you accelerate and catch up" (Steele, 2000). The goals are to avoid humiliating a student who may have had a steady diet of belittling attitudes about his/her intellectual capacities as well as to prevent the student from "dis-identifying" with the domain of school and higher education (Steele and Aronson 1995, p. 809; Steele 2000).

CONCLUSION

Minority faculty must often cope with complex interpersonal dynamics within their majority departments and campuses. These disadvantages, such as having their scholarship routinely devalued, were highlighted in chapter 1. But minorities also find that in the world outside academia, their professional credentials and hard work often count for *far less* than the same credentials and hard work of majorities. The negative mind-sets possessed by some majority power-holders are manifested in several ways: police harassment of certain minorities and their families; exclusion from powerful insider networks; and exclusion from government programs and labor unions that would help the faculty and their offspring accumulate real estate and wealth. Moreover, to earn their doctorates and become professors, many minorities have had to withstand the psychological and intellectual harm done by standardized tests and poor schools. The harm they have sustained is strikingly disproportionate to that suffered by majorities.

CHAPTER 3

EXTRA DISADVANTAGES FOR
COLONIZED MINORITIES

NOT ALL MINORITY GROUPS POSSESS the same standing and regard from the dominant group in power. Immigrant minorities, inside and outside academia, frequently enjoy higher status in the eyes of the majority group than do internal colonized minorities who are in this country because of force, not choice. This chapter will discuss *how* and *why* colonized minorities face greater disadvantages inside and outside academia. Again, I believe it is critically important that senior administrators and faculty attend to the different cultural contexts and histories inhabited by their new faculty hires and indeed by all their colleagues and students. Only willful naïveté would permit one to think that everyone is dealt the same context and status.

Listen to the following observations made frequently in high schools, colleges, universities, and newsrooms throughout the country. These remarks throw into relief how certain groups of minorities can be so differently regarded and treated, particularly in academic settings.

- *Why can't our domestic minority faculty—whose people have been here for ages—do as well as our international faculty? The international faculty I've known never complain; they work hard; they're polite and show old-fashioned deference to authority figures. They're models, in my mind. No wonder my department prefers to have them as faculty colleagues and graduate students.*
- *Hector, who has been here in Texas only five years, came from Guatemala with absolutely nothing and didn't even speak English. Well, he has done terrifically well in my college program. If*

> *he can do it, why can't our local Mexican Americans even man-*
> *age to stay in high school and graduate? What's going on here? I*
> *don't get it.*

- *I grew up in an affluent Connecticut suburb in the 1960s. Secure*
  behind old stone walls and trimmed hedges, safeguarded by bur-
  glar alarms, this was a world far removed from any discussion of
  race. It was a world of good schools, safe streets and perfect teeth.
  . . . In this world, people of color were the ones who came to your
  house to work, and they worked hard . . . [but] the better jobs
  went to the plumbers, the electricians, the painters: people from
  the ethnic white working class of the town, most of them Italian.
  . . . There were also a few Black kids at the school, but almost no
  one knew them. . . . Everyone liked them, wondered how they did
  it, but most thanked God every day that they had been born white
  (Correspondents of *The New York Times*, 2001, pp. 335–36).

- *Well, I'm from Jamaica and at first I wondered why most*
  African-Americans I met here were sort of shell-shocked. But let
  me tell you, now that I'm confused with them, I've had a taste of
  non-stop discrimination and diminishment for three years as
  an assistant professor. My confidence is definitely slipping as a
  scholar and teacher. How do you think I can reverse this feeling?

- *My folks came from Cuba but I've always lived in America. I*
  honestly don't think I've really been discriminated against on
  this or any other campus. I don't know why Puerto Ricans have
  such a big chip on their shoulders. I sometimes think they should
  stop all the complaining and just work harder.

- *The blacks from Africa [international students] on campus . . .*
  had deep contempt for their American black brothers. At that time,
  to be anything was better than being Negro. The college commu-
  nity, too, showed deference to the more exotic blacks from Africa.
  They took them home as houseguests, to restaurants. . . . These
  amenities and opportunities given African-born blacks only rein-
  forced their negative attitudes toward American blacks who were
  denied these experiences (Moore and Wagstaff, 1974, p. 20; also
  see C. Williams, 2001, p. 26, for a description of the disdain that
  African students often held for African-American students).

A. NOT ALL MINORITY GROUPS SHARE THE SAME CULTURAL STATUS AND CONTEXT: DIFFERENCES BETWEEN COLONIZED AND IMMIGRANT MINORITIES

The above observations and questions underscore that not all minority groups are alike—even though a folk myth holds that they are. Why

are certain minority groups more likely to be accepted and respected by the majority group at our colleges and universities? Why do some minority groups encounter higher obstacles and more hostility than other groups? Why are some more likely to resent the inequities they see and experience in educational settings and other contexts? Why do teachers and professors often believe that students from some groups possess good prospects for future success and students from other groups decidedly awful prospects?

To begin grappling with these large questions, I will draw a distinction—based on the research and writing of a number of distinguished cultural anthropologists, economists, novelists, educational researchers, political scientists, lawyers, and sociologists—between *immigrant/voluntary* minorities and *colonized/involuntary* minorities. I rely on a number of thinkers, but especially on Berkeley sociologist Robert Blauner, who in 1972 published a stunning analysis entitled "Colonized and Immigrant Minorities." For the insights below, I also thank Alvarez; Berreman; Brown; Bruner; Carter and Segura; Cruz; Cummins; DeVos; DeVos and C. Lee; Fischer et al.; Franklin; Gibson; Grosfoguel and Georas; Jacobson; Y. Lee; Markus, Steele and Steele; Martinez; Matute-Bianchi; Montero-Sieburth; Nieto; Ogbu; Oquendo; Powell; R. Rodriguez; Shibutani and Kwan; Shorris; Steele; Suarez-Orozco; Takaki; Vélez-Ibáñez; Waters; C. Williams; Wu; and Yetman (complete citations are in the bibliography). Even though these experts and a host of other novelists, scholars, and journalists have reminded us that the immigrant model for this country is shortsighted and obscures the stigmatized status of several minority groups, the model continues to be invoked, especially by U.S. presidents who claim "we are all immigrants" and all enjoy the fruits of American democracy and strive for the American dream.

Immigrant, Voluntary Minorities

Voluntary minorities are immigrants who have *chosen* to relocate in the United States—or any other society—because they desire a better future: more money, more opportunities for themselves and their children, higher social standing, safety and relief from political war or religious persecution. Immigrants believe they are making a fresh start. They typically possess an abundance of *hope* despite encountering, at least at first, daunting economic exploitation from the majority group in power. Examples of voluntary minorities in the United States include immigrants from Africa, China, India, Japan, Korea, India, Central and South America, and the Caribbean (Jamaica, Trinidad, and the Dominican Republic).

As immigrants, voluntary minorities predictably contrast their lot in the host country with the troubles and economic deprivation they left behind. Despite the sometimes enormous struggles tied to resettling and deciphering how to establish oneself in an unfamiliar and not always welcoming society, immigrants are usually pleased to be in the new country and show willingness to adopt some of the majority group's behaviors and mind-sets in order to succeed in school and the workplace. Typically, the children of immigrant minorities are deferential to school authorities. Yet these minorities (especially the parents) usually draw a line at some point and resist giving up what they regard as essential parts of their original culture. In short, if they have come to this country, for instance, they will usually *accommodate* but not *assimilate* to the majority European-American culture and its mores. Furthermore, immigrant minorities in the United States usually believe—with fierceness—that they or their children should acquire academic credentials in order to gain affluence and a better life. Their mantra holds that hard work, following the rules, and securing solid educational credentials will lead them to success.

In his autobiography, Colin Powell, U.S. secretary of state in President George W. Bush's administration and head of the Joint Chief of Staffs in the previous Bush administration, captures vividly the psychological advantage and cultural context he enjoys. Powell's parents voluntarily moved here from Jamaica. Although he himself was born in New York City, he—like his parents and his extended family—regards himself as an immigrant who takes great pride in having roots in the homeland of Jamaica. He explains:

> My Black ancestors may have been dragged to Jamaica in chains, but they were not dragged to the United States. Mom and Pop chose to emigrate to this country for the same reason that Italians, Irish, and Hungarians did, to seek better lives for themselves and their children. That is a far different emotional and psychological beginning than that of American Blacks, whose ancestors were brought here in chains. (1995, p. 23)

Colonized, Involuntary Minorities

By contrast, *colonized, involuntary* minorities are people who were originally brought into this or any other country *against their will*—through slavery, conquest, colonization, or forced labor—and who understandably interpret their presence as coerced on them by the majority group in the society. Think, for instance, of American Indians in this country. Many of their ancestors were subjected to physical and cultural annihilation. Those who remain are kept at the margins of the mainstream society and predictably encounter very high barriers to economic and political autonomy.

Colonization depends on conquest together with the powerful imposition of new institutions and the *denigration* of the conquered people's cultural practices and even humanity. Generation after generation, colonized minorities find that their ancestors' violent entry to this country continues to undercut their own status and relation with the majority culture and negatively influence their daily lives. Generation after generation, they feel oppressed and see their religions, their native languages, their intellectual abilities, and their substantial contributions to the development of the country underestimated or scorned. Colonized minorities routinely measure and compare their own economic and social status with that of majority-group members. In this comparison, they find that their status is almost always lower. If they are in the United States, they often feel that the American dream—upward social mobility and wealth—is for others but not for them. Their reservoir of hope cannot match that of immigrants. Contrary to the U.S. majority group's rhetoric about equal opportunity, internally colonized minorities see ample evidence that educational credentials will *not* lead *them* to attractive jobs and accumulation of wealth and status. Generation after generation, they hit a low ceiling that frustrates their advancement in academia and then in the workplace. While they believe that individual effort, education, and hard work are important, they also believe it is simply not strong enough to overcome built-in discrimination and oppression. Understandably, some children of colonized minorities can become depressed and oppositional in their attitude toward the majority group and its schools (Carter, 1970; Carter and Segura, 1979; DeVos, 1992; Cummins, 1986; Massey and Denton, 1993; Gibson, 1987, 1988, 1991; Ogbu, 1978, 1991, 1992; Steele, 1992; Nieto, 2000; Suskind, 1998; Suarez-Orozco, 1987; Waters, 1999).

Yet it is certainly true that some colonized minorities succeed in traditional institutions—despite at times crushing odds—and bring leadership to educational settings, the workplace, and various musical, religious, cinematic, philanthropic, and community-building arenas. Others channel their opposition and frustration into political activism: They seek to enlighten, protest, and organize in order to ensure that the United States lives up to its democratic ideals. Past and current examples include the antilynching campaigns mobilized by African-American churches and sorority women; the creation of minority-serving schools and colleges; the establishment and work of the National Association for the Advancement of Colored People and the Urban League; the mutual aid societies organized by Mexican Americans; the Chicano, Native Hawaiian, and American Indian political and student movements; the campaigns for Indian tribal sovereignty;

the struggle to unionize Mexican-American garment workers, miners, and agricultural workers; the mentoring of male youth by members of the numerous "100 Black Men of America" chapters; the political efforts and lawsuits to secure monetary reparations from corporations that benefited from slavery; and of course the civil rights movement. Still other minorities transform the pain and adversity they face into a visionary and poetic wisdom. This wisdom, according to Professor Ricardo Stanton-Salazar at the University of Southern California (personal correspondence, 2001), "has been best described by Gloria Anzaldúa in her book, *Borderlands* [1987], as a '*mestiza* consciousness.' Such a consciousness produces enormous creativity and the ability to see beyond old paradigms of thinking and behaving."

In the United States, colonized minorities include several groups: American Indians; Alaska Natives; Native Hawaiians; Mexican Americans, the original settlers of the American Southwest; Puerto Rican Americans; and African Americans. In other countries, examples include Algerians in France; the Catholic Irish in Great Britain; the Burakumin caste in Japan as well as Koreans living in that country; the Maoris, aboriginal people in New Zealand; and Maya Indians in Mexico (DeVos, 1967a-b, 1992; Gibson, 1987, 1988, 1991; DeVos and C. Lee, 1981; Y. Lee, 1991; Matute-Bianchi, 1989, 1991; Ogbu, 1978, 1991, 1992; Ogbu and Simons, 1998).

Cross-cultural studies have shown that it is far more psychologically draining for minorities to live in the same country where the dominant group has invaded, subordinated, decimated, or colonized their ancestors and where they themselves continue to have painful interactions with their former colonizers or enslavers. Puerto Rican Americans have had to live with such a legacy. In his splendid book *Latinos: A Biography of the People*, Earl Shorris explains: "Puerto Rico has been a colony for almost five hundred years ... in no remembered, recorded time did the people of Puerto Rico control their destiny; they have always belonged to someone, been a possession." Following the U.S. invasion of the island in 1898, Spain transferred its colonial dominion over the area to the victor. Becoming a possession-by-force of the United States did not, of course, allow Puerto Ricans to escape "the monolith of their history" and "the prison of colonialism." Their travel back and forth between the island and the mainland, while voluntary, cannot be characterized as immigration. They "remain colonized" as second-class citizens (Shorris, 1992, p. 144). Like other oppressed groups named above, they were engulfed by the dominant group; Puerto Ricans "became an underclass, systematically perceived and treated as a conquered people" (Oquendo, p. 70; also see Grosfoguel and Georas 2000).

In startling contrast, refugees and immigrants from nearby Cuba enjoyed preferential treatment and enviable status when they entered the United States. They were not, of course, colonized by the majority group. On the contrary, they were welcomed to the American dream with open arms. Because of the cold war and the U.S. government's fierce competition with communism, federal officials took unusual steps to ensure that the highly educated Cubans fleeing Fidel Castro's Communist regime would succeed impressively here. The Cuban refugees received subsidies (such as generous European-like welfare payments, special Small Business Administration loans, and special housing) that were *never* extended to Puerto Ricans, African Americans, and others. The U.S. government deemed it vital for Cubans to acquire substantial social capital and social mobility so that their success could be quickly broadcast to the world (Grosfoguel and Georas, 2000).

Is the United States the only country where colonized, involuntary minority groups can be found? Unfortunately, no. Looking to another part of the world will give us valuable cross-cultural insights. It may be surprising to learn that Koreans are treated as involuntary, colonized minorities within Japan, despite the popular notion that the two Asian cultures and peoples are similar in many ways. While Koreans settled in the United States, China, or elsewhere enjoy immigrant status, in Japan they have a far more difficult status: They are colonized and stigmatized minorities because of their past history as forced labor at the hands of the dominant Japanese. In 1910, Japan colonized Korea and quickly and systematically began to suppress the Korean language and culture. Hundreds of thousands of Korean men "were dragooned to work in mines and factories" in Japan; Korean women and girls were kidnapped to work as "sex slaves" for the Japanese military (Brender, 2001, p. A40). Although that sad time has passed, the Japanese are still brought up to treat Koreans living among them as outcasts. In schools in Japan, Korean students face low expectations and discrimination from Japanese teachers and contempt from Japanese students. The Korean culture is portrayed as unremittingly inferior in Japanese textbooks. As adults, Koreans face the same discrimination and negative mind-sets from the majority group: They cannot complete for desirable jobs in Japan on the basis of their training and abilities and have an almost impossible task in economically advancing themselves. In fact, in order to get jobs or rental housing, many Koreans adopt Japanese names with the hope that they will "pass" for Japanese (Y. Lee, 1991, p. 155; also see Brender, 2001).

Similarly in the United States, Mexican Americans have been assigned an outcast position. The Mexican-American war in the middle of the nineteenth century transformed the original settlers living in the northern part of Mexico (now California, Texas, Nevada, Utah, Arizona, New Mexico, and portions of Wyoming, Colorado, Kansas, and Oklahoma) into a conquered and "colonized" group within U.S. territory (Martinez, 2001, p. 5; also Alvarez, 1973). Following the war, the Treaty of Guadalupe Hidalgo slyly required the original Mexican owners to defend their land ownership in land courts run by their enemies. According to Vine Deloria Jr., Native American leader and University of Colorado professor, "The Court of Private Claims, established in 1891, by a variety of legal technicalities dispossessed almost all the landowning Mexicans and eliminated the common lands of villages that had been their heritage for centuries." Mexicans lost one half of their homeland. Systematically and ruthlessly, corrupt European-American lawyers and judges used devious means to deprive the natives of their farms and ranches in the Southwest. Usually in one generation, the people were diminished from large and small landowners to "seasonal serfs" working on the farms and ranches of the conqueror (Deloria, 1981, p. 95). In effect, the original settlers became "foreigners in their own land," a theme of dispossession that remains strong today in Mexican-American writings, according to John Chavez in *The Lost Land: The Chicano Image of the Southwest* (1984, p. 43).

To countenance such dispossession, leaders such as Texan Sam Houston embraced the doctrine of Manifest Destiny and argued that Mexicans, like Indians, were patently inferior and thus European-Americans were justified in pushing them off their land in the same methodical and ruthless way they had done to the Indians. To cut back Mexican Americans' political rights, legislators of the majority group hastily passed racial-restriction citizenship laws that reserved U.S. citizenship to whites or those who could pass for white. Mexican Americans, like American Indians and African Americans, were ruthlessly denied their political and civil rights and subjected to Jim Crow segregation laws; the majority group characterized them as polluting and dangerous to associate with. "Ironically, the political privileges [and citizenship] that the Spanish and Mexican governments had previously given people in the Southwest were abolished by the U.S. racial laws. The Mexican *mestizos* and Indians entered a new racial caste-like order," asserts anthropology professor Martha Menchaca (1998, p. 392). Up to the present day, both Mexican Americans living in the Southwest and Mexicans going back and forth across the U.S.-Mexico border have been reduced to the lowest level of worker: *disposable* migrant labor that is first pulled and then pushed according to the needs of the dominant European-American ranchers, farmers, miners, and industrialists. In summary, Mexican Americans occupy a low castelike position wherein they have suffered "economic exploitation, occupational segmentation, social segregation, miseducation, political and legal mistreatment, and cultural and linguistic erasure" (Vélez-Ibáñez, 1996, pp. 86–87; also see Alvarez, 1973).

The following summary captures the essence of what *colonized* minorities and their succeeding generations must deal with:

> Members of a minority, many of whom were brought to the country as slave labor, are at the bottom of the social ladder. They do the dirty work, when they have work. The rest of the society considers them violent and stupid and discriminates against them. Over the years, tension between minority and majority has occasionally broken out in deadly riots. In the past, minority children were compelled to go to segregated schools and did poorly academically. Even now, minority children drop out of school relatively early and often get into trouble with the law. Schools with many minority children are seen as problem-ridden, so majority parents sometimes move out of the school district or send their children to private schools. And, as might be expected, the minority children do worse on standardized tests than majority children do. (Fischer et al., 1996, p. 172)

Most readers would guess that the minority members being described in this passage are African Americans who were brutally dragged to the United States as slaves. In fact, the above details prototypically describe *any* colonized minority in any society. The passage, actually a composite portrait of *Koreans living in Japan*, appears in a book written by several Berkeley sociologists and arises from studies by Yongsook Lee, Changsoo Lee, George DeVos, and Thomas Rohlen. The passage could be applied, in general, to involuntary minorities wherever they are found. Blauner explains: "The colonized became ethnic minorities *en bloc*, collectively, through conquest, slavery, annexation, or a racial labor policy." Their cultural practices and ways of life are to varying degrees decimated, exploited, degraded, and controlled, generation after generation (1972, p. 151).

Implications for U.S. Society Distinctions between colonized and immigrant minorities must be understood because "they have repercussions for the way each group functions in U.S. society," according to Virginia Commonwealth University professor Dulce Cruz (1995, p. 95). As a result of their oppression, colonized minorities have a cultural history and cultural context that is in opposition or resistance to the majority group in the society. Caught in opposition, being on guard against further oppression and devaluation by the majority group and especially its majority schools, and yet eager to make a mark in the world—all this often creates a complex psychological and intellectual maze for involuntary minorities to navigate.

Stanford psychology professor Claude Steele explains that "non-immigrant minorities like blacks and Native Americans have always been here, and thus are entitled, more than new immigrants, to participate in the defining images of the society projected in school." Yet non-immigrant minorities' contributions and leadership in the society are not part of the positive images found in mainstream schools. Therefore Steele says, when schools expect these groups to assimilate in the same ways as immigrants do, they view this expectation as "*a primal insult* [emphasis added]: it asks them to join in something that has made them invisible" (1992, p. 121). Because immigrant minorities lack such an opposing and complex cultural history and context, they usually can approach school and the workplace in a simpler fashion and rightfully expect hard work to pay off in some dependable way (Bruner 1996; Ogbu 1978, 1991, 1992; Kain, 1969; Gibson, 1987, 1988, 1991; Carter and Segura, 1979; Caplan, Whitmore, and Choy, 1989; DeVos 1967a & b, 1992; Franklin, 1991).

Castelike Demeaning of Colonized Minorities   The majority group, according to sociologist George DeVos, predictably insists that colonized minorities are innately flawed and possess "some unalterable biological, religious, social, or cultural inferiority." Conquerors probably rationalize their oppression of others in this way to somehow lessen their own culpability and cruelty. What is even worse, the dominant group sees the conquered group as contaminated. In fact, "the pollution barrier is the most distinguishing feature of any caste society," according to DeVos, who defines a caste society as a "system of institutionalized inequality." The pariah groups are considered innately polluted and prone to moral depravity and intellectual dullness; they can contaminate any "pure" bloodline they marry into. By contrast, the superior group supposedly has more purity and capacity in intellectual, aesthetic, and moral pursuits and must diligently "protect itself" from the inferior group (DeVos, 1967, pp. 266–67).

Castelike Exploitation of Colonized Minorities   Caste systems not only psychologically stigmatize members of the lower castes—they also structurally segregate and economically exploit them. For those at the bottom, there is no social and economic mobility but instead rigidity. Those in the majority take steps to protect themselves from association by raising high barriers to intermarriage, integrated housing and education, and co-equal participation in businesses and the professions, especially at the middle and top levels, according to social anthropologist Gerald Berreman.

In a caste system, the superior group has decidedly greater access to goods, services, and other valued things. Berreman offers a chilling summary of how broadly a caste system reaches: "The ability to influence the behavior of others, the source of one's livelihood, the kind and amount of food, shelter, and medical care, of education, justice, esteem, and pleasure—all of these things which an individual will receive during his life—and the very length of life itself, are determined in large measure by caste status." He continues: "Who may be one's friend, one's wife, one's neighbor, one's master, one's servant, one's client, one's competitor, is largely a matter of caste" (1967, p. 50).

By design, colonized, castelike minorities are kept on the bottom rung of the labor force and the social order. They are not permitted to compete fairly as individuals for any type of job to which they aspire and are educationally qualified; they are viewed as seriously flawed in morals, judgment, and intellect. Remember that Koreans attending Japanese schools are treated as a conquered and despised people. The educational credentials they manage to earn do not bring them proportionately rewarding jobs (Bruner, 1996). In fact, the higher the Koreans' educational attainment, the less their financial payoff. Less than ten percent of Korean college graduates manage to find employment in Japanese companies because the discrimination barrier against them is virtually impenetrable. About fifty percent are employed in financially shaky, small companies owned by Koreans. The remaining forty percent work as laborers, inherit their families' modest businesses, are self-employed, or are unemployed (Y. Lee, 1991). In short, Koreans are trapped in inequality, not only educationally but also socially and financially. This is the *prototypical* situation for castelike minorities, including African Americans, Native Americans, Puerto Rican Americans, Native Hawaiians, and Mexican Americans in this country.

B. ASIAN AMERICANS: IMMIGRANT MINORITIES

Are Koreans and other groups of Asian descent—who now live *in the United States*—immigrant or colonized minorities? The answer, I believe, is immigrant. Certainly Asian Americans have endured intense economic, political, and social discrimination at different times in this country's history (including internment of Japanese Americans in camps during World War II). Nevertheless, those of Asian heritage have usually benefited from being viewed as immigrants and from possessing "extravagant dreams" about what America would hold for them.

Beginning in the middle of the nineteenth century, Chinese and Japanese workers began voluntarily coming to the United States as immigrants intent on acquiring money to send back or take back to their homeland. There is no evidence that they were kidnapped and brought here against their will to work in gold mines in the West, on fruit and vegetable farms, or on construction of the transcontinental railroad, according to Professor Ronald Takaki, a preeminent scholar on Asians and other U.S. immigrants (1987, 1989, 1993). There is, however, abundant evidence that the first Chinese, Japanese, and Korean workers were not only overworked and mistreated by railroad barons and other employers but also taunted verbally and violently by "nativists" in the majority group and in labor unions who resented the new arrivals. Yet the Asian immigrants and their offspring mostly did persist and mostly did succeed economically. In fact, the first Asian workers were capitalists because they willingly chose to come and they brought money with them (albeit small amounts) to invest and parlay into greater wealth (Takaki, 1993, 1989). In addition, some of them formed among themselves their own rotating credit associations, as they had done in their homelands. This was "their principal device for capitalizing small business" and acquiring real estate (Light, 1987, p. 84). The Japanese and Chinese newcomers "found themselves free for new associations and new enterprises" in the new country. "Like the immigrants from Europe, many Asians saw America as a place for a fresh start" and a place to realize their "extravagant dreams" (Takaki, 1989, pp. 18, 66).

From the beginning, Asian Americans in the United States were viewed as immigrants and avoided the *stigma* metaphorically burned onto the foreheads of Mexican Americans, American Indians, and African Americans, who were by force relegated to the lowest rung of the caste system. This point is underscored in *Majority and Minority: The Dynamics of Race and Ethnicity in American Life* (Yetman, 1999) as well as in *Yellow: Race in America beyond Black and White* (Wu, 2002). Asian immigrants, like Italian, Irish, Jewish, Russian, and other immigrants, benefited socially and economically because they were viewed (or came to be viewed) as higher on the chain of being than African Americans and other colonized minorities. When the number of African Americans migrating to the western states during and after World War II far surpassed that of the small Asian population, Asians ironically experienced a lessening of discrimination that "facilitated Asian American socioeconomic mobility." Of course, there was a concomitant increase of discrimination against African Americans that prohibited their advancement (Yetman, 1999, p. 267; also see Wu, 2002).

The first Asian-American chancellor of a leading U.S. university, Chang-Lin Tien of the University of California–Berkeley, has eloquently described how his immigrant background boosted his self-confidence and professional achievement. He explains: "For me, America is the land of opportunity. This is not merely a dream, but my experience. No other nation in the world has welcomed immigrants like me to its shores, offered us first-rate schooling, and then accepted our professional contributions." Climbing the ladder of academic administration, Tien says he "relied on the grand American tradition of democracy and the extraordinary emphasis on equality among women and men as my foundation" (1998, p. 35).

Likewise, the first Chinese-American governor of Washington State, Gary Locke, habitually stresses the greatness of America, where he and his family have thrived despite hardships. "He [the governor] noted in his inaugural address that his grandfather had worked as a houseboy less than a mile from the Capitol grounds. 'It took a hundred years to go one mile,' he said. 'But it's a journey that could only take place in America'" (quoted in Correspondents of *The New York Times*, 2001, p. 121). By contrast, Locke's opponent in the gubernatorial election—Seattle mayor Norm Rice, of African-American ancestry—carefully avoided talking about his origins because voters feel guilty and defensive about slavery. Privately and ruefully, he remarks, "I have a great story about how my family came to America. As good as Gary's. *We just happened to have different travel agents* [emphasis added]" (quoted in Correspondents of *The New York Times*, 2001, p. 126). Governor Locke feels sufficiently comfortable to play up his ethnic pride: European-American voters in his state mostly subscribe to the positive stereotype that Asian immigrants are "clever, diligent or shrewd." But the negative stereotypes about African Americans block Mayor Rice from doing so. In fact, Rice believes he must constantly downplay his background (Correspondents of *The New York Times*, 2001, p. 127), as do "several top-ranked African-American business executives" who refused to be interviewed by the *Times* journalists (Correspondents of *The New York Times*, 2001, p. 330). These two political leaders, Governor Locke and Mayor Rice, illustrate the different cultural contexts inhabited by voluntary, immigrant minorities and by involuntary, colonized minorities.

Intermarriage patterns reflect another important aspect of the Asian-American story. "In California in 1980, the rate of marriages to whites for Japanese was thirty-two percent, Filipinos twenty-four percent, Asian Indians twenty-three percent, Koreans nineteen percent, Vietnamese fifteen percent, and Chinese fourteen percent" (Takaki, 1989, p. 473). Asian Americans, "more than any other group," are intermarrying with European Americans (Yetman, 1999, p. 252); the

2000 Census confirms that this intermarriage continues to rise dramatically ("Impact of Census' Race Data," 2001 pp. 1A–2A). As one Asian-American educator joked to me, "You know, we are treated like honorary whites." In fact, intermarriage is one major way that *race-to-ethnicity conversion* takes place or at least is signaled: Perceived differences due to immutable racial differences get converted to perceived differences due to culturally based (and far less important) ethnic differences (Sanjek, 1994). By contrast, the intermarriage rates of involuntary minority groups with the majority group remain much lower, especially for African Americans (Patterson, 1998a; Yetman, 1999; Wu, 2002).

Housing patterns and college enrollment data also shore up positive pronouncements about Asian-Americans' advancement. "In striking numbers," according to the *Boston Globe*'s analysis of 2000 Census data, Asian Americans are moving into suburban and affluent neighborhoods where they are being accepted by the European-American majority. Upendra Mishra, a well-educated immigrant from India who owns two successful Indian newspapers, explains the family's residential choice: "When we were looking to move, we looked at SAT scores, the dropout rate, the percentage of graduates who go on to college. When we saw that every kid who graduated from Weston High School went on to college, without exception, we said, 'This is perfect. This is where we are going to live'" (quoted in C. Rodriguez, 2001, p. B3).

Professor Takaki points out that Asian-American students—with ancestral roots in India, China, Korea, Japan, and so on—currently are doing exceptionally well in academia (1989). Accounting for three percent of the U.S. population, Asian Americans make up five percent of college and university students and thirty percent or even more of enrollment at highly selective campuses such as Stanford, Berkeley, UCLA, and the Ivy League. Yet attention must be paid to a crucial cultural and political context: Most *recent* immigrants with Chinese ancestry, for example, have been middle class and highly skilled, according to Brown University history professor Evelyn Hu-DeHart (1999). Howard University law professor Frank Wu concurs that these highly skilled immigrants luckily arrived "during an economic boom period" (Wu, 2002, p. 66). Further, they arrived during an auspicious political era, explains Hu-DeHart. They "were perfectly positioned to benefit immediately from affirmative action—originally enacted in the mid-1960s to help African Americans overcome centuries of slavery and racial segregation—because eligibility for the program was extended to all other 'minority' groups just as these Asian immigrants were arriving in large numbers." Given such head starts and advantageous positioning, "many new Asian Americans have managed to attain the American Dream in far less than a generation's time" (Hu-De-Hart, 1999, pp. 7–8). This, of course, has not been the case for colonized minorities. Moreover, much slower advancement in likely for the newest arrivals from Southeast Asia (the Vietnamese, Laotians, and Cambodians): These Southeast Asians are usually penniless and uprooted *refugees* who suffered significant traumas in their homelands, as will be discussed shortly. Nevertheless, because they possess traits of immigrant minorities, they are not denied the American dream.

The "Model-Minority" Problem for Asian Americans and Other Minorities

Given their relative success in American society, Asian Americans currently have a rather odd problem: They are held up as the "model minority" group because of their academic and economic success. The positive academic stereotype has important downsides. It is true that Asian Americans often choose quantitative fields of study, such as accounting, computer science, mathematics, and engineering. Such fields especially draw *new* immigrants from other countries because the disciplines require relatively few verbal and written English-language skills. But equally important, teachers and guidance counselors channel Asian and Asian-American students into subjects where they assume they can do very well—science and math—and away from those subjects where they assume they will not—humanities and social sciences (Kiang, 1992, p. 107). Although the students ought to be encouraged to have interests and competencies in a variety of subjects, they are frequently pigeonholed into technical fields.

To remedy this, schools and campuses must help Asian Americans see the richness of academic options they might choose—otherwise, the students' potential is shortchanged. So, too, is the future development of their communities, suggests University of Massachusetts–boston professor Peter Kiang. He worries, "What are the social consequences, for example, if these students concentrate overwhelmingly in business, science, and engineering, when the communities, in fact, desperately need bilingual lawyers, health care providers, policymakers, writers, filmmakers, teachers, and organizers?" (1992, p. 109).

A vivid story—told by an Asian-American student at a University of Massachusetts–Boston conference I recently attended—captures this narrowness of occupations. The student acted out the gasps and stunned expressions on the faces of his high school teachers and guidance counselors when he told them he wanted to be not an engineer but a *stand-up comic.* Nevertheless, his story and the stereotype are no joke. As Kiang explains, "Although discredited by many schools, the stereotype of Asian American students as super-achieving whiz kids nevertheless continues to define them on campus and hides the reality of sacrifice that characterizes daily life for so many." The erroneous assumption—that Asian-American students are self-sufficient and always succeed—translates into their being unable to find tutoring, academic as well as mental health counseling, and other institutional support. The needs of first-generation Southeast Asian refugees, in particular, go unrecognized and "unmet" on most campuses (Kiang, 1992, p. 102). Further, the positive stereotype that all Asian Americans are successful "permits the general public, government officials, and the judiciary to ignore or marginalize the contemporary needs of Asian Americans" (Chang, 1993, p. 35).

The model-minority stereotype has a third downside. Princeton University political scientist Jennifer Hochschild, in *Facing Up to the American Dream: Race, Class, and the Soul of the Nation,* points out that "newspapers have a seemingly endless supply of rags-to-riches stories" about Asian-Americans but the stories forget to point out that "not all Asians escape poverty, crime, and discrimination." Held up monolithically in this way, Asian Americans are being symbolically and pointedly used to *embarrass African Americans* who have not achieved the American dream to a comparable extent (Hochschild, 1995, p. 34). Takaki agrees that Asian Americans are "again being used to discipline blacks. Shortly after the Civil War, southern planters recruited Chinese immigrants in order to pit them against the newly freed blacks as 'examples' of laborers willing to work hard for low wages." The current argument unfolds this way: "The triumph of Asian Americans affirms the deeply rooted values of the Protestant ethic and self-reliance. . . . If Asian Americans can make it on their own, conservative pundits like Charles Murray [author of *The Bell Curve*] are asking, why can't other groups?" (Takaki, 1993, p. 416). Berkeley professor John McWhorter, in *Losing the Race: Self-Sabotage in Black America,* asks a question very similar to Murray's: Why can't African Americans perform as well in school as "new immigrants" from Africa or the Caribbean? (McWhorter, 2000, p. 115).

First, such a question is built on an unexamined assumption: that there has been the same level playing field for all immigrant groups, "without due consideration to varying social origins, unequal degrees of opportunities available in the United States, and different levels of exposure to discrimination" (Martinez, 2001, p. xxiv). Remember that the first Asian workers were capitalists because they willingly chose to come and they brought money with them (albeit small amounts) to invest and parlay into greater wealth (Takaki, 1989, 1993). The direct answer to McWhorter's question, of course, is that the cultural context and status of immigrant minorities is far *more conducive* to academic and economic success than the context inhabited by colonized, caste-like minorities. The cultural context of colonized minorities *relative* to other groups must be reckoned with. Hochschild warns that ignoring this all-important cultural context can add "yet another component to the nightmare of a failed American dream." She memorably describes the morass: "Members of a denigrated group are disproportionately likely to fail to achieve their goals; they are blamed as individuals (and perhaps blame themselves) for their failure; and they carry a further stigma as members of a non-virtuous (thus appropriately denigrated) group" that usually fails (1995, p. 245).

Promulgating the myth of Asian Americans as a model minority also hurts economically poor whites and other minorities "who are blamed for not being successful like Asian Americans." This blame is then translated into a justification for less government intervention and fewer social services targeted to these "undeserving" minorities and poor people as well as a justification for eliminating affirmative action measures for such "undeserving" beneficiaries. "To the extent that Asian Americans accept the model minority myth, we are complicitous in the oppression of other racial minorities and poor whites," according to Loyola University law professor Robert Chang (1993, p. 361).

Southeast Asian Refugees

Vietnamese, Cambodian, and Laotian refugees, unlike immigrants from Japan and China, did not choose to come to America for a better life. They were forced from their countries. They fled war, famine, and chaos; they endured the intense trauma associated with uprooting, violence, loss of family members, relocation in refugee camps, and then confusing resettlement in strange places. "I'm happier here [in the United States] in a way," one Cambodian refugee muses, "because I can look for a better future. But in spirit, no. In Cambodia, I would feel shoulder to shoulder with the people. Even if I were a farmer, I would be proud; I would be qualified. Here, I feel so bad spiritually" (quoted in Kiang, 1992, p. 103).

Indeed, refugees often feel trapped in their new country. "Unlike the Chinese, Japanese, and other Asian immigrants to America, they cannot go home. . . . More so than the earlier groups of Asian immigrants, the refugees are truly the uprooted" (Takaki, 1989, p. 471; also see Wu,

2002). Nevertheless, refugees are a type of immigrant minority because they do *not* have a cultural history of oppression by the majority group in this country. Contrasting the situation they fled in their home with their new situation here, they often feel gratitude. They can safely believe that the American dream is for them. This point is reinforced by the study *The Boat People and Achievement in America* (Caplan, Whitmore, and Choy, 1989), which reveals how the Vietnamese usually trust public school officials and optimistically believe they can achieve social mobility despite the language and cultural hurdles they encounter. In short, these new people are regarded as immigrant minorities and view themselves in the same way.

C. WOMEN AS A COLONIZED GROUP?

In a discussion of colonized and immigrant minorities, the question arises in my mind and perhaps the reader's: Are women, as a group, colonized and stigmatized? Yes, I believe, in some ways. Consider that women in some areas of the globe have been and are still regarded as polluted or polluting. In other cases, men characterize their wives and daughters as their property and treat them as subhuman. Born into certain cultures severely oppressive to their gender, a trickle of women are currently escaping and seeking *political asylum* in other countries. In cultures and groups not as extreme, many men nevertheless demonstrate—through their daily behavior and attitudes—that they believe themselves inherently superior to women. Preordained assumptions hold that women are inferior.

In the United States, women have historically been treated as inferior to men. Research has documented that until very recently, women were forbidden to vote, to own property, to establish credit and control their own money, to have police protection against domestic violence, to live where and with whom they chose, to obtain a college education, to join unions and enter the skilled trades, or to be accepted as professionals in fields such as law and medicine.

Even today, women struggle against subliminal assumptions that they are innately less competent than men. Many find it difficult to earn equal pay for equal work, to be fairly evaluated and promoted, to gain membership in labor unions, and to obtain institutional support for their roles as working mothers. Glass ceilings continue to prevent women from securing leadership positions in the professions, despite their credentials and achievements. Their recognition and promotion are much slower than that of comparably qualified men, according to Judith Glazer-Raymo in *Shattering the Myths: Women in Academe*

(1999). Why are assumptions about the inferiority and low value of women so difficult to eradicate?

In her book *Why So Slow? The Advancement of Women,* Hunter College psychology professor Virginia Valian focuses on middle-class *majority* women in the United States and shows that gender *schema* are more inclusive and neutral than gender stereotypes and perhaps harder to identify and overcome. Schema are hypotheses that we all share, men and women alike, about what it means to be male or female; schemas assign different psychological traits to males and to females. Men are thought to be innately more aggressive and independent—therefore, it is expected that they would assume important, high-risk jobs and professions outside the home. By contrast, majority women are thought to be more emotional, expressive, and nurturing—therefore, these women are expected to stay at home and tend to their domestic duties (Valian, 1998a and b). But remember that many other women from minority backgrounds and different social classes have not been expected to tend only to their domestic duties and the hearth.

These gender schema influence supervisors to hold strong assumptions about women, especially women seeking professional and managerial posts and promotions. In a male-dominated workplace, women are predictably underrated and men overrated (Wenneras and Wold, 1997 and 2000). Experts on organizations and interpersonal communication have repeatedly shown that women, when compared with men, have a harder time keeping the floor in public meetings and receive more negative reactions to what they are saying (Valian, 1998a and b). Women are typically granted less authority than men. Well-known studies sponsored over the years by the National Science Foundation, the Modern Language Association, and other organizations have shown that an article submitted for publication, if possessing a woman's name as the author, will invariably receive fewer points from a review panel than the same article with a man's name. Likewise, a résumé with a woman's name at the top will consistently be thought to belong to an assistant professor. But with a man's name on the same résumé, the title magically rises to the rank of associate professor.

Being underrated, women find it much harder, Valian argues, to accumulate small advantages and recognitions that finally amount to large advantages and promotions. By contrast, men—because they are predictably overrated or given the benefit of the doubt— find it much easier to accumulate advantages and build leadership niches for themselves. They are viewed as natural-born leaders and professionals, with pictures and stories in newspapers, television, and other media relentlessly reinforcing this male-centered world on a daily basis.

At Stanford University, as Frances K. Conley, M.D., (a European American) made her solo way in the European-American male-dominated domain of medicine and surgery, she found that her intelligence, skills, and hard work were insufficient. "In addition, I would need to wage a lifelong battle to overcome imprinted cultural expectations, especially those defining a woman's limits, and be willing to persist in the face of misogynistic antagonism" (Conley, 1998, p. 10). Her accomplishments as a tenured professor and accomplished surgeon and researcher were trivialized by her male colleagues; she was treated as a cute mascot; her leadership and public recognition were sabotaged. Like a colonized minority, she was psychologically belittled at every turn.

When Professor Conley charged Stanford's school of medicine with rampant sexism and sexual harassment, eleven male and female members of the biochemistry and developmental biology faculties wrote a public letter explaining that "many other women on the faculty and staff at Stanford can sympathize, having felt the same pain at various times. . . . Women still feel distressed by many incidents, each seemingly too trivial to mention but cumulatively devastating. Ambitious women feel their progress restrained by some men's demeaning attitudes and many never reach their legitimate goals" (quoted in Conley, 1998, p. 141). A similar finding of distress was uncovered in a 1990 study at Johns Hopkins University's department of medicine, where seventy-five percent of women faculty said they felt that their male colleagues were unwelcoming and did not treat them and their careers with serious regard (Fried et al., 1996).

Even women who have become members of the distinguished American Academy of Science and other elite groups can face harmful assumptions and instrumental exploitation, both of which slow down their career advancement. For example, at M.I.T. in 1996, sixteen of the seventeen tenured women faculty in science documented that they (in comparison with their 194 tenured male colleagues) received less lab space, lower research funding from the institution, and fewer promotions to leadership roles, such as department chair—despite their equal qualifications with male faculty. The women's salaries, of course, were also lower. Something resembling a caste system is surely at work.

The women science faculty described how they were marginalized, deemed "invisible," excluded from having a voice in their departments and occupying positions of any real power, and kept down by a glass ceiling. Even though there were no bigoted verbal or written put-downs of the women faculty by male faculty or administrators, there was nevertheless powerful gender discrimination in operation: "*The heart of the problem is that equal talent and accomplishment are viewed as unequal when seen through the eyes of prejudice.*" This prejudice blocks women's success, causes them "to be accorded less recognition" than they deserve, and creates a poorer quality of life for them. The M.I.T. senior women faculty worry that they are thereby rendered, in an awful way, as "negative role models for younger women." Their mistreatment signals to younger generations that they should avoid academic science (*MIT Faculty Newsletter*, March 1999).

The gender inequities in the United States are even greater, of course, for women belonging to castelike minority groups. Members of these groups are typically treated as conquered people. University of Wisconsin professor Nellie McKay underlines the plight of minority women who seek to claim a place for themselves in a male-dominated profession such as the professoriate: "Of all groups, as bona fide intellectuals, they [minority women] are the furthest removed from society's expectations of their 'place,' the least expected to succeed on merit, and the most vulnerable to insult" (1995, p. 59). A similar conclusion is found in a 2001 book, *Our Separate Ways: Black and White Women and the Struggle for Professional Identity*. While all the women analyzed in the book experienced—in their business and professional workplaces—constant questioning and undervaluing of their judgment, authority, and ideas, it should be no surprise that minority women fared the worst (Bell and Nkomo, 2001).

CONCLUSION

Colonized minorities in the United States include African Americans, Native Hawaiians, Puerto Rican Americans, Native Hawaiians, Mexican Americans, and American and Alaskan Indians. Unlike refugees or immigrants, they have been dealt a castelike status belonging to conquered, stigmatized minorities. Generation after generation, many of them relive and struggle against many of the same oppressions suffered by their forbearers. Many of them face a social rigidity that negatively affects both their academic and economic advancement. Many women, too, face a castelike rigidity when they attempt to enter and succeed in traditionally male-dominated businesses and professions.

Over the centuries, fascinating theories have been floated to explain why certain minority groups find it extremely difficult or even impossible to advance themselves. Some philosophers and poets have maintained that certain minority groups (or women as a group) innately possess low intelligence and excessive passion and emotion—therefore, they fail while the more gifted and reasonable groups succeed. Other writers and orators have said that self-help attitudes of the groups themselves are pivotal: Some families and cultures push their children to succeed in school and apprenticeships and to secure solid positions in the workforce, while others simply do not push their offspring. Linguists have wondered if some minorities' spoken and written language (its structure, grammar, etc.) adapts more easily to the standard dialect used in U.S. or other countries' schools—so perhaps linguistic advantage explains academic success. Looking to the *sun*, others have concluded that people from cold climates usually work harder and are more ambitious than people from warm climates who like to cavort and "be happy." Religious zealots have pronounced that God or some higher being has jinxed particular tribes and groups as punishment for their past sins: They are now stuck in a kind of miserable purgatory.

There are indeed explanations for why some minorities succeed more regularly in academia and in the adult workplace, but the reasons are *not* because of differences in culture or climate, disfavor with the gods, linguistic idiosyncrasies, or racial or genetic superiority or inferiority. The reasons are **contextual**: Different minorities have different statuses because of their distinctive and historical relationships with the majority group holding power in a given country. The status of a group impacts both its economic and academic advancement. Immigrant minorities, as well as members of the majority group, inhabit a relatively humane *class* system where they can sometimes move upward or downward. Colonized minorities, by contrast, all too often have to wrestle with a *castelike* system of exploitation and exclusion.

Understanding both the class system and the caste system are vitally important for faculty and administrators. Why? As power-holders possessing influence, financial resources, and admission and hiring responsibilities, they must exercise these powers wisely and carefully by taking into account the cultural contexts and histories of their colleagues and students. In addition, these power-holders must be on guard—in their thoughts, evaluations, and actions—against overvaluing not only members of the majority group but also visitors and immigrants from other countries. Simultaneously, they must be on guard against undervaluing those who are members of domestic minority groups, especially those identified with colonized groups. To produce fair evaluations and a level playing field, academic power-holders must learn to recognize and rise above ingrained mind-sets that add points to the worth of some groups and subtract points from the worth of others. I believe that campuses will not be able to diversify their faculties until these mind-sets, often operating unconsciously, are corrected.

2
Solutions

CHAPTER 4

GOOD PRACTICES IN RECRUITMENT

ON LARGE AND SMALL CAMPUSES throughout the country, one hears the following complaints and frustrations:

- *My department has spent a small fortune on advertising faculty vacancies, but we get only a handful of applicants of color, and we can't seem to hire any. Why?*
- *Over the past five years this campus has hired eight faculty of color, but they seem eager to move on. I'm not sure they even unpack their bags! What can I, as provost, do about this awful migration pattern?*
- *Our search committees invariably find minority candidates they say are less qualified or less desirable than majority ones. But those same minority candidates then turn around and land impressive jobs elsewhere. Does this bother us? Not much. We have an attitude problem about diversity, if you ask me. What can be done?*
- *I totally agree with whoever said that faculty hiring committees represent academia at its most dysfunctional. But what can we do to head off this dysfunction?*

I offer here twenty-seven Good Practices to address these complaints and frustrations and to remedy some of the academic inequities described in the earlier chapters. These Good Practices will improve the recruitment, evaluation, and hiring of minority faculty—if the practices are followed by colleges and universities and especially by their academic departments. Because these guidelines, in my experience, enhance overall hiring, evaluation, and decision-making processes, they will benefit majority faculty as well. The chapter is divided into two sections:

- **A-1 through A-19:** Good Practices for campus presidents, provosts, deans, and academic departments
- **A-20 through A-27:** Good Practices for academic search committees, with emphasis on cognitive mistakes to avoid

The avoidance of sloppy cognitive approaches (see A-27) is critically important. I would ask administrators and faculty to make sure they *themselves* are not falling prey to familiar cognitive mistakes, such as wishing to hire clones of themselves, seizing pretexts, making snap judgments with insufficient evidence, and allowing elitism to be a substitute for careful weighing of information. Only when administrative and faculty leaders can identify and rise above these mistakes are they ready to begin coaching search committees and other peers. I would admit that this process of self-correction can last a lifetime, as least for most of us.

The variety of guidelines set forth in this chapter are drawn from initiatives already under way in individual departments and campuses around the nation. They also derive from the expertise of practitioners, including myself, who see some of the gridlocks—on both an individual and an institutional level—that block faculty diversity decade after decade.

By numbering the Good Practices, presenting them straightforwardly, and highlighting key insights within them, I aim to make them *easy to discuss in meetings* of academic departments and divisions, deans and department chairs, search committees, mentoring-program participants, and key administrators and trustees. Further, the appendix to this book provides a checklist of all Good Practices, so that users can easily locate one or more guidelines. My hope is that some or all of these will be adopted, adapted, or improved upon.

GOOD PRACTICES FOR CAMPUS PRESIDENTS, PROVOSTS, DEANS, AND ACADEMIC DEPARTMENTS

To add diversity to the faculty ranks, senior faculty already established in academic departments must play, of course, the primary role. But departmental faculty are unlikely to exercise leadership in a sustained way unless they feel that their college or university regards inclusiveness and faculty diversity as a valued goal of the institution. Therefore, the campus president, provost, and academic deans—and their persistent commitment to faculty diversity—must be centrally involved. But far more than commitment—and at its worst, mere lip service—is required. Specific behavior and procedures must be followed by senior administrators, departmental faculty, and search committees.

A-1. Diligently avoid the following myths and easy excuses.

Before beginning the search for U.S. underrepresented minority faculty, top administrators as well as departments and their hiring committees must overcome self-defeating assumptions they may hold. Unfortunately, the following myths and excuses, I have discovered in my work, are *rampant* in academia.

- *No minorities would want to live here. The geographic location—or weather—or political climate—or pollen count—or whatever— is lousy.*
- *No minorities would settle for the paltry salary we can offer; Stanford and other well-heeled places will beat us out every time. We'd be wasting our time to even bother assembling a package of non-monetary benefits to attract minority candidates.*
- *No minorities or white women would want to come here because they would not have a critical mass of others like themselves with whom to build community.*
- *We'll never find qualified candidates for our department; the pool doesn't exist. That's the reason we have so few minorities right now across this university.*
- *Well, we have one minority colleague in our department, so that's enough diversity. One is enough, isn't it?*
- *Because majority men are having an awful time in the job market, why shouldn't we be giving* them *extra consideration? We really don't need to work at identifying and hiring women and minorities, because they are having their doors beaten down by recruiters.*
- *Because this campus is already a color-blind and gender-blind meritocracy, we really can't be extra aggressive in our faculty recruiting of white women and minorities. We have to continue to be color-blind and gender-blind in our actions.*

In my work, I have confronted every one of these myths. Claremont Graduate University professor Daryl Smith, too, has heard most of them. She and her research team interviewed three hundred former Ford, Mellon, and Spencer Foundation fellowship holders about their job-market experiences. Smith documents in her book (1996) how the myths stem from stereotypes and inaccurate perceptions maintained by majority power-holders engaged in the search process. In another study, funded by the Ford Foundation, University of Massachusetts–Boston education professor Bernard Harleston and Georgia State University law professor Marjorie Knowles (1997) uncovered similar myths, most especially the one maintaining that no or so few qualified minorities are available (the "pool problem"). Visiting eleven major research universities, the two researchers interviewed the president, the provost, other administrators engaged in diversifying the faculty, minority faculty, and minority graduate students on each campus. A further discovery—perhaps not surprising—was that the eleven well-known campuses as a group had granted doctorates to over one thousand Ford fellowship recipients but had, astonishingly, hired only seventy out of that number as faculty for their institutions. It is no wonder that faculty diversity is so difficult to achieve, with such a plethora of myths enshrouding the enterprise. The first good practice, I maintain, is to avoid these myths and refuse to accept facile excuses. What must also be avoided are cognitive mistakes (such as cloning, seizing pretexts, and making snap judgments) illustrated in A-27.

A-2. Departmental specialist should do year-round recruiting ("like a talent scout").

Recruiting, to be successful, has to occur all the time, not just when an actual job vacancy is at hand and job announcements are distributed. At least one faculty member in each academic department should be dedicated *year-round* to cultivating relationships with prospective candidates: Invite these prospects to the campus for special events and to interact with departmental faculty; build relationships with possible "sender" doctoral departments that produce a number of minority Ph.D.s; and construct what some experts have called a talent bank, to be continuously expanded with information on possible candidates, for each department and its search committees to consult. (To underwrite these extra recruiting efforts will require special funding from the provost's office, a topic to be discussed a bit later.)

When senior faculty attend professional conferences, the departmental specialist should encourage them to visit nearby campuses and meet with minority graduate students who might be persuaded to apply for faculty posts *in the future.* Further, senior faculty should contact their allies at graduate campuses and research institutes throughout the country, to let these allies know that their departments are seriously seeking to hire minority faculty. When the allies suggest a promising candidate, that candidate should be personally contacted and invited to come in and meet faculty and students in the department. The departmental specialist should keep records on all such candidates and make sure that follow-up is pursued.

In addition, it is wise to build long-term links to minority caucuses within national organizations and to minority organizations themselves and their Web sites. The specialist, together with departmental colleagues, should maintain a productive relationship with various minority interest groups that are included within professional societies and national educational groups. This is the advice of Professor Caroline Turner in her excellent publication *Diversifying the Faculty: A Guidebook for Search Committees,* released in 2002 by the Association of American Colleges and Universities (AAC&U). Examples of such societies include the American Chemical Society, the American Educational Research Association, the American Psychological Association, the AAC&U, the American Association of University Professors, and so on. Building a network with these societies' minority caucuses as well as with the national groups such as the Compact for Faculty Diversity, the Black Physics Students Association, the National Name Exchange, and the Mellon and Ford Fellowship Programs, the departmental specialist will be able to cultivate promising candidates for the future and invite them to apply for faculty posts when they become available in the department.

Such proactive activities have been termed "recruiting like a talent scout." In short, waiting and passively advertising for exceptional talent and skills are insufficient. A final strategy is to have a headhunter aid the hiring committee as a consultant. Such a consultant could probably devote more time than the committee to finding minority candidates who would be a good fit for the department.

Recruiting in innovative ways, *throughout the year,* is beginning to pay off for a number of campuses I work with. A former campus president has delineated what Canadian universities are doing differently. Intent on faculty appointments for women, aboriginal peoples, and international scholars, several lead campuses have become "much more aggressive and thorough in their approaches to recruitment." For example, the universities identify candidates and ask them to apply, instead of waiting; faculty members use personal and professional networks and work the corridors of professional conferences; the universities pay for spouses or significant others to accompany job candidates on the campus visit; campus leaders "actively sell their locations, lifestyles, and amenities" to job candidates; and university personnel organize focus groups so that they can find out what recent hires view as strengths and weaknesses in the university's recruitment campaigns. These proactive approaches are reaping success (Farquhar, 2001, p. 16).

A-3. Coach and monitor search committees.

Do not rely solely on an in-house handbook to guide search committees in their work. Most of these publications, unfortunately, have limited value because they highlight only the illegal questions about family, sexual preference, age, and so forth, that a hiring committee should eschew. The handbooks usually don't identify stereotypical thinking and other complex problems of decision-making and fail to provide concrete steps to the search committees for rising above these problems.

Instead of simply handing each committee member a guidebook, the provost or another high-ranking administrator should arrange intensive coaching for academic search committees—*before* they begin their soliciting, screening, and review of candidates. The coaching workshops should focus on several areas. First, what are the self-fulfilling myths (see A-1) we must avoid? Second, what are the departmental and institutional needs, short-term and long-term, to be met by the new hires? Each search committee, joined by the provost and division dean, should explore and come to closure on this question. Grappling with *programmatic needs as well as institutional needs* "promotes long-range planning and counters the tendency to replicate current [or retiring] faculty members" (Michigan State University, 2001, p. 14). The dean of engineering at the University of Washington, Denice Denton, agrees that an assessment of short-term and long-term needs is an essential first step for each department. She herself participates in these assessments and urges other top administrators to show their commitment by being involved with search committees *throughout* their work (conversation with the dean, 2003; also Denton, 2002).

Third, the coaching should help the committee members *recognize and then correct sloppy thinking* as they become engaged in searching for, interviewing, and evaluating candidates. Later in this chapter, in A-27, I will provide examples of distorted thinking and how to avoid or correct it.

Fourth, the coaching sessions for committee members should help them *recognize and move beyond gender and racial mind-sets* they may have. These mind-sets, usually in operation at the unconscious level, devalue the accomplishments and promise of white women and U.S. minorities. The dominant group in our society has taught all or most of us that women and certain minorities are not expected to be competent professionals (see chapters 1 and 3). But through prompting by the provost and other officials, members of search committees can indeed rise above the mind-sets that would lead them to automatically underrate certain candidates and overrate others.

Fifth, search committees should come to understand how *colonized minorities in U.S. society* are often treated as if they are indelibly marked at birth by intellectual and moral inferiority. Those enslaved, colonized, and conquered by a majority culture inherit and must struggle against far more institutionalized disadvantages and deep-seated prejudices than do immigrant minorities in a country. Examples of colonized minorities who are typically treated in castelike ways include Koreans in Japan; Maoris in New Zealand; Jamaicans in England; and *Mexican Americans, Native Hawaiians, Native Alaskans, Native Americans, Puerto Rican Americans, and African Americans in the United States.* Colin Powell, U.S. secretary of state, has underlined an important distinction between immigrant minorities and colonized minorities: "My Black ancestors may have been dragged to Jamaica in chains, but they were not dragged to the United States. . . . That is a far different emotional and psychological beginning [for me] than that of American Blacks, whose ancestors were brought here in chains." (See chapter 3 and Powell, 1995, p. 23.) The distinctions between immigrant minorities and colonized minorities, set forth in chapter 3, deserve careful attention in the coaching sessions for search committees. Otherwise, the committees may inadvertently overestimate the promise of international and immigrant job candidates and underestimate that of domestic minority candidates.

A campus and hiring department should recognize that diversifying its faculty by hiring international and immigrant job seekers may be desirable and even essential in some academic divisions, but it is *not* a substitute for hiring domestic African-American, Hispanic-American, and Native American faculty (Piore, 2001). If we truly want to reflect American society in our classrooms, laboratories, and intellectual communities, we must deepen our resolve to recruit and retain our own native-born scholars whose families have been in this country for decades and centuries.

Monitoring the progress of each search committee is important, as engineering dean Denice Denton maintains. At Duke University, for instance, there is "ongoing oversight from the provost and a small committee that monitors efforts and results" (personal correspondence with Vice Provost Judith Ruderman, 2003).

A-4. An academic department should construct its retention plan for new faculty hires even *before* recruitment begins.

A retention plan (including, for instance, assigned mentors for all new hires, professional-development sessions, and community-building events) is essential for all new faculty coming to campus but especially for non-majority faculty. The several elements of a successful retention plan will be discussed in detail in the next chapter. But the overarching point is this: When a department requests consideration of new positions and budget lines, the department should also have to submit for provost approval a retention plan designed for its anticipated new colleagues.

When meeting the job candidates, the department's academic search committee should review this approved retention plan with each of them, so the prospective newcomers recognize that careful thought and resources have been committed. Seeing a well-crafted retention plan in place reassures job candidates that their well-being, success, and professional growth do matter. Such reassurance, I tell the minority doctoral scholars I advise, is far more important than their pressing for another one or two thousand dollars during salary negotiations.

A-5. Diversify within each search committee. Add a diversity advocate within each committee.

Make sure that every committee itself is diverse and has at least one woman and one minority faculty member. If the department cannot draw on such diversity within, then it should ask women and minority faculty from other departments to serve or invite in outside business and civic leaders. Having gender and ethnic/racial *diversity within the search committee* usually helps majority members become more aware of and rise above the stereotypical mind-sets they often hold about those different from themselves.

Also consider including on every search committee a senior faculty member from outside the hiring department whose role is to serve as *an advocate for diversity* and/or a senior faculty member from the campus-wide affirmative action committee.

Both strategies are successfully used by a number of campuses. According to Tom Lascell, the director of human resources at the State University of New York–Canton, the two special, full-voting members on the search committee help to "ensure the hiring process remains on track" at his campus and is "not compromised by inappropriate questions or considerations." Further, these two special members help each committee avoid tunnel vision and thereby prevent the hiring department from cloning itself (Lascell, personal correspondence, 2001).

In the alternative, some campuses—such as the University of Washington's engineering school and Middlebury College in Vermont— have had success in including the dean or associate provost on some or all search committees.

A-6. Language in job ads should underscore the desire for diversity.

Regarding the language to use in the advertising of faculty vacancies, consider an adaptation of the following example: "The college is committed to increasing the diversity of the college community and the curriculum. Candidates who can contribute to that goal are encouraged to apply and to identify their strengths or experiences in this area." Or: "Because of the importance of cultural diversity and richness on this campus, candidates should explain how they have been and could be involved in these areas." (Versions of such language are used by Colorado College, Michigan State University, and a number of other institutions.) Simply putting in the lip-service assertion, at the bottom of the advertisement, that "this campus is an equal opportunity employer" is insufficient. Moreover, make sure that your campus's mission clearly states that the institution values cultural diversity within its student body and faculty ranks and subscribes to the educational value of diversity. The job advertisement, of course, should be congruent with the mission.

Caroline Turner has additional advice: In the job announcement, describe qualifications as *preferred* instead of *required*, in order to cast a wide net. Further, in the ad make sure to underscore that you are looking for candidates who have *experience with a variety of teaching methods and/or curricular perspectives* or *previous experience interacting with communities of color* or *experience in cultures other than their own* or *interest in developing and implementing curricula that address multicultural issues* or *demonstrated success in working with diverse populations of students* (Turner, 2002, pp. 17–18). One or more of these phrases can be appropriately used in *any* disciplinary announcement, from physics to physical education.

But please remember that passively advertising is usually insufficient. Proactive identifying and cultivating of talent—all year long—will be needed, as was described in A-2.

A-7. Make sure departments and divisions are offering equitable salary and benefit packages to new hires.

Most women and minorities will usually not negotiate as aggressively as most majority men (Valian, 2000a & b). My experience in coaching hundreds of women and minority doctorates reinforces this pattern. Therefore, the provost and president should set the expectation that, within each department, the salary and equipment packages for new hires will be very similar. Data on these packages should be monitored by the provost and president. Otherwise, those in the favored majority group will predictably start out with better packages and be able to quickly accumulate new successes and advantages. The reverse will hold for those in the less-favored group.

A-8. Constantly monitor the recruiting and hiring processes and outcomes in all departments—to make the system more transparent.

Provosts and presidents should gather data on new hires and on start-up packages offered to them in various academic units and divisions. Moreover, top administrators should have their appropriate representatives undertake exit interviews with those hired *and* not hired, to discover the strengths, weaknesses, and possible inequities of the hiring process. Only through *constant* monitoring and assessment can inequities and biases be detected and then eliminated, a view shared by the California state auditor, who is moving to eradicate gender inequities at campuses in the California university system. Such quality-control monitoring has been recently adopted by M.I.T., in reaction to reports from the campus's tenured women faculty in science documenting widespread gender discrimination. Besides gathering data and undertaking monitoring, the campus president and provost have pledged to move women faculty into leadership roles as department chairs and deans—roles they have previously been shunted away from (*MIT Faculty Newsletter*, 1999).

A-9. Have the chair and dean do the final choosing and hiring of candidates.

At some campuses, the search committee sends an *unranked* list of its final job candidates to the dean and department chair, who then do the actual selection and hiring (also see A-26). In other words, the committee recommends but does not take the final step. Yet another approach calls for the provost or dean to be an active member of each search committee.

A-10. Hold deans and chairs accountable for faculty diversity.

In their annual job-performance reviews, deans and chairs should be penalized or rewarded for the faculty-diversity outcomes within their jurisdictions. Such accountability would keep these key leaders centrally involved in the work of their departments' hiring committees. While the search process itself can always be improved (and must be), the real question to answer is: How many non-majority faculty did your department or division actually hire this year? A merit pay increase should hinge on a positive answer. While corporations for years have tied diversifying of personnel to a manager's annual review, colleges and universities are just beginning to do so. Rensselaer Polytechnic Institute, under the leadership of President Shirley Jackson, is moving to adopt this approach. (Dr. Jackson, a physicist, formerly headed the Nuclear Regulatory Commission.) Without such accountability for chairs and deans, there will always be easy excuses for why faculty diversity is not being attained.

A-11. Provide sufficient financial resources and staff support for diversifying the faculty.

The president's and provost's offices will need to provide funding to underwrite some or all of the following:

- Extra staff support for search committees, beyond that supplied by the usually overworked departmental secretaries. Unfortunately, a dysfunctional practice calls for faculty members to undertake their search duties as an add-on, with no reduction in their other committee assignments or departmental duties. Under these circumstances, committee members often resort to rapid screening and sorting of job candidates. They lack the necessary time as well as staff support to implement outreach campaigns, cultivate potential candidates, and perform genuine *searches* for excellent prospects, especially those from minority groups. Provosts, deans, and chairs should try to reverse this dysfunctional custom.
- "Target of opportunity" incentives and "bridge" grants, to help those departments that are prepared to hire non-majorities. (But note: Some campuses deem it unwise to offer such special-category funds and insist that the hiring department, following standard procedure, should provide all the funds for the hire.) If targeted funds will be used, should the non-majority candidate be informed of this fact before accepting the job offer? In my consulting, I answer yes to this question often posed to me by academic leaders. The job applicant should be able to ask informed questions about the duration of the special funding and understand that such funding may be seen as suspect by some colleagues in the hiring department. I maintain that it is the job of the chair and provost to prepare the department for appropriate use of targeted funds, in order to prevent a boomerang effect on the non-majority hire.

- Release time for the one faculty member in each department who is dedicated to year-round recruiting—as well as travel funds to be used by this departmental specialist for identifying and cultivating prospective candidates two or more years *before* they will be ready to apply for a position (this is recruiting "like a football coach").
- Incentive or supplemental grants to enable divisions and departments to do *cluster hiring* of several minority faculty during the same time period.
- Support of a greater number of minority speakers, visiting scholars, and dissertation scholars-in-residence on campus.

A-12. Assist with spousal job hunting.

Your campus's recruitment outcomes will improve if your central administration can offer genuine assistance to the candidate's *significant other*—as that partner seeks an attractive job in your geographic area. If the candidate can be sure that his or her partner will have meaningful employment (either at your campus or somewhere nearby), your likelihood of securing that candidate as a faculty member is considerably enhanced. Even *before* the candidate musters the courage to bring up this two-career topic, the academic hiring committee should anticipate it by saying something to the candidate along the lines of: *"Our campus [or our provost's office] makes it a habit to offer assistance to a candidate's 'significant other' in securing meaningful employment in this geographic area. Is that something you might be interested in?"* Obviously, before this statement can be made in good faith, the provost's office should have *already* inventoried nearby businesses, nonprofit organizations, and other academic institutions in order to be ready to help the spouse or significant other reach out to the right contacts, quickly. Moreover, the provost's office should be up-to-date not only on current employment opportunities on campus, but also on possibilities in the near future that might interest the spouse or significant other.

The University of California–Santa Cruz operates a "dual-career service" where office staff and a constantly updated Web site give assistance to partners and spouses in finding employment in the geographic area, including information and links to academic, corporate, and government employers (http://www2.ucsc.edu/ahr.dcs/). Several campuses in the Bay Area, including UC–Santa Cruz, have also have formed the Higher Education Recruitment Consortium, which shares information about academic positions currently available at fifteen community colleges, four-year colleges, and comprehensive and research universities in the geographic area (http://www2.ucsc.edu/ahr/dcs/herc/). More informally, several campuses I work with help one another with spousal hiring by having their affirmative action officers keep in touch with their counterparts at neighboring campuses, to stay informed about employment opportunities that spouses or partners might seek.

A-13. Pay attention to the lifestyle concerns of job candidates.

During its interviews of job candidates, each hiring committee should *initiate* discussion of lifestyle concerns the candidate may have. Concerns—related to housing and mortgages, spousal hiring, the composition of communities, K–12 schools, cultural and musical offerings, and social-life opportunities and limitations—matter far more than in the past, according to the findings of Harvard researcher Kathy Trower who surveyed 700 beginning faculty members and 2,000 doctoral students. Trower discovered that while lifestyle issues are at the *top* of candidates' lists, hiring departments have been slow to appreciate this fact (personal conversation, 2002). One exception, Wheaton College in semirural Massachusetts, recently has been effective in hiring minority faculty. Their hiring committees made it a point to find out, *before* the campus visit, what the job candidates were worried about so they could deal with those concerns. For those candidates hesitant about living in a mostly white small town, for instance, "we introduced the candidates to Providence, Boston, and Cambridge." For a creative writer with an interest in theater, a search committee arranged "a backstage tour of the top-notch repertory theatre in nearby Providence." Yet another candidate was introduced to an art historian with similar interests at a nearby university, in order to begin networking. Going the extra mile in these ways showed the job candidates how much they were valued and, without a doubt, gave Wheaton a leg up in recruiting (personal correspondence with Professor Paula Krebs, 2002).

A-14. Provide housing assistance to new hires.

Some campuses have built faculty housing to offer for sale or rent to new hires. By doing so, institutions can ensure that at least some of their minority and majority faculty and their families live in inclusive, multicultural residential areas. Other campuses have worked with lending institutions to offer innovative loans for house mortgages. In areas with high-cost real estate, such as Boston, San Francisco, and

New York, campus assistance will be essential to enable new faculty to enter the area's housing market. To secure talented newcomers, campuses will have to stand ready to lend a hand.

A-15. Promote cluster hiring.

Departments and divisions should hire more than one minority faculty member or one majority woman at a time. Clustering is easier on everyone and *will prevent the "solo" phenomenon, which can be excruciating,* as chapter 1 suggests. Make sure minority job candidates know that the college is working hard to hire a cluster of minorities, in order to prevent the isolation and extra burdens typically faced by the solo.

In 1998, the University of Wisconsin–Madison began an innovative Cluster Hiring Initiative that is yielding some success in the hiring of African-American and Latíno/a faculty for tenure-track posts. The university, according to Linda Greene, professor of law and associate vice chancellor of academic affairs, has created and funded cross-departmental areas and informal centers that especially attract intellectuals from *minority* backgrounds (both emerging and established leaders). Some of the areas include Environmental and Global Security; Urban Ecology and Ecosystem Dynamics; International Gender Policy Studies; Family Policy and Law; Poverty Studies; Visiting Artists; American Indian Studies; and the African Diaspora. As an alternative to conventional hiring by separate departments, the Cluster Hiring Initiative opens up new research tracks and hiring opportunities while expanding curricular offerings for students. Choosing the interdisciplinary areas for the next cycle of funding is done by various faculty advisory committees, with "lead" deans then creating and working closely with the search committees. The new hires do not replace faculty searches already authorized or under way in the various academic departments endorsing and supporting the new interdisciplinary areas for cluster hiring (Greene's personal conversation with author, 2002; in addition, see UW–Madison's Web site).

A-16. Also hire senior faculty members.

Besides hiring pre-tenure women and minorities, campuses and departments should recruit tenured faculty who already have positions at other universities. These senior faculty, with their professional standing and wide networks, usually improve the recruitment of other non-majority faculty and students by the campus.

A-17. Bring to campus visiting scholars from underrepresented groups.

Visiting or adjunct minority professors, on campus for a year or more, will enrich the intellectual enterprise for students and faculty and probably attract additional underrepresented faculty and students to the campus. Equally significant, a steady stream of visiting scholars will help to *reduce the novelty* of having minorities in the departments and across the campus.

A-18. Include non-majority speakers in every lecture and seminar series.

In departmental and campus lecture series and intellectual forums, make sure that a sizable (not a token) number of U.S. minorities and women are featured. Again, reduction of novelty will be hastened by the presence of these speakers. When underrepresented scholars visit, extend to them a warm welcome and a meaningful introduction to your departments and campus. Above all, let them know how genuine are the departments' and campus's determination to diversify its faculty and student body. Some of these visitors will become handy allies who recommend promising candidates to you throughout the year. Such *word-of-mouth promotion* of your departments' and campus's strengths by a credible authority is exceptionally valuable and will increase the effectiveness of your recruiting.

A-19. Start a visiting dissertation scholars-in-residence program on campus.

With such a program in place, a college or university plays host to one or more minorities close to receiving their doctorates from other doctoral campuses. These advanced graduate students receive a stipend from their hosts, spend twelve months or so completing their dissertations while being visiting scholars-in-residence, and undertake a very light teaching assignment (usually one course in the spring semester) for the host department. The visiting scholars typically make a presentation about their dissertation work at a formal campus forum sponsored by the president's or provost's office; the scholars also attend a few informal pizza parties during the year, where they share tips with students on campus on how to succeed in graduate school.

The *get-acquainted period* of twelve months often results in the host departments hiring the scholars as assistant professors. Having launched and directed such residency programs for many years, I find that the visiting scholars value not only the support while completing their dissertations, but also the chance to learn more about the geographic area and the host campus and department. Many of the scholars come to appreciate the host campuses and departments in ways that few of their peers would be able to do.

Similarly, campuses have found it helpful to operate postdoctoral programs for minorities. Typically, the postdoctoral position combines research and teaching and gives the host department and the recipient valuable time to become acquainted.

GUIDELINES FOR SEARCH COMMITTEES

The following Good Practices, some of which were already discussed in the previous section, should be observed by all search committees. Especially give attention to A-27, which illustrates examples of sloppy information-gathering and decision-making.

A-20. Avoid easy excuses and self-fulfilling myths about how difficult it will be to hire minority and women faculty.

The myths and excuses make up a sizable list. Here are examples: *Minorities wouldn't like this campus's location, or weather, or pollen count, or conservative lifestyle, or whatever. We don't have the money to woo diverse faculty candidates because Stanford will always be the top bidder and beat us out. Because this campus and community don't have a critical mass of minorities, I don't see how we'd be that attractive. We can't find any qualified minorities. Majority men are getting to be an endangered species; I think we should spend extra time hiring them. I don't think we can do anything differently in our faculty hiring because it would be illegal to do anything resembling affirmative action to hire more minorities and women.* For more details, see A-1.

A-21. Recruit year-round "like a football coach."

Collaborate with the dedicated faculty member in the department to identify and bring to campus promising job candidates, both for current job vacancies and future ones. Do not rely on passive advertising to meet your hiring goals. Tap into various networks (such as minority caucuses of professional societies), and build bridges to those doctoral departments where a goodly number of non-majorities earn doctorates. More details can be found in A-2 about how a talent scout constantly seeks and cultivates new recruits.

A-22. Receive coaching from the provost.

Before beginning its work, the search committee should confer with the provost and assess programmatic and institutional needs to be met by the new hire(s). Above all, the search committee should receive coaching from the provost or outside consultants, to help its members move beyond gender and racial mind-sets as well as understand how and why colonized minorities usually grapple with more prejudice than do immigrants.

Search-committee members should be prepared and practiced so that during the search process, they are able to exercise critical thinking and avoid stereotypical and sloppy thinking. Fallacies to be avoided are detailed in A-27. Chapter 9 provides scenarios that search committees can use to practice and test themselves on bad and good practices related to recruiting.

A-23. Ensure diversity in the search committee's membership.

The committee itself should have U.S. minorities and women as members. When none is available inside the department or campus, women and minority business and science leaders from outside should be brought in to participate in the search process. Another effective move, followed by many campuses, is to designate one (willing) committee member as the advocate for faculty diversity.

A-24. Use detailed language about faculty diversity in the job advertisement, not merely boilerplate statements.

Simply saying the campus is an equal opportunity employer is insufficient. The ad should have language similar to the following: "This campus and department are committed to student and faculty diversity and value the educational benefits flowing from such diversity. Candidates should make known their experience and leadership in this area." Additional suggestions can be found in A-6.

A-25. Follow key pointers for campus visits and interviews of job candidates.

Before the final candidates arrive for the campus visit, phone and ask them what life-style concerns they may have about the campus, the environs, and so on. And then do your homework, with the assistance of the provost's office or another central office. Be ready to trumpet the quality-of-life benefits of your campus, neighborhoods, and the like. Once the candidates have arrived on campus for their interviews:

- Ask the candidates if they would like the provost's office to assist with spousal or "significant other" hiring.
- Arrange for minority and women job candidates to meet privately with minority and women students and, especially, faculty from across the campus.
- Be very cordial and professional to all job candidates. Realize that the committee itself is representing the campus and the department as it interacts with job candidates; the committee should not generate ill will and bad publicity.
- Offer equitable start-up packages to the final job candidates.

A-26. Send an *unranked* list of final candidates to the dean and department chair, for either their input or their decision.

At Virginia Polytechnic Institute and State University, the dean and department chair, after sifting through the recommendations from the search committee as well as through the information they themselves have gathered about the finalists, make the actual decisions about which candidate to hire. This approach is already followed by a number of campuses. While the appropriate dean and chair at Virginia Tech receive from the search committee a summary on each finalist (concerning qualifications, potential contributions to the campus and department, and so on), the search committee does *not* numerically rank the finalists. The presumption here is that all finalists would possess the minimum qualifications and achievements for the faculty opening or they would not have survived to the final stage of the hiring process. The non-ranking is a key element, according to Myra Gordon, former associate dean for diversity and curriculum at Virginia Tech's College of Arts and Sciences, because it requires the search committee to do careful homework and think through the case to be made for each candidate (personal conversation, 2002). Dr. Gordon is now associate provost for diversity and dual career development at Kansas State University.

At other campuses, the custom is to factor the evaluations of the provost or dean into the decisions made by the search committee. And, as previously mentioned, at some institutions the provost or appropriate dean is involved from beginning to end with the search process and the search committee.

A-27. Throughout the search committee's work, its members should avoid sloppy, biased thinking and decision-making (bad practices).

Typical mistakes—of serious consequence—often hamper the functioning of search committees. Below is a list of mistakes that are likely to surface as the committee reviews the paper credentials of the job candidates; interacts with applicants during job talks and interviews; evaluates their perceived strengths, weaknesses, and potential; and considers how the candidates could enrich the department, the students, and the campus.

The provost, an outside consultant, or an appropriate academic leader should prepare search committees, at the beginning of their work and at several intervals during their search process, so they are able to identify and then *rise above* the following fallacies. (The discussion scenarios in chapter 9 can be used as aids in the coaching sessions organized by the provost or others.)

To coach and steer these committees toward critical thinking and evaluation is, I believe, the most important task of provosts, departments, and those committed to diversifying the faculty. A number of studies have uncovered rampant subjectivity and sloppy decision-making often occurring within the processes (Twombly, 1992; Wade and Kinicki, 1995). As one example, in thirteen searches for administrators at Ohio State University, when committees came to discuss the candidates' professional style and interaction with others as well as their image, body language, and so-called fit with the institution, the racist and sexist assumptions rushed in. Only majority male candidates resembling the membership of the search committees were deemed safe, comfortable, and professionally appropriate for the majority university. These candidates, but not women and minority candidates, were spared probing and offensively personal questions about their families, lifestyles, and so on. Not surprisingly, the committees expressed reservations about the dress, demeanor, accent, values, or whatever of those who did not resemble them. And finally, the committees typically trusted only information about candidates offered to them by colleagues they *already* knew at other campuses (Sagaria, 2002). Such a closed system and such outrageous behavior must end. Given the gatekeeping function performed by search committees, it is imperative that they learn to identify and rise above the following cognitive mistakes.

BAD PRACTICES AND COGNITIVE FALLACIES

Avoid cloning, as manifested by these behaviors:

- Undervaluing a candidate's research area because it is not familiar to one or more committee members (e.g., a search committee member remarks: *This candidate's research approach is so different from what we usually do around here*)

- Undervaluing a candidate's educational credentials and career path to the professoriate because they are not the same as most of those on the hiring committee (e.g., *Have we ever hired anyone with a doctorate from Howard University? By the way, where in the world is Howard?*)
- Seeking candidates who would be mirror images of one's self or of one's colleagues, current or retired (*Francisco will stick out in our department, as I'm sure everyone here senses. He's just too different to be a good fit*)

Avoid snap judgments and seizing of pretexts:

- Making judgments quickly about job candidates, with insufficient evidence (*A doctorate from Michigan is golden for me. What else do we need to know?*)
- Quickly labeling one candidate as the "best" and ignoring positive evidence about the other candidates (*Eric stands head and shoulders above all the others; I hate wasting time with the other applicants*)
- Giving excessive weight to something trivial, in order to justify quick dismissal of the candidate (*Didn't Raquel seem nervous during the first five minutes of her job talk—so why keep her in the running?*)

Avoid elitist behavior:

- Downgrading on the basis of the candidate's undergraduate or doctoral campuses, regional accent, dress, jewelry, social class, or whatever (*She's so southern—I'm not sure I can stand the accent and mannerisms. And one of her reference letters is from a university located in the great unwashed Midwest no less.*)
- "Raising the bar"—increasing the qualifications for women and minority candidates because their competency doesn't strike you or other committee members as trustworthy (*Don't we need more writing samples from Latorya?*), or expressing suspicion about the authenticity of the non-majority candidates' credentials or recommendations (*Dewayne's letter from Berkeley seems excessively positive to me. Something is fishy*)
- Feeling uneasy and defensive because a minority colleague will somehow, in an overall way, lessen the quality and prestige of the department (*Well, we always have to ask if a particular faculty hire will bolster our standing in the* U.S. News and World Report *rankings*)

Avoid wishful thinking:

- Insisting that racism and sexism no longer exist (*Every civil right* imaginable *is now legally protected; the bad old days of overt and covert discrimination are over and gone*)
- Arguing that affirmative action policies are repugnant and that extra efforts should not be devoted to identifying and inviting in underrepresented job candidates (*We have to hire the way we always do and let the candidates fall where they may; we have no other choice. If that means we're reproducing ourselves, so be it*)
- Believing that America and its colleges and universities are a meritocracy where whom you know and what status and privileges you hold are immaterial (*There is no subjectivity involved when we seek merit and excellence in candidates. We should be proud that all our hires are from Harvard. Nothing has been rigged*)

Avoid disingenuous and willful innocence:

- Insisting that a department and its search committee can be and must be gender-blind and race-blind in its recruiting (*It really doesn't matter to me whether a candidate is black, white, green, or purple. In fact, I don't really see gender or race in people. Really—I don't*)
- Ignoring people's backgrounds and insisting that treating everyone the same is the only way to treat them fairly (*Isn't that what we should do if we hire Garcia? Just treat him like everyone else? Otherwise, life becomes too complicated for me*)
- Feigning personal innocence (*I myself have never perpetrated discrimination against women and minorities on this campus. So what is there to remedy, and why should we give minorities any breaks here?*)
- Feigning personal ignorance about institutional and societal inequities (*I myself have never seen or heard genuine instances of minorities and women being devalued or excluded. Really, I haven't*)
- Equating current efforts to promote the greater inclusion of women and minorities with reverse discrimination against majority men (*I thought we were supposed to stop pushing one group over another. Soon white men will be the endangered species. Is that what we want? I move that we hire the white guy*)
- Exaggerating how majority men are hurt by affirmative action taken on behalf of underrepresented minorities and women

(*White guys are losing out on jobs, right and left. If affirmation action keeps going, white males will soon become the lowest caste and they'll be blocked from prestigious professions and universities and trapped in unskilled jobs. Why should they be shoved to the political and economic bottom?*)

For more discussion of such disingenuous stances and wishful, noncritical thinking, consult Patricia Williams's *Seeing a Color-Blind Future: The Paradox of Race* (1997); Robert Dahl's *How Democratic Is the American Constitution?* (2001); Bryan Fair's *Notes of a Racial Caste Baby: Color Blindness and the End of Affirmative Action* (1997); Ellis Cose's *Color-Blind: Seeing beyond Race in a Race-Obsessed World* (1997); Lani Guinier's and Gerald Torres's *The Miner's Canary: Enlisting Race, Resisting Power, and Transforming Democracy* (2002); and Ronald Takaki's contributions in *From Different Shores: Perspectives on Race and Ethnicity in America* (1987), a book also edited by Takaki.

Valuable, too, is Frances Rains's article "Is the Benign Really Harmless?" wherein she analyzes the insistence by majority power-holders that "I really am color-blind; I don't see color." Such an assertion, according to Rains, "trivializes the substance and weight of the intertwined histories of Whites and people of color" since the beginning of the U.S. democracy. Further, this color-blind assertion glosses over the abominable treatment that many minorities encounter daily. By claiming to be innocent and color-blind, speakers seek to "absolve" themselves of any responsibility whatsoever for these daily inequities or any responsibility for working to level the larger playing field (Rains, 1998a, pp. 93–94).

Finally, those claiming to be color-blind may be expressing the desire to remain aloof and far removed from people of color, due to aversive racism. That is, they may feel ambivalence: They still hold negative beliefs about the capabilities of certain minority groups, but they also want to regard themselves as liberally upholding the equal-opportunity rhetoric of the U.S. Constitution. Torn by such ambivalence, they try to ignore minorities and minority issues because they feel unease, confusion, and discomfort (Gaertner and Dovidio, 1986).

CONCLUSION

This chapter has emphasized both *institutional* and *cognitive* Good Practices—for senior administrators, departmental units, and search committees—that will improve the hiring of faculty on predominantly majority campuses. Clearly that improvement in recruitment will require substantial long-term efforts from many parties. There is no quick fix.

The cognitive mistakes and self-fulfilling myths highlighted in A-1 and A-27 will probably take the most concentration and ongoing attention. To identify and then void these deviations from critical thinking, in both one's self and one's colleagues, will be a constant struggle. These mistakes and myths will be present in most situations involving evaluations of: job candidates; colleagues for tenure, promotion, and merit pay; and students, faculty, and staff nominated for awards and other recognition. But we must make the struggle to overcome these deviations; otherwise, faculty diversity will remain only a slogan.

CHAPTER 5

GOOD PRACTICES IN RETENTION

GIVEN THE TIME AND MONEY expended in the recruitment of new faculty, it seems exceedingly wasteful for colleges and universities to remain passive while newcomers, especially colonized minorities, struggle alone with the multiple stresses and confusions of their new jobs. Many business corporations, by contrast, invest heavily in family-friendly and professional-development measures for their employees, such as providing child-care, elder-respite, and after-school-for-older-kids centers at the place of employment; generous family leave; support groups on parenting, professional issues, and so on; consistent mentoring by experienced "wise owls" in the organization; flextime and compressed workweeks; leadership and multicultural training; and evaluation of managers partly based on their hiring and advancement of nontraditional employees. (*Working Mother* and other magazines regularly survey and rank corporations' investments in their employees and workplaces.)

Clearly, higher education has much to learn. The following twenty-one Good Practices should be widely adopted, for they will improve the daily lives and professional achievements of both minority and majority faculty. The chapter is divided thusly:

- B-1 through B-13: Good Practices for key campus leaders and mentoring programs
- B-14 through B-21: Good Practices for academic departments

GOOD PRACTICES FOR CAMPUS PRESIDENTS, PROVOSTS, DEANS, TRUSTEES, AND MENTORING PROGRAMS

B-1. Implement a formal campus-wide mentoring program.

On some campuses, the offices of the provost and/or dean of the faculty assign a two- or three-person mentoring committee to *each* faculty newcomer, whether minority or majority. I applaud this practice. All of the mentors are senior professors; one is drawn from the newcomer's own department, but the other two are from outside that department. A typical campus-wide mentoring program for new hires can be organized this way: Senior faculty in various departments volunteer or are nominated to be mentors; they receive cross-cultural and cross-gender coaching to improve their skills. (In chapter 6, I provide pointers and caveats for mentors as well as their mentees.) The mentoring committee and its mentee agree to meet informally at least once per month, with lunch perhaps paid for by the provost's office. The once-per-month meeting requirement must be rigid, according to faculty-development expert Boice (2000), or else the new faculty hire will probably become a no-show when s/he succumbs to the frenetic and overwhelming *busyness* of the first year.

Every three months or so, the various mentor-mentee groups meet to build more collegiality with one another and to review tricks of the trade that are working for the new faculty. A seasoned administrator should oversee the operation of this formal mentoring program and intervene, if necessary, to help solve problems that may arise. Each new hire should be asked to present to his/her mentoring committee a catalog, summarizing research projects and teaching experience to date and outlining future plans. With this document in hand, the committee can give specific advice and leadership to help the junior faculty member achieve his/her goals and fill in gaps in professional development.

Another variation: The Great Lakes College Association has had success with assigning *a mentor from one member campus* to a mentee newcomer possessing similar scholarly or research interests from *another* campus in the consortium (Wylie, 1990). A third variation: The *same three* specialized mentors are assigned to *all new* faculty hires. One mentor deals with teaching skills and problems; one assists with understanding and meeting the requirements for tenure; and the third focuses on the newcomers' grant-writing skills and scholarship. Each mentor could hold small-group meetings with some or all mentees as well as give one-to-one attention. (Mentoring programs are also discussed in B-20 below. Chapter 6 sets forth Good Practices for mentors as well as self-help strategies for mentees.)

B-2. Sponsor career-development workshops for faculty throughout the year.

The office of the provost or dean of the faculty should sponsor such workshops for new and established faculty. Topics of perennial interest include

- Writing Proposals to Secure Research and Travel Support
- Improving Your Teaching (comraderie could result if both senior and junior colleagues participate in these workshops)
- Managing Dual-Career Families (both spouses attend)
- Managing Commuter Marriages (both spouses attend, *if possible!*)
- Becoming a Productive Writer
- Improving Your Research
- Getting Your Work Published
- Developing Skills in Cross-Cultural Communication, Problem-Solving, and Negotiation
- Managing Your Finances
- Reducing Stress
- Managing Time and Tasks
- Balancing Your Career with Your Private Life

Special invitations to these workshops could be issued to all new hires and to the mentors and mentees involved in formal mentoring programs.

B-3. Provide child-care facilities on campus.

Providing this service on campus would eliminate one major stressor during the child-rearing years: making the frenetic rush across town to pick up your small children before day-care workers put them on the street at 5:30 p.m. Higher education should follow the lead of businesses and guarantee child care on the premises of the workplace.

B-4. Allow family leave.

Slowing down the tenure clock, for both male and female faculty involved in child rearing, is desperately needed. Child rearing, whether by two adults or by a single parent, can be enormously stressful if family and work/tenure schedules conflict at every turn. Provosts and presidents must check to see that there are *no penalties* for faculty who make use of such family leaves. It is still the case that pre-tenure faculty often hesitate to make use of such leaves because some senior faculty intensely disapprove.

B-5. Ensure leadership positions for non-majority faculty.

M.I.T.'s provost and president have pledged that women and minority faculty will receive their fair share of leadership posts. Most departments on this campus have always been headed by European-American male faculty, even though the campus's tenured women faculty have been recognized by the American Academy of Science and other societies for their exceptional achievement and competence. Likewise, the chronic absence of women faculty as chairs, deans, and other top administrators at the Johns Hopkins University Department of Medicine is being remedied, thanks to a long-term intervention initiative (Fried et al., 1996; also personal conversation with Professor Fried, 2003). All campuses must seek ways to move non-majorities into leadership posts that have been forbidden to them in the past.

B-6. Hold critical-thinking workshops for department chairs, senior faculty, and tenure and promotion committees on a regular basis.

Because annual job-performance assessments and tenure decisions regarding non-majority faculty are likely to be unconsciously corrupted by gender and racial/ethnic schema often held by majority power-holders (Wenneras and Wold, 2000; also see chapter 1), strategies must be followed to overcome this corruption. Simple reminders of these schema combined with pep talks to majority faculty to rise above them are necessary but, in my experience, not sufficient. The president and provost must provide a series of sessions where faculty and various gatekeeping committees can learn to recognize and *overcome* their sloppy and/or stereotypical thinking. And check-ins with faculty and committee chairs should take place at regular intervals. The point is that evaluations must be monitored and fine-tuned, on an ongoing and long-term basis. The material in chapter 4, especially on avoiding myths (A-1) and cognitive mistakes (A-27), should be incorporated into these sessions.

B-7. Provide mentoring training for department chairs, senior faculty, and new associate professors.

Special sessions for department chairs and senior faculty should enable them to become more effective monitors and mentors of pre-tenure faculty. Moreover, newly minted associate professors with tenure in hand should be cordially invited to these sessions so they can become mentoring leaders. The special training should cover the duties of the mentor and mentee; how the mentor can be instrumentally helpful in the advancement of the mentee's career; problem-solving skills; cross-cultural communication and sensitivity; and active listening. The National Centers of Leadership in Academic Medicine (sponsored by the Office of Women's Health within the Department of Health and Human Services) provides at its Web site excellent recommendations for how to prepare both faculty mentors and their pretenure mentees. In chapter 6, I present insights and materials for use by mentors, mentees, and mentoring programs.

B-8. Reward senior faculty for their attentive mentoring of new faculty.

The rewards could take the form of a course release, extra professional travel money, new lab equipment, a supplemental stipend, and so on. Those senior mentors—who are helping new hires and pretenure faculty to expand their competencies and establish themselves as productive members of the campus community—deserve genuine thanks from the provost and department chairs. In fact, the provost and other key leaders should routinely remind their colleagues of the great value being added through the mentoring of pre-tenure faculty.

B-9. For faculty newcomers, arrange campus-wide orientation sessions and cordial visits with the dean.

Campus-wide orientation sessions, mandatory for all new faculty, should begin prior to newcomers' first semester and occur every two months thereafter for the entire first year. Issues and problems arising from teaching and learning, scholarship and research, relations with colleagues, and so forth, should be addressed, along with time-management and stress-reduction strategies. What will not suffice is the conventional two-hour explanation of the campus's pension and health-insurance plan, by a bored and boring personnel officer!

Because the sessions are campus-wide, juniors will be able to connect with similarly situated colleagues from all corners of the campus. Assisting with the orientation sessions should be friendly senior faculty, from across the campus as well as more advanced pre-tenure faculty, who would act as peer mentors and lead discussion within small clusters of new faculty with kindred interests and concerns.

The good news is that the orientation sessions should *be short and sweet*. The first one, occurring prior to the beginning of the semester, features an informal lunch followed by four mini-workshops of twelve minutes—on Teaching; Obtaining Grants; Becoming a Productive Scholarly Writer; Managing Time and Stress—which preview the in-depth workshops that will be offered over the academic year. Each of these later in-depth workshops, mandatory for all new faculty, should not exceed two hours and should provide additional reading recommendations (Boice, 1992b).

In addition, each dean should take the initiative to spend at least one hour with every new faculty hire in the academic division. I have worked with a number of deans who believe that a cordial, one-on-one connection with each newcomer is well worth their time and attention and is an important part of the campus's retention plan.

B-10. Sponsor community-building events for new hires and pre-tenure faculty.

Sponsor a reception during fall semester that includes not only the campus's junior faculty, but also junior faculty from other campuses in the state or region. Such a community-building event is *especially critical for minorities*, who will appreciate meeting others who are in similar token situations on majority colleges and universities. Retention depends on new faculty building meaningful relationships both within and outside the home campus. Responsibility for organizing the fall gathering could rotate among the provosts' offices at the different campuses involved.

B-11. Bring in speakers chosen by junior faculty.

Under the sponsorship of the Smith College provost Susan Bourque, pre-tenure faculty apply for "Connections" grants that enable them to *bring to their new departments impressive scholars whose work keenly interests the junior faculty* or closely parallels their own research topics or methodologies. As a result of this innovative speakers series, the department and campus are enriched; the pre-tenure faculty add the visitors to their own professional network; and the senior visitors—rather than the pre-tenure faculty—bear much of the intellectual weight of introducing and explaining unconventional or controversial approaches (personal conversation with provost, 2002). (At times, the senior visitor is a new hire's dissertation adviser or research collaborator.) Other campuses should experiment with such an innovative speakers series driven by pre-tenure faculty.

B-12. Develop a campus culture that is working to level the academic playing field, value multicultural diversity, and build community.

As University of Southern California professors Estela Bensimon and William Tierney have persuasively argued in their book *Promotion and Tenure*, senior faculty and administrators as well as academic departments and divisions must become adept at using gender and race/ethnicity as "lenses" through which they can analyze, in new ways, their business-as-usual practices, assumptions, and procedures. Using such lenses, these leaders will be able to see, probably for the first time, how their practices and customs disfavor non-majorities and favor majorities. More importantly, these leaders should put in place good practices (such as those set forth in this chapter) that will equalize the playing field for their faculty and enable non-majorities in the academic community to thrive and feel they belong (Tierney and Bensimon, 1996, p. 81).

It is useful to consider the predictable stages of development a campus must go through to become multicultural. For instance, in the monocultural and "exclusive-club" stages, campuses merely improve limited access for non-majorities and add a few as token power-holders. By contrast, an "affirming organization" not only works to increase the chances that non-majorities will succeed but also encourages all employees "to think and behave in a non-oppressive manner, and the organization conducts awareness programs toward this end." A higher evolution is reached by the "redefining organization" that is moving to "distribute power among all of the diverse groups in the organization." As the highest level of evolution, "the multicultural organization" draws on the contributions of diverse cultural and social groups not only in its mission, but also in its day-to-day operations and in the goods and services it produces. Further, this organization makes sure its representatives from diverse cultural and social groups are full partners in decision-making to change and shape internal policies and procedures. Not only inside but outside its walls, a multicultural organization and its members continually work to eradicate social oppression in their society (Jackson and Hardiman, 2003, pp. 1–2; also see Banks and Banks, 1989).

Ensuring the multicultural content of college and university courses occupies the intelligence of scores of faculty and administrators across the country. Trustworthy publications to guide such reform include *Multicultural Course Transformation in Higher Education* edited by San Diego State University professors Ann Morey and Margie Kitano (1997) and various works on curriculum change by University of Massachusetts–Amherst professor Maurianne Adams and other scholars. Another important step is to add one or more diversity course requirements to the general education core for undergraduates; many campuses have already taken this step. To find updates on what campuses are doing to develop into multicultural organizations, one can periodically check Diversity Digest within the Web site of the American Association of Colleges and Universities.

B-13. Encourage and develop senior faculty who serve as champions for diversity.

In my consulting, I recommend that provosts and deans identify senior majority faculty in various disciplines who are attempting to be "bridge leaders" (C. Williams, 2001, p. 21) and advocates for diversifying the student body and faculty ranks. Working behind-the-scenes as well as at times stepping up on the bully pulpit, these advocates often have palpable influence on some of their colleagues and students. With deliberate coaching and encouragement by outside consultants and internal leaders, these advocates can heighten their influence and build alliances with other diversity champions across the campus. It behooves provosts and other leaders to constantly enlarge such a cadre of champions not only because they can be prime movers in creating a multicultural campus community, but also because they can provide wise counsel and assistance when backlashes and boomerang effects arise because of diversity efforts. As I quip in my consulting work, administrators such as provosts come and go quickly, but senior faculty *endure and endure.* Because senior faculty have such significant and lasting power, they must be engaged in important diversity initiatives.

GOOD PRACTICES FOR DEPARTMENTS
B-14. Prepare members of the department for the new hire's arrival.

Prior to the minority newcomer's arrival, the department as a whole (perhaps with the dean or provost included) should discuss the explicit and implicit customs observed in the department and then seek the professional and personal reaction to these customs by non-majority faculty in other departments or at other campuses. As a result of this assessment, some departmental practices will probably need to be replaced because they would deliberately or inadvertently exclude or hamper the career development of non-majority hires. As Brown University professor Evelyn Hu-DeHart (2000) has compellingly argued, a majority department typically—and egocentrically—expects a new non-majority hire to adapt to the departmental culture. But the departmental culture itself must also change, to ensure that the new hire is treated as a valued colleague who will receive nurturing and collegial support in order to thrive.

For one example, the department should recognize that members of the majority group usually receive more *instrumental mentoring* than minorities within the same department (Fried et al., 1996; Turner and Myers, 2000). Instrumental mentoring occurs when senior colleagues take the time to critique the juniors' scholarly work, nominate them for career-enhancing awards, collaborate on research or teaching projects, and arrange for them to chair conferences or sessions and submit invited manuscripts. Less instrumental mentoring for minorities can translate into a significant and cumulative professional disadvantage. The department as a whole must become aware that the experiences of majority newcomers are likely to be very different from those of minority newcomers and that accumulating professional strength and advantage is usually easier for majorities (see chapter 1). In fact, accumulating professional advantage may be the most difficult of all for members of colonized minority groups, as I demonstrated in chapter 3. Not only should the department be mindful of these facts, but it should also develop strategies to ensure that non-majority hires receive instrumental mentoring and guidance in leveraging small successes into larger ones.

During the faculty meetings prior to the new hire's arrival, the department chair should lead discussion on how affirmative action strategies and diversifying the faculty will enhance (rather than dilute) the excellence of the department and its value to students and the campus. The new colleague must not be undervalued and belittled as an "affirmative action hire"; it is the department chair's responsibility to be on guard and to preempt any such negativity about the new hire. It would be truly ironic for the new hire to have to face such negativity from one or more senior colleagues, given that European-American males have enjoyed *invisible* affirmative action and political and economic monopolies since colonial times (see no. 9 in chapter 1 and Dahl, 2001).

B-15. Supply newcomers with essential information about departmental operations months before their arrival on campus.

Three months before the newcomer's arrival, the department chair (aided by other faculty and the departmental secretary) should provide essential information to ease the transition. For example, details should be given about the newcomer's course load, typical number of office hours for a departmental member, anticipated class size, and academic level and preparation of students. Sample syllabi should be sent, together with sample book lists for the newcomer to review, e-mail addresses of faculty who have taught the courses and are willing to chat with the newcomer, and a description of student-advising duties for the newcomer. Any faculty or personnel handbooks should be included.

In addition, the new hire should be informed about his/her office and computer equipment; clerical support that will be available; travel and research funds that can be requested; and the possibility of research or administrative assistants and how to secure them. Finally, the department or the institution's personnel office should supply information about housing, schools, day-care centers, transportation options, cultural and sporting events, recreational opportunities, and so forth. Easing the transition is a *critically important process*. Invaluable checklists and tips can be found in *The Department Chair's Role in Developing New Faculty into Teachers and Scholars* by Estela Bensimon, Kelly Ward, and Karla Sanders (2000). A caveat: If any of the equipment or support mentioned to the newcomer fails to materialize, then the chair or a designated senior faculty member should immediately and apologetically inform the newcomer prior to his or her arrival. What should be avoided is a lapse or omission that might be construed as a personal or professional slight by the understandably nervous newcomer.

B-16. Introduce and warmly promote the new faculty member to students at the beginning of the semester, as well as to other faculty colleagues.

To heighten the newcomer's sense of belonging, the chair or a designated senior faculty member should visit the newcomer's classes on the first day of the semester, to briefly and enthusiastically explain to students why the department is so pleased about its new addition. This courtesy to the new hire will also help students better appreciate the new faculty member. In addition, the chair can underscore to the dean and faculty colleagues how valuable the newcomer is to the department.

B-17. Senior faculty in the department must become persistently friendly and instrumentally helpful to newcomers, especially minority ones.

Merely smiling and being vaguely cordial is insufficient in light of the extra stresses and taxes that most minority and women newcomers must bear. For instance, senior faculty could introduce junior faculty to informal and useful Internet networks and to helpful colleagues near and far; collaborate with the juniors on research or teaching projects; and consistently invite newcomers to lunch or cultural or sporting events. In short, *persistently reach out*—or isolation will set in.

Senior faculty must realize that doing no harm to minority faculty is not enough. Countless times I have had majority faculty explain to me that they themselves are on their best behavior: "I am cordial and invariably ask how our new hire is faring." I respond that being pleasant is insufficient, in light of the extra taxes and burdens that minorities face in a majority academic setting (see chapter 1). What must senior faculty do? They should be exceedingly and *repeatedly friendly* to newcomers (especially to non-traditional faculty such as white women and minorities) and make sure they feel welcome and comfortable. For example, on *day one* include them in lunch, bowling, skydiving, or whatever! If senior faculty themselves feel uncomfortable and awkward around newcomers whose gender, race, or ethnic background is different from their own, then the seniors should consider taking one or more communication skills workshops focused on multicultural concerns. Usually these sessions build new skills and approaches in a very short time for those ready to learn. I have talked with dozens of senior faculty who recommend such workshops because of the confidence and competence generated.

Senior faculty should informally introduce their pre-tenure colleagues to information and Internet networks of value to them. Seniors can co-teach and collaborate with junior colleagues and/or review their scholarship, writing, and teaching and make light-handed suggestions. They can *appreciate and learn* from the newcomers' unique abilities and approaches; they can care about the new hires' satisfaction and success. In short, they can be magnanimous colleagues and, hopefully, mentors. Just as there are productive ways in business organizations to be "one-minute" mentors who quickly dispense valuable praise and guidance, there are ways to be one-minute senior mentors in academe. I have used the following preparation for senior faculty: First remember how you yourself in your recent or hoary past have been affected by a positive remark or suggestion, made in passing by a senior person, perhaps on an elevator ride. Now cultivate "mindfulness" of such one-minute mentoring so that you are ready, in passing, to give similar quick encouragement and pointers to junior colleagues at opportune times. (I do admit that some mentoring experts would prefer to call this exchange "elevator *coaching*" rather than "one-minute mentoring.")

Here is an example of a senior faculty member *reaching out* to befriend junior faculty. Professor Ronald Wakimoto, in the forestry school at the University of Montana, typically asks newcomers in his department to give him very brief advice regarding a troublesome part of a manuscript he is working on or regarding a teaching or mentoring problem he has encountered. (He deliberately asks the new hires for guidance where they are strong.) By helping the senior professor and knowing that he will return the favor when they have a writing or teaching problem, the newcomers become connected and have the opportunity to participate, if they wish, in a reciprocal and constructive relationship. This has proved an effective way to begin valuing and appreciating newcomers' unique abilities, approaches, and competencies (personal conversation, 1999).

B-18. The department chair and senior faculty should protect junior faculty, in particular minorities, from excessive teaching, advising, and service assignments.

A chronic overtaxing typically occurs when minority and women faculty are asked to serve as the "diversity" member for numerous campus-wide or departmental committees, as no. 5 in chapter 1 explains. It is the chair's and mentoring committee's responsibility to "run interference" and prevent not only an overload of committee work, but also an overload of student advising. Help the newcomers wisely choose committee assignments that will bring them in contact with other faculty important for them to know and possibly to collaborate with on scholarly enterprises—this, too, should be a task of the chair.

For all new faculty hires, the department and its chair should assign a reduced teaching load during the newcomers' first year and also ensure that the courses to be taught are very familiar ones. These steps will help newcomers avoid a frenetic and stressful launch of their careers (Fink, 1984). In addition, the newcomers should be encouraged to apply for summer research grants rather than accept summer teaching assignments.

B-19. Actively work to help new faculty make scholarly connections within and outside the department.

It is insufficient for the department chair to merely introduce the newcomer to departmental and campus colleagues, one by one. During the first year especially, the chair or his/her designee should act as *a broker*, to help the newcomer make scholarly connections with colleagues inside and outside the department that could further research and teaching productivity and foster collegiality. Both newcomers and old-timers can be cued to the possible overlapping of their intellectual interests. In addition, the newcomer should receive a detailed summary of faculty colleagues' interests, especially if the department he/she is entering is large.

B-20. The department chair and senior faculty (making up a review committee) should assess and monitor pre-tenure faculty as they work to meet the tenure requirements for teaching, research, and service.

Each pre-tenure faculty member must receive an *annual job-performance review* as well as feedback about tenure requirements. Nothing can be as bewildering as wondering "how am I doing?" and "what are the tenure goals I should be focused on?" These questions must be answered.

Conventional wisdom holds that the department chair should serve as the primary monitor of performance for new faculty. I don't believe this arrangement is feasible, given the current practice in many departments of rotating their chairs every two to three years. In order that pre-tenure faculty have long-term continuity of mentorship and monitoring, in case the original chair is replaced by another professor, I suggest that the *chair and two other senior faculty make up a review committee* for all new hires. (The committee is sometimes called a career-development committee.) This special committee would make sure newcomers and pre-tenure colleagues understand the protocols and idiosyncrasies of the department and especially the procedures and expectations regarding tenure. Additionally, the chair and other two seniors should monitor the junior members as they work to meet the requirements for teaching, research, and service and approach the time for possible tenure and promotion.

Any teaching difficulties and concerns underscored in student evaluations of a new faculty member should be surfaced; the committee should discuss ways to remedy the difficulties. It would also be helpful to ask each new hire to prepare his/her three-year or five-year plan for scholarship and publications (if these are expected). Reviewing this plan, the committee can determine if departmental resources such as money, clerical help, research assistants, and the like can be allocated to support execution of the plan. In the Education Department at Louisiana State University, a review committee ensures that new faculty understand the requirements for tenure and are working satisfactorily toward that goal. The high success rate of those monitored and mentored shows how productive junior faculty can be when they receive feedback and are no longer mystified and bewildered by the hidden rules of the game, according to Kofi Lomotey, a former professor at L.S.U. and now president at Fort Valley State University in Georgia (personal conversation, 2003).

B-21. Assign senior faculty the responsibility for actively mentoring newcomers.

Before each new hire (majority or minority) arrives in the department, the provost's office should appoint for the newcomer a mentoring committee composed of three enthusiastic senior faculty, as I discussed in B-1. Studies suggest that two of these mentors should be from outside the newcomer's department because such faculty will not be evaluating the newcomer for contract renewals and tenure decisions. The third, from the new hire's department, should be appointed by the department chair. This mentoring committee's tasks are to *actively* coach the newcomer; share tricks of the trade regarding time management, teaching, research, and publishing; and protect the new colleague from overloads of either student advising or committee assignments.

A schedule of monthly meetings between the mentors and the newcomer should be set (perhaps meetings over lunch, with costs underwritten by the provost's office). Every three months or so, several mentoring committees and their protégés can meet with one another, again to build collegiality and share insights. Bob Boice, the preeminent faculty developer, has interviewed hundreds of pre-tenure faculty over his career. He has concluded that departments and institutions must take deliberate steps to ease the transition for newcomers, particularly with the help of trustworthy mentors. If these steps are not taken, then *negative incidents and isolation*, occurring very early in the faculty career, will undermine retention of newcomers, most especially non-majority new hires (Boice, 1993a).

What should/could mentors discuss with their brand-new mentees? Because the start-up of a mentor-mentee relationship can be uncomfortable until people come to know one another, I have found it essential to share several guidelines and pointers with mentors that will help them initiate the new relationship cordially and competently. These Good Practices will be provided shortly, in chapter 6. Also included in the next chapter will be a number of *self-help strategies for minority faculty* to enhance their professional success and satisfaction on majority campuses. My recommendation is that mentors and mentees *together* consider these self-help strategies and explore ways that the mentors can be useful and encouraging as the mentees activate their own plans of action.

An Illustration of a Comprehensive Retention Program

Comprehensive Good Practices at the departmental level can undeniably improve the department's culture, protocols, and customs—and benefit all faculty, not just minority faculty. At Johns Hopkins University, the Department of Medicine in 1990 instituted a *fifteen-year program of comprehensive interventions* (what I would call departmental Good Practices) designed to shrink and finally eliminate gender-based salary inequities and career obstacles for women faculty there.

A fascinating article in the *Journal of the American Medical Association*, by Professor Linda Fried and several others (Fried et al., 1996), summarizes those interventions and their outcomes. For instance, workshops on mentoring help to ensure that senior male faculty provide *comprehensive* career-advancement mentoring, not just to pre-tenure men faculty but also to pre-tenure women faculty. For all pre-tenure faculty, the department now guarantees annual job-performance reviews and salary reviews while the department's Promotion Committee provides suggestions on how to strengthen one's case for tenure and promotion. Two or more women faculty are now appointed to each academic hiring committee in the department.

To reduce psychological isolation, the department moved medical grand rounds, "held on Saturdays for 100 years," to Friday mornings so that more faculty and medical residents with family obligations can attend. Further, the department organizes special career-development workshops for women faculty and women fellows in all medical divisions, which also serve to produce for the women a gratifying "sense of critical mass" with others throughout the large department. As a result of these interventions, the number of women holding tenure at the associate professor rank moved from four in 1990 to twenty-six in 1995, with no changes being made in the criteria for promotion; three times as many women now say they expect to stay in academic medicine; the proportion of associate professors among women faculty increased from nine percent in 1990 to forty-one percent in 1995, comparable to the proportion for men faculty; and morale and job satisfaction among *all* junior faculty rose, according to surveys of both male and female junior faculty (Fried et al., 1996). In my conversation in summer 2003 with Dr. Fried, she reported that the department (now with eleven women full professors and seven women in senior leadership roles) is undertaking other cultural-change interventions over the next several years, to eliminate or at least reduce cultural biases and mindsets, to recruit more women into high-level leadership positions, and to improve the decision-making processes throughout the department so they are more inclusive of women faculty.

CONCLUSION

The Good Practices in retention in this chapter, along with the Good Practices in recruitment from the previous chapter, can be experimented with and adapted to the discipline-specific characteristics of a department or division. What makes sense is to first become mindful of sloppy evaluation processes, ingrained presuppositions, and unexamined customs already in operation (perhaps for a hundred years, as at Johns Hopkins). Then, assess the effects—intentional and especially unintentional—of these practices and premises, with the assistance of senior and junior faculty, students, and outside experts. Third, replace antiquated or harmful customs and practices with new ones, drawn from the examples provided in this chapter on retention as well as the previous one on recruitment.

CHAPTER 6

GOOD PRACTICES IN MENTORING

THE PREVIOUS CHAPTERS SET FORTH Good Practices—in recruitment and retention—for adoption by provosts and other administrators, academic divisions and departments, and academic search committees. This chapter focuses solely on the essential steps to be taken by two other key parties: the senior, power-holding mentor and his/her pretenure mentee, who will be considerably less powerful but eager to learn the ropes. Before we start, I offer this working definition. Mentors typically provide to mentees both psychosocial support and instrumental assistance with career advancement; by contrast, advisers just give advice and information, often for the short term.

I recommend that each mentor-mentee pair or each small group composed of a mentoring committee and mentee(s) take time—*together*—to discuss the pointers and practices below. By doing so, readiness and trust will develop, the mentoring relationship will deepen, and perennial problems will receive attention. Moreover, discussion of parts or all of this chapter can serve as an icebreaker, helping mentors and mentees launch their relationships efficiently. (For additional details about how mentoring *committees* function, see B-1 and B-20 in chapter 5.)

I know that for non-majority faculty working in majority settings, the self-help strategies (in the second half of the chapter) are vital. Invariably, such faculty express relief when I—and others—identify and demystify the crosscurrents and obstacles they are contending with. They appreciate when I and others outline specific steps that they, as agents, can take to lessen or resolve their stressors as well as enhance their success and satisfaction with their profession. But please note my recommendation: Both the mentee *and* mentor should be involved in activation of some of these steps. It would be inhumane to expect the junior faculty mentee, all alone, to launch and sustain an action plan. Such a sink-or-swim arrangement must be avoided.

The practices and strategies in this chapter can serve as a core curriculum for campus-wide or division-wide mentoring programs. Such programs are invaluable. In my view, effective mentoring should be guaranteed for *all* pre-tenure faculty—minority and majority—as well as *all* new faculty hires. It is also my hope that senior departmental faculty, provosts and deans, and campus trustees will choose to discuss this chapter in their own meetings—to better understand the challenges and demands being faced by newly hired and pre-tenure faculty and then explore how they, as power-holders, can create a more welcoming and nurturing environment for these colleagues.

GOOD PRACTICES FOR SENIOR MENTORS

As I discussed above, the insights in this section should be read by mentees as well as mentors.

C-1. Recognize the hesitation of some mentees and try to move beyond it.

As a mentor, you should realize that some minority and women faculty *may not feel entitled* to the attention and protection of senior mentors. Typical protests and puzzling demurs you may hear include: *I didn't want to bother you because I knew you were preparing for your big conference; Well, I did call once, but I didn't want to make a pest of myself; I didn't e-mail you with this problem because I thought I should be able to figure it out for myself; Well, I didn't want to seem needy, so I just kept going on my own.* Mount Holyoke College chemistry professor Sheila Ewing Browne (recipient of the Presidential award for science mentoring from the National Science Foundation) often warns minorities and women that this assumption—that they do not deserve a mentor—can be a "self-fulfilling prophecy" (personal correspondence, 2003). Professor Browne believes mentors, in the first few meetings with mentees, should frontally address this assumption and try to banish it. Otherwise, the assumption can obstruct the beneficial development of the relationship.

Moreover, mentors should take the lead in constructing a schedule of mentor-mentee meetings (perhaps once per month, over lunch). Because most new hires will feel overwhelmed with their teaching and other duties from time to time (or most of the time), they will be tempted to skip scheduled meetings with the mentor. *Important note to mentees:* Such skipping or canceling would be a *mistake!* Frequently talking and checking in with your mentor is critically important in ways you cannot know at this point in your career. Protect the time you have set aside with your mentor.

C-2. Disclose some of your own failures and confusions.

As a mentor, you should disclose to your mentee, fairly soon in the mentoring relationship, *some failures and confusions that you* yourself *have experienced* as a student and now as a professional. (Come on, now, you can surely think of a *few!*) If you do not disclose some of these low points, junior faculty will probably put you on a pedestal and come to suspect that you are superhuman—while they, of course, are decidedly not. Ironically, the suspicion that you are superhuman could have a chilling effect on the mentee's own ambitions and self-confidence. Those being coached know that they stumble and are often off balance. But they also need to know that you have such moments—yet you have persisted and kept going. *Persistence* is a key lesson for a mentor to transmit. My advice would be to tell personal stories and testimonials to help mentees grasp this lesson rather than lecture abstractly to them about persistence and resilence with Aristotelian quotes sprinkled in.

C-3. Address critical incidents experienced by mentees—and assist with damage control.

No later than the first week of the mentoring relationship, the mentor should be light-handedly insistent that mentees discuss hurtful or confusing *critical incidents* they may be experiencing as they execute their various duties as a new professor and interact with students and colleagues. For example, mentees may be ignored in a departmental faculty meeting. Or they may find that their offices are not ready for occupancy, even though the new semester has begun. Several students may be acting hostilely or sarcastically toward the mentees (this often happens with non-traditional faculty, as I will explain below). Senior colleagues in the department may not be including the new faculty in their lunches or collaborative projects or even jokes at the watercooler. Unless these hurtful or bewildering incidents are ventilated and put in perspective, they can fester and prompt the mentee to resign, figuratively or literally (Boice, 1993a). I have repeatedly seen this pattern of resignation threaten to take shape early in a newcomer's career. Interventions must interrupt the pattern. Encouraging the mentee to talk about these critical incidents, the mentor should give empathetic support and guidance; the mentor might also consider working behind-the-scenes to reduce the harm done by the incident.

C-4. Understand the typical cumulative disadvantages for those viewed as "outsiders" and "tokens."

Non-majorities who are viewed as outsiders and pioneers often are given signals by some of their senior colleagues that they are not fully qualified and competent and actually don't belong in the department or academe (see chapters 1 and 3). Discomfort may be felt by these senior colleagues when they interact with a faculty member (such as a woman or minority person) whom they view as so different from themselves. Such interpersonal discomfort is likely to block the established colleagues from offering inside information, tricks of the trade, and encouragement to the newcomer viewed as different—hence the term "chilly climate." Moreover, tokens (the numerically few) may receive unfairly low evaluations of their job performances because they are being subjected to others' global presumption of their inferiority and strangeness. For example, some students have difficulty accepting the intellectual authority of someone who looks and sounds different from the traditional faculty member; women and minorities, as new professors, find that their course evaluations by such students can be especially critical. Academic departments must become sensitive to how and why such evaluations of non-traditional instructors can be skewed in contrast to those of traditional faculty (TuSmith, 2001).

The mentor should be alert to and empathetic with any undervaluing and chilliness that may be experienced by the mentee. But the mentor should also try to help senior colleagues rise above their discomfort or resistance as well as coach the mentee in appropriate self-help strategies to deal with negative behavior aimed at them.

C-5. Understand the extra disadvantages for members of colonized minority groups.

Faculty mentors should be aware of the special stresses that *colonized* minorities often contend with. Colonized minorities in this country include Puerto Rican Americans, Mexican Americans, African Americans, American Indians, Native Hawaiians, and Native Alaskans. Having been reared in the United States, members of these minority groups probably have had to deal with a steady barrage of belittling comments and attitudes about their intellectual abilities (see chapter 3). This barrage can take its toll on one's self-confidence. I believe that you mentors should be prepared to offer *more encouragement and ego boosting* to them than you ordinarily offer, in a routine manner, to others. "I see a critical part of my role as mentor being to persistently bolster the confidence of my mentees," explains Christopher K. R. T. Jones, Guthridge Professor and Chair of Mathematics at the University of North Carolina–Chapel Hill (he is European American). "This is particularly important in mentoring women and minorities as I have been struck by how often and to what extent they underestimate their intellectual abilities" (personal correspondence with author, 2002).

C-6. Help mentees learn how to self-promote.

Self-promotion may be a difficult strategy for some women and minorities to adopt. While senior faculty know all too well that promotion of one's work and one's intellectual competency are essential in academia, they are puzzled as to why some students and junior faculty sometimes shy away from blowing their own horn. In the first place, people who are introverted understandably get sweaty palms just thinking about self-promotion. For introverts, a mentor can suggest behind-the-scenes ways to ensure that one's work gets its due. In the second place, new faculty often resist self-promotion because they feel that their tribe or culture or family upbringing prohibit the obnoxious self-promotion they observe, at times, in academic settings.

By naming this prohibition and candidly discussing it with mentees, you mentors should be able to help them outline a variety of different ways to self-promote that are not obnoxious and distasteful to them. For example, one Native American professor I know makes it a point to promote his Native American colleagues, and they likewise promote him. This arrangement circumvents the tribal frowning on self-aggrandizement.

C-7. Undertake *instrumental, proactive* mentoring.

Mentors need to provide psychological bolstering and also *career-advancement interventions*. For instance, mentees should receive inside information about the real workings of academic departments; what the unspoken rules are; how one methodically builds a track record of achievement by leveraging a new success from a previous one; and how one methodically expands a professional support network. Mentors can introduce their mentees to influential leaders who can open new doors of opportunity for them. Having mentees *collaborate with mentors* on intellectual projects can help the juniors hone their research, publication, and networking skills—such collaboration is the center of a formal mentoring program sponsored at the University of California–San Diego School of Medicine for pre-tenure women faculty (personal conversation with epidemiologist Deborah Wingard, 2003). Above all, mentors can give honest feedback in a tactful manner about the mentee's academic work, so that the mentee stretches and grows.

C-8. Observe some ground rules when *arguing* with mentees.

Of course, there will sometimes be disagreements between you mentors and your mentees. If the argument becomes intense, make sure you consciously shift gears and start sentences with *"I" rather than "you."* For example, you might say: "I'm really concerned by something you said yesterday" or "I wonder why you spent so little time on your departmental presentation last week." Beginning with "you" can escalate the tension and preclude problem-solving with your mentee, or in fact, anyone. Consider for a moment how inflammatory or hurtful the following might sound to the recipient: "You are vague and scattered this morning" or "You're taking the easy way out with those multiple-choice exams." Likewise, avoid "always" and other overgeneralizing adverbs that can escalate an argument beyond control. In short, when you feel yourself getting hot under the collar, switch to "I" messages or arrange to talk at another time.

C-9. Rise above gender and racial/ethnic stereotypes.

Be mindful of gender and racial schemas and stereotypes you may have internalized from having lived in this society (see chapters 1–3). The first step is to *catch yourself* employing these stereotypes and mind-sets that underrate the competence and leadership of women and members of certain minority groups—while, at the same time, they overrate European-American and Asian-American men. The second step is to consciously *overcome* these mind-sets. Conscientiously going through these two steps may well be a strenuous, lifelong process.

C-10. Avoid the temptation to clone.

Be careful not to impose your own career path on the mentee. If you were an early bloomer (for instance, at age seven you knew you wanted to be a rocket scientist), don't devalue the experience of someone who took longer to make that decision. If you didn't have children until after you were established in your career, don't assume that everyone else will imitate your timing. If your mentee started at a community college while you went to Harvard as an undergraduate, do not assume that you're more talented, or even better prepared academically. There are many kinds of brilliance, and they can manifest themselves at various times. Cultivate tolerance and indeed appreciation of *unconventional career paths and timetables* so that you welcome so-called late bloomers into your discipline and into your campus community.

C-11. Realize that you are providing invaluable guidance and collegial support.

Mentors can make a tremendous difference in showing junior colleagues the ropes, reducing their loneliness and bewilderment, applauding their strengths, and shoring up their weaknesses. In a score of national studies and in my own work with pre-tenure faculty, the importance of mentors always ranks highly.

POINTERS AND STRATEGIES FOR PRE-TENURE FACULTY MENTEES

As I discussed at the beginning of the chapter, this section should also be read by mentors.

A handful of job stressors affect almost every new faculty member. While adjusting to a new position and maximizing one's enjoyment of it are usually not easy, you newcomers can do better if the process is demystified. If no one has "told the truth" and clued you in to the crosscurrents and struggles you will probably experience, you are likely to waste psychic energy being bewildered. By being clued in, you can make better use of your personal and professional resources. Because minority and women faculty often confront additional taxes and stressors that majority newcomers do not (as discussed in chapters 1 and 3), these will receive extra attention.

This chapter, however, does more than identify and describe the typical stressors. A variety of self-help strategies are presented. These have been successfully used by majority and especially minority faculty to reduce the stressors and to achieve greater satisfaction in their teaching, scholarship, service, and interaction with colleagues. Many insights here are drawn from my monograph *Demystifying the Profession: Helping Junior Faculty Succeed* (Moody, 2001). Another concrete and valuable publication is the 2002 book *Tenure in the Sacred Grove: Issues and Strategies for Women and Minority Faculty* (edited by Joanne Cooper and Dannelle Stevens).

For the reader's convenience, I have highlighted in bold font some key insights in the text below. This second part of the chapter will lend itself to discussion by newly hired and pre-tenure faculty together with their senior mentors, their department chairs, or their mentoring committees. These seniors should be involved in helping the junior faculty activate some of these self-help strategies. In addition, junior faculty may wish to discuss and share some of these strategies and caveats with their peers and members of their professional support groups.

TYPICAL STRESSORS—AND WHAT TO DO ABOUT THEM

D-1. Lack of collegiality

New faculty typically report that in their new department, they enjoy "very little" intellectual companionship with their colleagues. Indeed, their biggest surprise is discovering how lonely and intellectually understimulated they are at first at their new campus. In a way, these new faculty grieve for the social and intellectual circle of friends, colleagues, and mentors they enjoyed in graduate school. In graduate school, "people worried about me and I about them." But leaving that cocoon, new faculty have to start all over in a new setting where some of the senior faculty can be standoffish; absorbed in their own worlds; caught up in gossip and departmental or campus politicking; and uninterested in welcoming new faculty and helping them adjust and succeed in their demanding new roles. "I was at first totally stunned by how little community I saw or experienced in this department," recalls one newcomer who must remain anonymous.

How serious is this? It is a major source of stress and frustration, according to University of Massachusetts–Amherst associate provost Mary Deane Sorcinelli (1992; Sorcinelli and Near, 1989); veteran faculty developer and SUNY professor emeritus Robert Boice (1992a & b, 1993, 2000); University of Oklahoma faculty developer Dee Fink (1984); and a half dozen other researchers. Loneliness and intellectual understimulation can easily and quickly undermine the newcomer's enjoyment of the job. New faculty complain that senior faculty don't reach out to them and offer friendliness, encouragement, and pointers. But researchers hasten to add that most new faculty are very passive and rarely seek out help, advice, and mentoring from within their department or from others on campus.

What to do? New faculty must be proactive and repeatedly reach out to junior and senior faculty colleagues, inside and outside their department. According to the splendid coach Bob Boice, new faculty who thrive and succeed typically **spend about five hours per week networking and building collegiality** through face-to-face visits, letters, phone calls, and e-mail with colleagues near and far.

- They attend colloquia and lectures given by esteemed colleagues and dare to initiate cordial conversations with them.
- They track down accomplished teachers on campus and at other campuses and learn what they can from them—as well as enjoy the collegiality that results.
- They don't hide their own scholarship away: They talk, talk, talk about it and ask informed others for their reactions (whether these others are on or off their campus and whether they are peers or way up the hierarchy).
- They reach out and persuade others, on and off campus, to join with them on collaborative writing, teaching, research, or fund-raising projects.

Studies of productive science and social science researchers reinforce Boice's points: These successful scholars maintain regular contacts with colleagues with similar research interests; they circulate papers among themselves; they help one another find bibliographic references; they brainstorm about the implications of each other's hunches, failures, theories, and discoveries. They find that such **personal interaction is far more important than merely reading journals and even presenting formal papers** at meetings. Of course, working the crowd at a conference can be important: Talk to people at science poster sessions, presentations, and panel discussions; ask for their papers and reprints, and get back to them with your feedback. This is how you create allies for yourself.

Admittedly, the constant reaching out to new and old colleagues, for the purposes of collaboration and networking, will demand more energy and willpower if your personality leans more toward introversion than extroversion. But your investment will pay dividends.

One last piece of networking advice comes from chemistry professor Sheila Ewing Browne, winner of mentoring awards from the National Science Foundation, the Compact for Faculty Diversity, and other organizations. She urges mentees to **be on guard against "terminators,"** meaning those one or two colleagues in any organization who should be avoided because they delight in causing others pain and frustration. In short, do not network with such dangerous individuals but instead stay far away (personal conversation, 2003).

D-2. Negativity

In graduate school, chronic complaining seems to be an unfortunate part of the landscape. A former New England dissertation scholar-in-residence in anthropology, Ken Marty, recalls: "I didn't expect to find so many graduate students with severe anxieties and low self-esteem. Many students constantly talk about stress, pressure, inse-curity, and the difficulty of writing" (quoted in Moody, 1996, p. 15). If any of you while in graduate school picked up the virus of chronic suf-fering and complaining, then please realize how much psychic and in-tellectual energy are being drained from you.

What can you do to counteract this tendency? Successful new fac-ulty **take an optimistic approach** to their students, their colleagues, and their campus. These "quick starters," as Boice terms them (1992b), try to avoid people who specialize in being bad-mouthers and "stress carriers." They say they dislike gossip about their colleagues and try to stay away from it. David Schuldberg, a psychology professor at the University of Montana, underscores this point: "Avoiding gossip is a wise strategy and a feature in the careers of some of my most success-ful colleagues throughout the country" (personal conversation, 2002). Quick starters also dislike wasting time listening to others' chronic complaining and horror stories. As a junior faculty member confided to me: "I hate *ain't it awful* litanies and try to find some excuse to leave when someone starts up."

On the other hand, do indeed talk with your mentor if you have ex-perienced a confusing and hurtful slight that continues to bother you (such as the perceived snub of a senior colleague or the aggressive stance of several of your students). These are critical incidents that need to be ventilated and put in perspective with the help of your mentor. Do not hide away such incidents, out of a sense of embarrass-ment. You will need wise guidance in dealing with these incidents, which happen to everyone from time to time.

D-3. Unrealistic expectations

Sorcinelli reports that studies of first-year faculty members show "newcomers feel a great deal of self-imposed pressure to perform well on every front." She quotes one insightful novice: "It's been very stressful to try to do everything and do it well. I'm not coping very well and I work every living, breathing moment I'm awake. . . . The problem is that I could live with less than a perfect job as a student but not as a profes-sor" (1992, p. 30; also see Fink, 1984). Boice (1992b) repeatedly cautions against this sort of perfectionism. To compound the mistake, some deans, senior faculty, and department chairs expect the newcomers to "hit the ground running"—an unrealistic and even cruel expectation.

How can you cope? First of all, please listen carefully to the "self-talk" going on inside your head. Are you pushing yourself inhu-manely? Are you berating yourself and accusing yourself of being an impostor? If so, try to change what's going on in your head. With the help of friends and mentors, give yourself credit for what you've already accomplished. Next, set priorities, construct realistic expectations, and compliment yourself for methodically working to realize these. Concentrate on important tasks that are a part of your game plan, and try to resist being drawn off into the performing of urgent—but frequently trivial—tasks.

Perfectionism may be the biggest trap and anxiety producer. An accomplished practitioner and writer on mentoring, professor of sociology Charles Willie (in Harvard's Graduate School of Education) says that learning to be less than perfect in some tasks is a difficult lesson for junior faculty. But if they don't learn it, they can "tie themselves in knots" (personal conversation, 1998). Organizational psychologist Joan Tonn (associate professor of management at the University of Massachusetts–Boston) agrees. In her workshops on stress management, she urges, "stop punishing yourself for not being a perfect person; instead encourage yourself." Accept joyfully that "everything worth doing is not necessarily worth doing well—no matter what your grandmother insisted" (personal conversation, 1998).

D-4. Not enough time

This stressor afflicts junior faculty not only in their first year but also in all their years leading up to tenure. (At some campuses, the tenure decision comes in the third year; at others, in the sixth or seventh, or later if family or another kind of leave has been granted.) For instance, because instructors' preparation for their classes can't be put off, what usually suffers is attention to other tasks like research and writing that may be important to the new faculty members and/or their departments.

What can you, as a new faculty member, do? Talk in concrete ways to other junior faculty and to senior faculty inside and outside your department, both about how to teach more efficiently and effectively and about the organization of your scholarly projects. Concrete talking will probably yield insights that enable you to adopt new time-management and time-saving habits and to feel more in control of your workweek. Additionally, concrete talk will help you reach out and build new relationships with colleagues; these will provide you with social and psychological support and reduce your loneliness and isolation.

Here's another step to take: Set up a task-management and time-management regimen for yourself that maintains *balance* among your teaching, your research and writing, and your building of professional networks. A sense of balance will usually dampen anxiety and stress. Another way to keep stress under control is to sign up for a relaxation and/or exercise program and stick with it. Your physical and mental health demand it.

Finally, even though you have a multitude of tasks to execute, you must **resist becoming a workaholic.** Never forget to reserve time for the things you enjoy and treasure. If you keep your head down, frantically work every waking moment, sacrifice your private life, fail to cultivate new friendships and mentoring relationships, and neglect your intellectual networking with colleagues near and far, then you are positioning yourself to be counterproductive. With such an approach, you will likely spin out of control and feel that precious parts of yourself are being lost.

D-5. Lack of experience in teaching: Lessons from quick starters

Teaching can overwhelm you because most junior faculty have failed to receive either careful supervision of their teaching or coaching in the tricks of the trade. If they had received these in graduate school, they would begin their careers as more effective, efficient, and comfortable teachers. Because they are usually unprepared as they take their first job, they can feel intense anxiety about their duties in the classroom. As their research and writing are put off, their anxiety intensifies.

What can a new teacher do? Some new faculty express remarkable satisfaction with and enjoyment of their teaching and receive high ratings for their teaching effectiveness from students and expert observers. These new faculty, whom Boice dubs "quick starters," exhibit many of the following traits (Boice, 1992b, 2000).

Quick starters are student-friendly. Arriving early to their classes, quick starters chat informally with their students. Showing interest in their students, they work hard to learn their names. Quick starters hand out very informal class evaluations early in the course, to find out anonymously what students are finding most helpful and least helpful thus far about the course, the class discussion, and the like. The quick starters then review these anonymous points in class, encourage students to react, and explain what refinements and modifications, usually minor, will be made as a result of this evaluation and ensuing discussion. Students usually appreciate this invitation to give feedback. In the class discussion prompted by it, the students come to better understand the professor's pedagogical goals and strategies, better comprehend how they can improve their own class participation, and sometimes better grasp the dynamics of groups and group discussion. Finally, quick starters enhance the classroom experience of all students by dealing with students who may be obstructing productive class discussion. Quick starters don't shy away from cordially "defanging" (in a way) troublemakers and cordially "dampening down" monopolizers.

Quick starters regard their teaching as somewhat public and continuously improving. These wise individuals refuse to have preparation for classes take up their whole workweek, to the near exclusion of scholarship/writing and professional networking/collegiality. Instead, they take the initiative to seek teaching advice and tricks of the trade from junior and senior colleagues in their own and other departments. Visiting colleagues' classrooms, inviting others to theirs, experimenting and at times briefly co-teaching with diverse colleagues—these are typical moves. Another is to track down the exceptionally accomplished teachers on campus and consult with them. Such treating of teaching and learning as open-ended and *public* enterprises (rather than closed, private, and proprietary) should become more widespread, according to the American Association for Higher Education, the Pew Charitable Trusts, and other reform-minded groups.

The Internet is quickening this reform, because faculty can now communicate about their teaching problems and successes via several bulletin boards sponsored by the American Association for the Advancement of Science, the National Science Foundation, the Sloan Foundation, and several disciplinary societies. Talking, reading, and thinking about their teaching and their students' learning are enjoyable to quick starters; they say they plan to experiment even more to increase effectiveness and stimulation for both themselves and their students.

Quick starters take their time in the classroom. Boice notes that going too fast through lectures, discussions, problem solutions, and the assigned materials are predictable mistakes made especially by nervous beginners. Furthermore, slow starters believe lecturing is the only way to teach. Delivering perfect "facts-and-principles" lectures is their consuming goal. They present too much material too rapidly in the classroom. They try to ignore the bored and sometimes hostile reactions from students. Overpreparing for their lectures, they teach defensively so to avoid being accused of not knowing their material. Above all, they fear being exposed as an impostor. They have few plans to improve their teaching beyond improving the content of their lectures and making student assignments and tests easier.

Quick starters, on the other hand, realize they must slow down their class presentations and in various ways check to see that the students are not being left behind. Early on, quick starters try to promote critical thinking by their students; they make sure that their students are preparing for class and that they, not just the instructor, are doing intellectual work during the class period. In their courses, they spotlight some of their own specialized research interests and projects: Both the students and the instructor usually enjoy this examination of something fresh and new, and usually a few students will be drawn in as apprentices to the instructor as a result of this intellectual sharing.

Determined to generate productive student interactions, **quick starters also experiment with a range of discussion techniques** until they find what works for them and their unique personalities. According to Duke University professor Anne Firor Scott, an "important part of a teacher's responsibility is to plan classroom experiences that promote a sense of discovery." The point is "to activate an intelligence to begin learning on its own . . . and help students learn how that knowledge came to be and how it can be used to think through problems and organize concepts" (1995, p. 187).

How can the professor, junior or senior, become more comfortable and competent in promoting students' discussion and critical thinking? In her article "Why I Teach by Discussion," Scott shares her tricks of the trade regarding how to do this: First, carefully design the syllabus for an active-learning course; conceptually ready the students for active learning; ensure students' class attendance; be ready to jump-start student discussion and to deal with occasional "dead silence"; keep discussion on track; summarize frequently; model mannerly and respectful behavior during spirited arguments; and design appropriate examinations and evaluations for an active-learning course. Conceptually, the approach in Scott's classes is to **cover less** (material) and **discover more**—an approach I recommend to the doctoral and dissertation scholars I coach who are preparing to be college professors. Scott concludes: "Keep thinking about the educational process, what it ought to accomplish, how one can make it work better" (1995, pp. 190–91).

For helpful pointers on how to use case studies to nurture class discussion and a learning community in the classroom, check the Harvard Business School Press's *Education for Judgment: The Artistry of Discussion Leadership* (Christensen, Garvin, and Sweet, 1991). Writing case studies for one's own classes is within the realm of possibility. Try it! It can be fun. Here's another tip. In a large lecture class, stop the class once or twice per meeting; pose a question (try to make it funny sometimes) and ask for a show of hands for one of three answers; then ask each student to take five minutes to convince a neighbor of the "correct" answer; then, after the five minutes, ask for another show of hands. Minds can change through animated talking. Harvard professor

Art Mazur has documented that his students comprehend and retain more when he uses this technique in his large lecture course (*Teaching Science Collaboratively* videotape). There are many more such techniques; ask your colleagues, near and far, what works for them.

Finally, a new teacher must concentrate on learning to be efficient and wise about the use of time. A memorable analogy is offered by Assistant Professor Kim Needy in industrial engineering at the University of Pittsburgh. She observes: "Teaching preparation can be more like a gas than a liquid or a solid. In other words, it will fill all the space available to it if you let it. You can always add a case study, improve an overhead, and revise a handout. At some point, you have to put a box around it and say, 'enough'" (quoted in Reis's Listserv, March 16, 1998).

D-6. Obstacles to writing and networking

Slow starters—whether junior or senior faculty—are marked by busyness, procrastination, and binges. These faculty think the ideal time for writing is when they have a big uninterrupted period, such as a summer or semester off. And they think that they can write only when they are fully prepared, ready to do the perfect paper, and not so busy. Because *they stay very, very busy*, they put off writing, month after month. Procrastination sets in because writing becomes too big a deal, becomes too important, and requires too much effort and just about perfect conditions.

By contrast, the same people who are described as quick starters in teaching also demonstrate fast starts, according to Boice (1992b), as scholarly writers/researchers and networkers. During most work-weeks, quick starters in humanities and social science **make time to do scholarship**, usually four to five hours per week, and they spend as much time on professional networking as on writing—because the two activities feed and reinforce one another. They **write in brief, non-fatiguing, daily sessions** lasting about an hour, and they hardly ever write in the evenings or on weekends. Effective and efficient writers push themselves to get an outline of their project done quickly and to methodically write and fill in gaps. Such writers accept the fact that several revisions will be necessary. Very little writing and thinking flow cogently and elegantly from anyone's pen or laptop on the first try—though we all wish it would happen this way!

Senior faculty who are accomplished writers also follow this writing-in-moderation approach, according to a Modern Language Association study of one hundred such humanities professors (Jarvis,

1991). Similarly, John Creswell in *Faculty Research Performance: Lessons from the Sciences and the Social Sciences* (1985) reports that productivity in research and publications peaks when scientists, junior and senior, spend about one-third of their workweek on research. Going beyond that seems counterproductive. Boice (2000) explains why this writing-in-moderation technique works so well:

- A one-hour-per-day writing regimen *minimizes tension and fatigue.*
- This regimen keeps the writing fresh in the author's mind and thus *minimizes warm-up or catch-up time.*
- The schedule coaxes writers to *get over their perfectionism* and begin writing before they have the ideal block of time and the ideal preparation. Holes must be left in the imperfect, ongoing work and then filled in later.
- The regimen helps new faculty feel that their scholarship is under way. Because procrastination takes a lot of energy (isn't this so?) and generates anxiety, getting on with the writing brings *some relief and satisfaction.*

Efficient writers also strive to **learn the tricks of the trade regarding publishing** in their field from more experienced practitioners. Quick starters learn how to interact productively with editors and publishers. They seek advice from wise owls about when they should laboriously revise to please an editor or peer reviewer and when, instead, they should immediately send their work to another good prospect. Learning another shortcut, they have several scholarly projects going at the same time in order to enrich creativity and efficiency.

Quick starters also devote about one hour each day to **networking**—such as phone calls, visits, and e-mail—wherein they discuss their teaching, talk about their writing and research projects and ideas, and map out plans for future projects with other scholars and even with students. These conversations add to the feeling of collegiality and usually bring new ideas and insights to your writing projects.

Quick starters in *science-related* fields must often raise funds to support all or part of their research projects and subsequent publications if they are employed at research-oriented campuses. New science faculty often feel "overwhelmed and don't break their funding ideas down into discrete pieces," observes James Henkel, professor of medicinal chemistry and associate graduate dean of the Graduate School at the University of Connecticut. Henkel advises new faculty to talk with mentors and peers about how to **subdivide a research project.** Then begin work on one part, even if it is only jotting down stream-of-consciousness insights, hunches, and questions on the back of an envelope. "The important thing is to **get something down on paper**. This breaks through the writing block or the procrastination that has you stalled."

Setting milestones is more good advice. Using perhaps a large timeline sheet taped to your wall, "you post the external deadlines you face for your grant proposal or conference presentation and then you work backwards, writing on the timeline sheet what specific tasks have to be done by what date." Clearly, this strategy will help to reduce the feeling of being overwhelmed and immobilized. Henkel adds magnanimously, "Even the most organized person sometimes misses deadlines. **Don't be terribly hard on yourself**, and think your career is ruined when you make mistakes like the rest of us. **You'll recover**" (personal conversation, 2002).

D-7. Inadequate feedback

Ironically, academia is marked by a conspiracy—almost—of silence: Essential knowledge one needs to succeed is kept unspoken and hidden. (Sternberg, 1998; Tierney and Bensimon, 1996). For junior faculty, mystery enshrouds how to get all of one's demanding work done while keeping some sanity, joy, and balance. In particular, mystery enshrouds what exactly is required to secure a favorable evaluation at tenure time; there is far too little "show and tell" about tenure hurdles offered by departmental chairs and senior colleagues (Trower, 1999). Being in such a bewildering fog is guaranteed to create insecurity and stress for the academic newcomer. Until the enlightened day when your department makes its tenure requirements clear and its tenure review process transparent, **what can you do?**

As a new faculty member, you should proactively **cultivate mentors** inside and *outside* your department. These allies can help you improve your performance by giving you feedback about your teaching or scholarship and helping you establish networks. These mentors will also give you essential social and emotional support and encouragement. Having mentors outside your department means you don't have to worry about impressing them all the time, the way you might if your mentor is in your department and potentially on your tenure-review committee. (If you are lucky, your provost or academic division will have organized a mentoring committee for each new faculty hire, with probably two of the committee members being drawn from outside your home department.)

It will be necessary for you to spend time cultivating mentors: They unfortunately don't just knock on your door and sign up for the job.

Because there is an art to such cultivation, here are a few tips. After becoming familiar with some of the scholarship, novels, paintings, or other projects done by prospective mentors, you can engage these folks in conversation. Who doesn't like to talk positively about what is important to them? From such a cordial conversation can flow others that may add up to the development of a mentoring relationship. In addition, try becoming extra friendly with one or two colleagues you admire who serve on a campus or departmental committee with you. My overall advice is this: *You* must take the extra steps. You can't afford to be shy—you need mentors, so reach out for them.

You can also **take the initiative in seeking feedback** from senior faculty in your department about how your work is being evaluated. Construct a kind of portfolio that contains your completed, ongoing, and planned writing projects as well as your teaching philosophy, plans to improve, and student evaluations. (Samples of teaching portfolios can be ordered from the American Association for Higher Education in Washington, DC.) After improving your portfolio with the help of your closest colleagues (and your mentoring committee, if you have been assigned one), show the portfolio to your chair and other senior faculty, on an annual basis, and seek their opinions as to whether your work is leading you toward tenure.

Faculty developer Bernice Sandler (1992b) and others in this field suggest that you also **develop a five-year plan** that will guide your progress as a scholar, teacher, and colleague. If you specify what resources (travel funds, teaching workshop, a semester off, research assistant, clerical help) you need to accomplish your goals, you are then well positioned to seek assistance when you meet with resource-holders—also called *deep pockets*—on your campus. First, show your draft plan to your allies and mentors. This process will guarantee you systematic feedback and get you thinking early on about how to successfully clear the tenure bar. Then, when you're ready, show your revised plan to your chair, dean, and other resource-holders.

You also should **request formal feedback** about your job performance on an annual basis from the chair and other senior faculty. It is dangerous to assume that no feedback means no problems! Annual reviews of new faculty members are, happily, becoming more widespread in departments. When there are negative points in the formal and informal evaluations (and there will be), discuss with the chair and other senior faculty what you need to do to improve.

Finally, **keep careful records** from day one of your activities and accomplishments as a teacher, writer/researcher, and colleague: These make up a large part of your tenure file, and you don't want to forget anything. When a significant compliment comes your way about any of these three roles, pleasantly ask the admirer to write you a short letter for this tenure file. If you wait years to ask for these testimonial letters, the details will be sparse and unconvincing. Here is some helpful advice from a publication of the American Historical Association:

> Keep class grade lists, course outlines, notes, and evaluations, if available. Keep copies of anything written for institutional business, publication, or public presentation, as well as reviews of your work. Inform the chair of the department whenever you apply for or get a grant, have something published, or appear on the program of a professional meeting—in fact, anything that contributes to your professional career. (Gustafson, 1991, p. 64)

In addition, keep records describing your contributions to all committees on which you have served as well as your involvement in student advising and mentoring programs. Also be prepared to describe *new initiatives* you have undertaken and provide evidence of *leadership* you have demonstrated in your department and college.

To document your teaching experiences and effectiveness, make sure you also **file documents** such as your course syllabi, your writing assignments, examples of a variety of student papers from your classes, in-class handouts, and any other written work that indicates your competency as a teacher. If you have a problem with a particular course, then you are advised to write an explanation to your department's personnel file that gives your perspective on the problem and what you are undertaking to prevent its recurrence. Make sure your department chair and personnel committee have an opportunity to discuss the explanation with you during your annual review.

D-8. Balancing work and life outside work

New faculty almost always lament that their work lives "negatively spill over" into their personal lives, sometimes severely hurting both their family life and their social and recreational activities (Sorcinelli and Near, 1989). Unfortunately, many colleges and universities across the nation cannot be characterized as family-friendly or even worker-friendly employers.

What to do? Make it a habit to **ask admirable people** how they are managing to balance their public and private worlds. Associate professor of chemical engineering Gilda Barabino, at Northeastern University, recalls that she had to learn "the hard way" to structure and guarantee herself quality time with her family. "I now make sure my husband and son are always on my calendar. For example, we often eat dinner together, and we exercise and read together. It's wonderful" (personal conversation, 1999). Agreeing with Barabino, professor of biological sciences and associate graduate dean Harold Bibb (University of Rhode Island) has this pointer for balancing career and family: "I find that sharing information about my family and personal interests with my professional colleagues is wise—so, too, is being sure my family has an appreciation for my professional commitments. Such a flow of information leads to an understanding by all that there are times when one set of demands must take precedence over others. The result is far less tension, and I am able to enjoy the various parts of my life" (personal conversation, 1998).

What other self-help tips can you try? First, **pay close attention to how you organize your workweek;** make sure all three professional functions (teaching, research, and service) receive quality investment. No one function, such as research and writing, gets put on the back burner (unless research and writing are not viewed as essential for the professor, department, and/or campus). In particular, limit the time you spend on lecture and class preparation so that this preparation doesn't consume the rest of your personal and professional time. According to Boice, effective newcomers to the faculty usually don't spend more that two hours of preparation for each classroom hour— and by the newcomers' third semester, closer to one and a half hours (1992b).

Next, **divide your day into segments.** Do trivial but necessary tasks when you're tired, suggests Carol Espy-Wilson (associate professor of electrical engineering at Boston University). She and her spouse and three children divide up household chores so they can then spend quality time together and enjoy their church activities. "Getting yourself on a regimen," Espy-Wilson says, "may help you manage career and family without shortchanging either one" (personal conversation, 1997). Those academics who want the summer totally free for family responsibilities should keep this in mind when they are job hunting. Investigate which campuses' schedules and expectations allow this freedom. Plenty do. For those who find their nuclear family is working them to a frazzle, there are options. If you no longer live near your parents and relatives, you can deliberately create an extended family composed of neighbors, friends, and co-workers. Extended families can provide psychological support; laughter; backup, emergency child care when your kid-sitter doesn't show up; and daily or at least frequent intergenerational interaction—which some medical experts believe is beneficial for physical and mental health.

Make sure you **complete important tasks, not just urgent ones.** Decide what things you will allow to slide. Work to become not only an effective teacher but also an efficient one. Naomi André, associate professor at the University of Michigan, discloses that she has found it invaluable to think through whether a task to be done is *urgent* or *important*. She explains "It's so easy to put aside important tasks and give all of one's attention to urgent and often trivial tasks" (personal conversation, 2003). To keep focused on important personal and professional tasks is to keep one's eyes on the prize. All of us can probably improve in this area; doing so will bring us closer to a sense of control and balance. And remember, balance is possible when one is striving for *competency* but probably never possible when one's hidden agenda is *perfection.*

COPING WITH THE SPECIAL STRESSORS FACED BY NON-MAJORITY FACULTY

All new faculty members typically experience, to some degree, the stressors discussed above. But if you are a white woman, U.S. minority, or international minority taking on your first professorial position in a predominantly European-American and male department or campus, then you may have to cope with one or more of the following additional stressors. These have been termed *cultural, racial, gender,* or *class taxes* that are exacted from non-traditional faculty fulfilling the role of pioneer, outsider, and token.

D-9. The extra taxes borne by faculty from *colonized* minority groups

A political overview is important: Certain U.S. minority groups—such as Native Americans, Puerto Ricans, Mexican Americans from the Southwest, and African Americans—often experience, generation after generation, castelike treatment by those inside and outside academia. These groups have been described as *colonized minorities* because their ancestors, against their will, were enslaved, dispossessed, or colonized by the European-American majority group. By contrast, *voluntary minorities (immigrants and international visitors)* have chosen to move to this country for a better life or special opportunities. While immigrants may indeed experience severe challenges as they settle in their new setting and adjust to their new academic home department and campus, they probably will not be treated, in a castelike way, as members of "conquered" and inferior groups. It seems clear that faculty from colonized minority groups in the United States usually have the weightiest burdens and stresses to bear. It also seems necessary to state this in an unvarnished manner. (See chapter 3 for more details.)

Members of colonized minority groups, like Professors Nell Painter, Raymond Padilla, and a score of others, underscore how "tiresome" it is to fight the never-ending battle to be accepted as competent and qualified by majority colleagues and the majority culture (see chapter 1). By contrast, Asian-American professors deal with the stereotype that they are super-qualified. The chronic (and usually unthinking) undervaluation of colonized minority groups can easily translate into an unfair evaluation of junior colleagues' teaching performance, scholarly production, or dependability as a departmental or campus citizen and leader. Not only the minority faculty members but also their senior mentors must recognize and be ready to deal with—and *counteract*—this chronic undervaluation.

D-10. Internalizing feelings of inadequacy

From my work, I know that minority and women students and junior faculty (especially those from colonized minority groups) sometimes internalize the denigrating attitudes about their abilities they have heard at times—or indeed most of the time—from authority figures and peers in the majority culture. Given this incessant belittling, they sometimes conclude that they deserve the *cumulative disadvantages* that have accrued to them because of their outsider status. A moving example of feeling like an *imposter* is found in the article "Peer Mentoring among Graduate Students of Color," wherein three male graduate students of color review why and how they formed a dissertation-writing group. One member of the group disclosed the following: "While the reality of being at a predominantly white university and being faced with an occasionally hostile environment was not new, it did not prepare me for the internalized fear and racial vulnerability I experienced as I struggled with the writing of my dissertation." Repeatedly, he would ask himself, "What is a working-class, New York Puerto Rican trying to do entering the ivory tower?" (Bonilla, Pickeron, and Tatum, 1994, p. 106).

If you experience this sort of self-talk, it may be a sign that you have internalized some destructive negativity. Focus on what you've already accomplished against heavy odds. Reflect on the ways in which your students and the academic community need you. Recall the intellectual excitement that brought you to academia. Consider the contributions that you can make to the development of your discipline. By cultivating optimistic, kind, and confident self-talk, you can replace the old destructive tape recordings that may be running in your head. (In chapter 8 are quotations from minority faculty about why they enthusiastically choose to stay in academia.)

Be aware, too, that studies have definitively shown that women often internalize failure. That is, when they do badly, they think, "It's my fault because I'm not intelligent enough." On the other hand, women frequently externalize success: "I got lucky and really don't deserve this." Males often do the reverse. Both genders are undoubtedly responding to their socialization in American society. But these societal tapes can be reprogrammed—and should be (Ginorio, 1995).

For instance, when you catch yourself falling back into negative self-talk and complaining (such as, "I'll never be able to do this because I'm just not good enough"), you must yell *STOP!* to yourself and try to get in the habit of being kind and supportive in your self-talk. One junior faculty member recalls: "Becoming aware of my self-talk has helped me become a lot more encouraging to myself. It was amazing to notice how often I was thinking about myself as a fraud. That's ridiculous!"

D-11. Being seen as an "affirmative action hire"

Non-traditional newcomers may have to deal with yet another complex and demoralizing social dynamic: Some members of the traditional group may belittle them, implicitly or explicitly, as political additions who were hired for what they symbolically represent rather than for their abilities and credentials. Yet those same naysayers ignore how many unearned privileges have been directed toward European Americans and especially males of that dominant group. The U.S. Constitution, we should recall, grants political and economic power only to white, male property owners; the legacy of that exclusionary tactic is still playing itself out in just about every realm of our society. The favored group has enjoyed a monopoly in education (over many generations, only members of that group could attend the University of Virginia, Harvard University, and so on); in the professions (only they could practice law or become college professors); in political arenas (only they could vote and lead); and in commerce (only they could own property, borrow money, and join unions).

I recommend that each department chair and each mentor circulate and then discuss with their colleagues no. 9 of chapter 1, which details how the favored group has been privileged and pampered. This action, of course, would not be necessary if no misguided grousing about affirmative action hires is taking place.

D-12. Finding a chilly climate within the department

European-American male faculty may behave in ways that seem very standoffish and distant with newcomers who are different from them. Accustomed to being surrounded by *"white sons,"* some of these senior males may feel hostile and angry because their old male order is losing ground (as a result, they believe, of affirmative action or political correctness). If this happens to you, try to keep a political perspective on the chilly climate you are encountering, and try to keep it from personally harming you. Talk with your mentors and then to the department chair or dean (whoever is likely to be more empathetic) about what they and you can do to have the climate warmed up. Realize that you may have to repeatedly solicit advice and inside information from your senior colleagues, even when you see that they offer these freely to majority newcomers. Despite such inequity, work with persistence and dignity (charm helps, too) to establish yourself and gain the coaching and essential information you need and deserve.

Admittedly, you will have to expend extra energy and concentration to navigate the complex dynamics of your department if you have been given the role of solo or pioneer. There may not be any role models "whom we can watch and figure out all the little questions about subtextual meaning, about how dress or speech or makeup are interpreted in this particular environment," points out University of New Mexico law professor Margaret Montoya (2000, p. 516). Nevertheless, forge ahead. Remind yourself that you have a right to be in academia. Give yourself credit for the cumulative disadvantages you have probably had to deal with (these are discussed in chapters 1 and 3). Take pride in your accomplishments to date and in those gifts and perspectives you bring to the professoriate. Remember that those possessing majority privilege who have succeeded usually feel proud even though they have been pampered with a large number of built-in advantages (see chapters 1 and 2).

What else can a solo do? Here is hard-earned advice from professor of education Aretha Pigford, recently retired from the University of South Carolina. Having spent three years being the first and only faculty member of color in her department and being vastly outnumbered by majority students and faculty on her campus (where in the recent past, because of her race, she could *not* have enrolled as a student), she described her reality:

- You will be placed in the spotlight; bask in it.
- You will have more responsibilities that many of your white colleagues; juggle them as well as you can.
- Your competence will be questioned; accept that.
- You will have the opportunity to help other minorities; help them.
- You may experience external and internal conflict; resolve it.

- Some people will expect you to make all problems racial; disappoint them (1988, pp. 76–77).

Seven years later as a tenured, full professor, Pigford takes stock again and adds the following pointers to her earlier ones:

- Find mentors.
- Build relationships with colleagues near and far.
- Stay focused on meeting the requirements for tenure—postpone some projects until after tenure is attained.
- Give back to your community, and whenever possible, efficiently connect your writing or research with your community service.
- Respect and value teaching.
- Direct your own path and decide what you do and don't want to do.
- Seek balance and don't neglect your family, church, community, and hobbies (Pigford, 1996; also personal correspondence, 2000).

D-13. Being given too little or too much attention

Non-traditional faculty in majority settings often report a puzzling phenomenon: They are treated at times as invisible and at other times as super-visible. Here is one example: "The paradox of *'underattention'* versus *'overattention'* experienced by women in general is often exacerbated in the case of Hispanic women." On the one hand, a Hispania's comments may be routinely ignored or downplayed in staff or faculty meetings (this happens to many women in public forums). On the other hand, she may be singled out to give the monolithic "minority" view or the "Hispanic view" (Nieves-Squires, 1991, p. 7; also see Ibarra, 1996). In other words, she will be assumed to be standing for and speaking for her entire tribe or group (see no. 4 in chapter 1). A similar experience happened in my first teaching post, where I was the first and only white woman in an English department of thirty-three white men. I was frequently (and at times sarcastically) called on to explain "women's lib[eration]."

Another obvious stressor is in store for non-traditional new hires: They will probably find *few if any senior women or minority faculty* in the department or elsewhere on campus who can share with them hard-won lessons for surviving and succeeding. And they may find that these seniors—if they exist—at times feel unwilling or unable to befriend them, for their own personal or political reasons.

D-14. Having your scholarship undervalued

Some senior faculty in mainstream departments, particularly in the humanities and social sciences, may *resist and undervalue scholarship about minority issues* or any issues unfamiliar to them. (Anti-intellectual behavior, you say? Yes, exactly.) For instance, American Indian scholars still find that some colleagues and some journal editors suspect their work and believe it is impossible for Indians to do objective scientific research on their own people (Stein, 1994). This has been termed the taboo against "brown-on-brown" scholarship. Yet European-American scholars are regarded as doing all kinds of objective and valuable scholarship on European-American topics and people— or anything else, for that matter. As another example, university presses are still lily-white and have yet to diversify and broaden their editorial ranks and their perspectives regarding what is important to publish (Shin, 1996).

D-15. Experiencing the acute sting of negative incidents

Because out-of-the-mainstream newcomers are often isolated and overtaxed (because of their gender, race, class, or cultural background), they can feel intensely the offense of a senior faculty member's negative remark about their scholarship; a junior colleague's lack of response to an overture of friendship; a student's barbed comment on a teaching evaluation; or another critical incident. My observation is this: Such negative moments hurt everyone but probably hurt *more acutely* a person who is already overstressed and overtaxed.

If you have a support system at hand or on the Internet, then the "critical incident" can be discussed with allies and put in perspective. Above all, I advise you to share details about the critical incident(s) with your senior mentors and to *involve them* in processing various components and implications of this incident. You don't want the hurt or dissonance you feel to go unattended. You don't want the incident to undermine your peace of mind and enjoyment of your profession.

D-16. Managing excessive committee assignments

Women and minority faculty often will be asked by the dean or department chair to serve as the "diversity" member on several campuswide or departmental committees. This committee overload can seriously cut into the new faculty's workweek, hamper their teaching and writing performance, and throw them off balance. What to do? **Seek protection** from your department chair or, if the chair is the problem, a trusted senior faculty member. Also **learn to say no** pleasantly but very firmly to this dangerous overload (for instance, "I am honored that you have nominated me to serve on Committee X and appreciate your confidence in me. But I must decline because I am already on Committee Y and am expected to finish Whatever Project in the next year").

D-17. Managing excessive student demands

Perhaps the day is gone when a European-American male student would walk out of class the first day when he realized a young African-American woman was the professor for the course (Pigford, 1988). Nevertheless, minority faculty can have their intellectual authority questioned repeatedly by majority students.

Minority faculty also experience other forms of student pressure. They may do more student advising than their colleagues—either because all non-majority students are sent to them or because such students gravitate to the non-traditional faculty member. To avoid being overwhelmed, you should appeal to your department chair (or a sympathetic senior colleague) for help. You should also practice saying no to some of these demands. On the other hand, if you are *eager* to undertake more than your fair share of diversity work and student advising, then discuss your availability with the department chair and determine if your annual job-performance review and tenure review can reflect your extra commitment. For example, you might have scholarship count for forty percent of your job duties, teaching forty percent, and diversity work and student advising twenty percent. The point is to get credit, recognition, and evaluation for the extra work you would like to do. But realize that your negotiation with the chair may not bring the revaluation and restructuring of your job duties that you wish; this is always a possibility.

D-18. Handling inappropriate behavior

In those situations where you choose to confront someone's offensive behavior or seek a clarification from them, how do you do this effectively? Many interpersonal communications experts suggest that you **avoid inflammatory messages, name-calling, and exaggerations**, such as "*You* are a jerk"; "*You* are a white supremacist"; or "*You* have never liked and respected me." Such "you" messages are guaranteed to escalate the argument into a contest where no one is listening and no one can learn anything. (Check books on the topic "dealing with difficult people" for other pointers.)

Also realize that messages beginning with "I" that express the emotions of the speaker have a good chance of being heard and give the other person room to act constructively. Here are examples: "I'm uncomfortable when you call me sweetie. I feel like you don't respect me or my work"; "I was puzzled by your behavior [or remark or silence] today when you———." An "I" message will usually provide valuable information and psychological room for the two people to **discuss and negotiate** rather than to immediately start pounding on one another.

There are other ways, of course, to confront troublesome issues. Here's another illustration. Currently professor of science at Roxbury Community College in Boston, Kyrsis Rodriguez felt culture shock when she moved from the University of Puerto Rico, where she received her bachelor's degree, to a university in the Midwest where she would earn a doctorate in botany. Rodriguez learned to **deal humorously** with the hurtful comments elicited by her cultural differentness in that context. "Where in the Pacific is Puerto Rico?" was answered by her this way: "Didn't you hear? We moved!" She muses: "Many people say offensive things out of ignorance—they just don't know. I use their comments as an opportunity to educate them while I stay calm and secure in knowing what I stand for. It works almost all the time" (quoted in Moody, 1996, p. 16).

D-19. Overcoming isolation

To guarantee yourself professional support and stimulation, **get into a career-advancement discussion group or writing group**. If this proves too difficult to find or organize, then ask the provost or faculty-development program officer on your new campus to help you find or start up such a group. The rewards of these are great, according to dozens of junior faculty from majority and minority groups I have interviewed.

Fight against isolation and succumbing to nonstop hard work. To succeed and to keep enjoyment in what you're doing, proactively network with others and learn how to **be interdependent**. Boice says again and again that majority and especially minority faculty thrive early in their careers if they have strong social networks, mentoring, and collaborative projects under way with colleagues near or far (1993a). The same point is valid for women scientists: "Those women who had networks, peer groups, or mentors were more likely to persevere than those women who were isolated" (Ginorio, 1995, p. 16).

D-20. Not feeling entitled to be in academia

Listen carefully to the internal conversations you carry on with yourself. Keep faith with yourself, and give yourself credit for the trailblazing you are doing. Remind yourself that the professorial line of work can be splendidly rewarding and that academia and the students need you. If you don't already feel entitled to be in academia, then work on cultivating this feeling. You belong there. Being a professor has clear benefits: "Academia is a route to social and political power; it brings automatic prestige, access to the media, access to political structures, and access to promising young minds who will shape society's future" (Bronstein, Rothblum, and Solomon, 1993, p. 28). In addition, academia acutely needs non-traditional faculty and students and the contributions they make to the intellectual and moral life of colleges and universities.

CONCLUSION

I trust that mentors and their mentees, often in tandem, will move to implement many of the Good Practices and self-help strategies offered in this chapter. Their actions are as essential as steps taken by departments, provosts, and other leaders to adopt and adapt the Good Practices of retention discussed earlier.

CHAPTER 7

OTHER REMEDIES: MACROCOSMIC AND MICROCOSMIC

GLOBAL AND LOCAL CHANGES ARE essential to eradicate the castelike features embedded in our nation's economic, social, and academic spheres. While chapters 4 through 6 set forth a number of Good Practices to adopt as well as bad practices to avoid, all of these are specific to higher education. Changes *outside* higher education, I readily admit, are long overdue and even more daunting. This chapter briefly sketches recommendations drawn from a range of thinkers and activists that are intended to erase or at least reduce rigid inequities.

A. STRUCTURAL AND INSTITUTIONAL CHANGES: DISMANTLE CASTELIKE ELEMENTS; CONTINUE TO ACT AFFIRMATIVELY; AND PAY REPARATIONS

1. A macrocosmic perspective holds that the economic caste system currently entrapping many colonized minorities must be dismantled, the low job ceiling lifted, and job segregation ended. When some progress is made in the all-important economic realm, far more minorities will have the incentive and the opportunity to devote themselves to academic achievement and occupational progression. Neither fixing the minorities' perceived personal deficiencies nor increasing their educational access and achievement will remove the *larger* financial and occupational handicaps they face after graduation. What is required is structural change in the *economic* system to level the playing field, equalize the rewards, and provide easy access for minorities to enter the gates of opportunity (Franklin 1991, Kain 1969, Ogbu 1978, 1991,

1992, Carter and Segura 1979, Gibson 1987, 1988, 1991). Because European-American males continue to dominate the key economic institutions (corporations, banks, federal regulatory agencies, labor unions, media outlets, and investment enterprises), they often make and enforce the policies that preserve their castelike privileges and advantages as well as those that enforce the castelike penalties and disadvantages reserved for "internal colonies" of stigmatized minorities (Blauner, 1972, p. vii).

Law professors Lani Guinier (Harvard) and Gerald Torres (University of Texas–Austin) envision a fairer redistribution of political and economic power brought about by the work of *cross-racial coalitions*, comprising various minority groups together with European Americans, not only poor and working-class members but also affluent social activists. These grassroots coalitions would be characterized by a politically constructive *opposition* to business as usual; their work would build community and political power among ethnic/racial groups that have usually been splintered from one another and denied the American dream (Guinier and Torres, 2002).

2. In a related way, "Americans' best chance for a future that we want our children to inherit," asserts political scientist Jennifer Hochschild, "is to insist that the practice of the American dream be made to live up to its ideology." She clarifies that this dream is "the promise that all Americans have a reasonable chance to achieve success as they define it—material or otherwise—through their own efforts, and to attain virtue and fulfillment through success" (1995, p. xi). The dream should not be only for European Americans and immigrant minorities.

3. In speeches throughout the country, Frederick Douglass IV (the great-great-grandson of the famous abolitionist and orator) calls for economic transformation for African Americans. He believes that American corporations benefiting from slavery—as well as the federal government—should pay reparations to African Americans, similar to the way Jews, Japanese Americans, and others have been compensated by governments and businesses here and in other countries for the internment, inhumane treatment, or partial genocide they have endured.

Acting as the steward of this payout to African Americans, a think tank of business and civic leaders and business school deans would invest the money and then lend out the proceeds to start up new African-American businesses, expand established ones, and generate decent jobs and wealth on a large scale for African Americans. Reverend Jesse Jackson, a national leader, predicts that the next stage of the U.S. civil rights movement will be African Americans' recovery from economic exploitation and their new leadership in capital formation, industrialization, and technology developments (Ryan, 2000). A similar reparations strategy and economic empowerment movement should be considered for other colonized minorities in the United States.

4. Another remedy—forming antiracism organizations that will take overt and covert actions to dismantle white racism—is already under way (O'Brien, 2001; Thompson, 1996, 2001; Thompson and Sangeeta, 1993). In a related vein, institutes and teach-ins are being held to uncover and unravel white supremacy, with the hope that some members of the majority group will become effective leaders for healing white racism and building a stronger democracy—in solidarity with members of minority groups (Garvey and Ignatiev, 1997; Feagin and Vera, 1995; Giroux, 1997; see also Jane Elliott's famous teach-in featured in the videotape *Blue-Eyed*, 1995). Everyone in society is developmentally stunted by caste and race-based structures, which uphold the following tenets: Some people are superior while others are inferior; some are more prone to criminal activity while others are not; some are polluted while some are not; some should be channeled into certain schools, jobs, professions, and residential neighborhoods while others should not; some groups may intermarry with one another while others should not. In the twenty-first century, the nascent worldwide movement to dismantle caste systems may grow in strength. Although the movement is now mostly focused in India, other countries certainly possess castelike structures and practices and should certainly be involved in the dismantling process.

5. Yet other activists and thinkers call for a new constitutional convention to forge a U.S. constitution of broader vision. Remember that the 1787 convention excluded women, African Americans, and Native Americans—who at the time made up *two-thirds* of the nation's population! A new convention in this century would be inclusive of all groups rather than exclusively limited, as it was in 1787, to European-American male landowners, slaveholders, and capitalists intent on protecting their own interests (Feagin and Vera, 1995). Calling for a more inclusive constitutional convention is somewhat similar to the current "gender parity" movement in France. A 1999 law, enjoying broad public support, requires French political parties to endorse an equal number of women and men candidates for municipal, legislative, and European elections. Thus in short order, France will have more female political leaders than even the Swedish Parliament with forty-three percent women and the Icelandic, with thirty-five percent. A second parity movement—with a business focus—aims to ensure salary equity and a proportional number of women in managerial positions in French corporations (Lambert, 2001).

6. Affirmative action in employment involves special efforts to identify and recruit non-majorities into majority-dominated businesses and professions. As someone succinctly put it, affirmative action is not about getting minorities in the door who can't compete—rather, it's about making sure that corporations allow *in* the door those who most certainly can compete, if given the chance. Even the archconservative John McWhorter, professor of linguistics at Berkeley, supports affirmative action in the workplace because he, as an African American, has seen that hiring and advancement are based "as much on personal contacts and social chemistry as merit." He maintains that European Americans currently in power, "if left to their own devices," will predictably hire and promote those who look like themselves (McWhorter, 2000, p. 225). Moreover, ingrained stereotypes and schema in this society tend to undervalue the professional or managerial potential and achievement of women and minorities while overvaluing the same in majority men, as pointed out in chapters 1–3. Without special interventions on their behalf, women and minorities, especially colonized minorities, are unlikely to break through these mind-sets held by those making the decisions about hiring and promoting (Graham, 1995, pp. 245, 253). A number of scholars, including political economist Michael Piore, urge affirmative action to be limited to non-immigrant, stigmatized minorities rather than to be unfairly stretched to benefit immigrants (Piore, 2001, p. 83; also see Hu-DeHart, 1999).

Harvard professor Orlando Patterson calls for a temporary fifteen-year affirmative action campaign to include "Afro-Americans, Puerto Ricans, second-generation Mexican-Americans, Native Americans, and Euro-American women." According to Patterson, merely increasing these groups' educational credentials is insufficient: "No ethnic group has ever achieved success in America by relying solely on education." What these minorities usually lack is access to jobs where they can gain inroads into majority-dominated networks—networks that could enable them to constantly enlarge their connections for personal and career development. At the end of the fifteen-year affirmative action campaign for non-immigrant minorities and women, Patterson advocates, the campaign should be transformed so that it actively assists economically disadvantaged citizens of any ethnic background. "The resulting class-based program should last as long as poverty and underprivileged classes exist" (Patterson, 1998a, p. 23).

7. To break through job ceilings, women and colonized minorities in midlevel jobs must receive career-enhancing mentoring; opportunities to develop into visible and influential players; and of course, long-term institutional commitment to remove job ceilings and make room for—and welcome—minorities and women at the top. Business expert Rosabeth Kanter advocates formal mentorship programs for outsiders in majority-dominated business settings. Managers, she suggests, should be evaluated on how well they promote the career development of women and minorities. "Artificial sponsorship"—that is, connecting women and minorities to senior people other than their immediate supervisors—should occur. And organizations should routinely include women and minorities in meetings and events where they will come into meaningful contact with power-holders (Kanter, 1997, p. 279). In a management-training program Kanter created in a large corporation, the few women in this male-dominated setting were guaranteed role models, potential sponsors, and allies. The program she established "tried to lay the groundwork for a support system and a power base that would help the women as well as the men succeed as managers." Training for male power-holders also focused on helping them recognize and then *overcome* the stereotypical, belittling attitudes they often held toward women peers (p. 281).

8. Power-holders must learn *how* to make their evaluations of people less subjective and biased; good intentions are insufficient. Virginia Valian, Lani Guinier, Charles Willie, Rosabeth Kanter, and other experts call for workshops and coaching so that decision-makers in academic and economic spheres can recognize predictable errors they make in interpreting and judging others' performance or promise, especially when those others differ in background or gender from them. It is essential that the decision-makers recognize and correct their own *sloppy and stereotypical thinking* and that of their colleagues as they proceed with information-gathering and evaluation processes as members of recruitment, promotion, and other important committees. In addition, power-holders must give special attention to the misperceptions and wrongheaded assumptions they often make about the solos, pioneers, and tokens in their department, division, or organization (see A-1, A-3, and A-27 in chapter 4; B-6 in chapter 5).

B. CREATE MORE DIVERSE STUDENT BODIES AND FACULTIES

9. National studies have demonstrated that substantial educational benefits flow to students of *all* backgrounds when academic institutions have a diverse student body and faculty. Mindful of this, many colleges and universities deliberately seek ethnic, geographical, socioeconomic, religious, and other kinds of diversity on their campuses. The campuses do so not so much to remedy past discrimination against certain groups of students, but to enrich all their students' educational experiences (Coleman, 2001; Bowen and Bok, 1998). But recruiting diverse students is only the beginning.

10. Educators at the institutions must "send an unequivocal message to all their students that the mainstream society encompasses multiple cultures and that all students have much to gain through contact with students of diverse backgrounds" (Gibson, 1991, p. 377). College and university leaders, by example and through their actions and words, "have the ability and obligation to act as moral compasses for their students" and help them understand how to *live* diversity. "Without guidance or a higher moral vision," many members of the campus community will stay trapped in their own homogeneous and distrustful enclaves and mind-sets (Graham, 1995, p. 218).

11. Predominantly majority institutions should recruit and retain a *critical mass* of colonized minority students and minority faculty, so that these minorities are not coping with the "solo" phenomenon. To be one of a few tokens can be exceptionally difficult and hamper academic progress. A more balanced ratio is essential. Further, majority institutions should pay close attention to the retention of stigmatized minority students and faculty, in light of the cumulative cultural disadvantages they may be coping with. (See chapters 1–3.) What *external forces* might motivate campuses to focus on good practices of retention? Cathy Trower and Richard Chait at Harvard University suggest surveying women and minority faculty at regular intervals in order to find what they rank as the "best departments" to work in (and, presumably, *awful* departments to work in). Because that ranking would be nationally publicized, it would give important information to job candidates and, of course, create competition among higher education institutions (Trower and Chait, 2002). In other forums, the two Harvard researchers have further suggested that the NAACP, Urban League, and other associations put outside pressure on those departments and campuses that have not yet made it a priority to diversify their student body and faculty ranks.

12. Colleges and universities should *deemphasize or eliminate* the use of standardized tests such as the SAT and GRE. Not only are these tests invalid, but they also have a pernicious effect on many students' self-confidence and ambitions, especially *highly motivated*, stigmatized minority students (Steele, 2001a and b; Gladwell, 2000). Many more colleges and graduate schools should scrutinize the correlation, if any, between their own students' scores on the SAT, GRE, and other tests and these students' later success, defined in various ways. Performing such a correlation study would wean campuses from using these tests (see no. 3 in chapter 2).

C. EDUCATE STUDENTS ABOUT UNEARNED ADVANTAGES AND DISADVANTAGES

13. Faculty and other leaders should help students, from majority and minority groups, better understand the psychological dynamics faced by immigrant and especially colonized minorities. Further, students should better understand the hidden privileges granted to members of the majority group and become proficient at "decoding" the hidden rules, advantages, and disadvantages that are inlaid in the academic and economic systems. If these dynamics and advantages/disadvantages are not understood, then students will continue to believe that their group or that each of them (as an individual) is either superior or deficient. They will miss the powerful defining forces at work in the larger society.

If women and colonized minorities possess a political, macrocosmic understanding of the U.S. economic and academic systems and their several castelike features, they are far more likely to push through the numerous barriers blocking their advancement. With a larger perspective, they can become more philosophical, thick-skinned, and resilient. Sheer ability and concentrated hard work are simply not enough for non-majorities, in my experience—political savvy is essential for self-protection; naïveté is dangerous.

14. Educators should also encourage majority students to explore and better understand their and their families' ethnic backgrounds—so that they come to realize that they are not part of a vague and disembodied norm but rather citizens possessing their own cultural contexts and histories. University of Washington American ethnic studies professor

Johnnella Butler frequently emphasizes that the ethnic histories, identity formation, and psychological and cultural constructs of European Americans deserve scholarly attention from faculty and students.

D. CREATE LEARNING COMMUNITIES IN COLLEGES AND UNIVERSITIES

15. University and college students should be able to enroll in several small classes each year where they can develop rigorous critical-thinking skills and participate in collaborative-learning communities with a mix of minority and majority students. The campus setting (or a subset of the campus) should be small enough so that students receive personal attention and frequent feedback about their work from their professors. Moreover, faculty should develop trusting relations with their students and impart to them "a sense of academic and personal worth" (Loo and Rolison, 1986, p. 70). Not only stigmatized minority students, but all students would benefit from such treatment.

16. The campus community should be reorganized so that the lives and cultures of all students are celebrated and affirmed throughout the intellectual life of the institution. All students would be encouraged to examine critically how their lives are shaped and molded by society's forces and also how these forces, when inhumane, can be resisted. In addition, University of Southern California professor William Tierney suggests, all members of the campus community should routinely analyze power relations within the organization and continually struggle "to transform the campus's hierarchical culture into a more democratic one" (1992, p. 41).

17. Faculty and administrators would be wise to help majority students understand the value of collaborative and small-group learning with those culturally different from themselves—and teach all students communication and conflict-resolution skills that will enable them to maximize the benefits of small-group learning. As most college professors know, merely sorting students into small groups is insufficient. The students need training in order to become productive and satisfied members of collaborative-learning groups.

18. Tutoring and other academic and psychological support should be available for all students on campus. Furthermore, students should be prompted about how to seek help and about how not to feel diminished when they do so.

19. Educators should be aware that the "model-minority" stereotype can reduce the options of Asian-American students by channeling them into technical fields and away from all others. Furthermore, the stereotype of the supremely competent Asian-American student can blind colleges and universities to the needs and vulnerabilities that these students may have, especially Southeast Asian refugees (see Kiang, 1992, and chapter 3, section 2).

E. CREATE K–12 LEARNING COMMUNITIES

20. In elementary and high schools, learning communities must also become the rule. First, the funding of elementary and secondary schools has to become far more equitable so that savage inequalities, to use Jonathan Kozol's term (1991), no longer exist between suburban schools and private schools on one side and inner-city and rural schools on the other. School districts must provide small schools and small class sizes at the elementary and high school levels where qualified teachers respect and enjoy their students and where the students can develop a sense of trust in their teachers.

Educator Deborah Meier has brilliantly shown how to convert a large and depressing inner-city school system in East Harlem into a network of several small, personal schools. In her schools (the latest is located in Boston's Mission Hill), African-American and Latino/a students constantly develop their critical-thinking skills in all subjects and can count on respectful and intellectual interactions with their teachers. Trust is constantly being built. At these small schools (modeled after the best small private schools catering to affluent majority students), the graduation rate is ninety percent and almost all graduates go on to college. Meier admits that even these extraordinarily effective small schools "cannot and should not be expected to close all the gaps between the haves and have-nots that the larger society seems bent on widening. But schools can, and should, use their limited time to prevent the disadvantages that kids come to school with from becoming more serious lifetime handicaps" (1999, p. 21; also see Meier, 1995).

21. To use high-stakes tests on elementary and high school youngsters is an *awful practice*. Such tests, purporting to measure students' intellectual worth, intensify the context of inferiority surrounding colonized minority students—and will hasten their self-screening, alienation, and dropping out of school, according to University of Texas professor Angela Valenzuela (quoted in Alicea, 2001). State legislators and school officials should find other ways to hold *schools* accountable and improve students' learning outcomes.

22. Educators must stop "tracking" (*segregating*) stigmatized minorities into intellectually stultifying and slow classes in junior high and high schools. Dozens of books focus on the damage wrought by this bad practice; see especially *Keeping Track: How Schools Structure Inequality* (1985) by Jeannie Oakes.

23. Minority students need *mentors outside the school system,* and these mentors can be found in college and university student organizations, nearby corporations, religious institutions, sororities and fraternities, and so on. In particular, students trapped in deadening school situations will benefit from a relationship with someone who is on their side and can give them extra attention and validation. As any mother or father knows, the constructive attention from an adult *other* than the parent can have a transforming effect on almost any youngster.

24. Classroom teachers should manifest their belief that *all* their students possess good prospects (Steele, 1992). In a steady fashion, teachers should incorporate into the curriculum contributions from minority cultures—and *avoid* cursory and patronizing observation of such contributions during a special-recognition week or holiday. The point is to demonstrate that minority cultures, communities, and identities deserve inclusion in the classroom and in textbooks. In the alternative, minority-focused academies are developing. For instance, Detroit has three academies for black male students, characterized by "an Afrocentric curriculum reinforced by building self-esteem and by high expectations, strict discipline, respect and love, and parental involvement" (White and Cones, 1999, p. 261).

25. Educators and community leaders should encourage colonized minority students to accommodate but not assimilate to school, just as immigrants typically do. That is, encourage colonized minorities to *keep the most precious parts of themselves,* even as in school they are expected to adopt and master new ways of thinking, speaking, and behaving (Gibson, 1988). But I hasten to add that until the castelike structures are dismantled, colonized minorities will have to continue to struggle in various ways against their treatment as conquered people at the bottom of a castelike system.

CONCLUSION

Not only macrocosmic but also microcosmic changes will be needed to ensure that the American democracy far more closely approaches its inspiring rhetoric. As the social philosopher Mary P. Follett has said, "we must *live* democracy" (quoted in Tonn, 2003, p. 301).

3

Items for Discussion, Analysis, and Practice

CHAPTER 8

MINORITY AND MAJORITY
FACULTY SPEAK

As an American Indian scholar, I feel that I'm on never-ending probation. Many of the majority folks in my department scrutinize me far more than they do more traditional colleagues.

Well, I admit I'm a passive bystander when it comes to diversity issues on campus. I guess I'm part of the problem. I really don't know how to be part of the solution.

Such observations—offered by faculty from both majority and minority backgrounds—are found throughout this book. Nevertheless, I believe that an entire chapter of quotations is justified to provide room for eye-opening and at times lengthy disclosures from faculty about how they see academia really working.

Some or all of the almost three dozen quotations below could serve as springboards to reflection and discussion, in meetings of faculty, administrators, and trustees. Organizers of orientation and mentoring programs for new faculty hires, especially minority hires, could use some of these quotations as items for consideration. In addition, classroom teachers might ask their students to *apply* appropriate Good Practices and principles set forth earlier in this book to one or more quotations found below.

For the reader's convenience, I have numbered the quotations and assembled them into the following categories:

- Why diversify the faculty? (quotations 1–5)
- Stresses and vulnerabilities (quotations 6–16)
- Different views of affirmative action in academia (quotations 17–21)
- Bad practices that must be replaced (quotations 22–26)
- New practices and new visions (quotations 27–34).

A. WHY DIVERSIFY THE FACULTY?

1. "We [minority faculty] are knowers, revising centuries of misperceptions of knowledge. As outsiders in traditional disciplines or insiders in our special cultural areas, we bring fresh perspectives to learning. The new areas we open up revise the entire structure of this civilization's knowledge base. Without us, this work would not get done. We are very important in our time and in the places in which we work." *American and Afro-American Literature Professor Nellie McKay, University of Wisconsin–Madison* (1995, p. 58)

2. "A diverse faculty is essential for the University's full engagement in the community of scholars. Cutting-edge scholarship and the growth of knowledge depend on discussion and debate incorporating multiple perspectives, theories, and approaches. . . . A diverse faculty enhances the University's reputation among other key constituents: students are attracted to an institution of higher learning that offers opportunities to learn from a diverse faculty; key funders, especially governmental agencies, place a high value on diversity; and employers increasingly demand graduates who have studied, confronted, and appreciated diverse points of views. Only by aggressively recruiting and retaining a diverse faculty can the University meet the demands of these important constituencies." *Provost James Maher, University of Pittsburgh* (at www.pitt.edu, March 29, 2002)

3. "I've defined my work as a teacher, advocate, and organizer across the fields of education and Asian American Studies. Much of my research and teaching centers on *sharing voices* (creating contexts in which immigrant voices, student voices, women's voices, Asian American voices can be expressed and appreciated); *crossing boundaries* (approaching problems and opportunities in a multidisciplinary way and crossing back and forth across disciplinary, bureaucratic, political, institutional, and cultural lines); and *building communities* (so that refugees/immigrants can feel they belong in the United States; so that my students feel connected to the wider university community). I'm always looking for ways to show that scholarship, teaching, and community work can be integrated." *Peter Nien-chu Kiang, Professor of Education and Director of the Asian American Studies Program, University of Massachusetts–Boston* (personal correspondence, 2003)

4. "Academia is a route to social and political power; it brings automatic prestige, access to the media, access to political structures, and access to promising young minds who will shape society's future. Thus, for individuals trying to address social, political, and economic inequities, an academic career can provide the means." *University of Vermont Clinical Psychology Professors Phyllis Bronstein and Esther Rothblum and graduate student Sondra Solomon* (1993, p. 28)

5. "When I explain myself, explain my Latina context in the classroom, I extend the invitation to engage in a particular critical consideration of text or theory or practice. Such cultural positioning enables students, the inquirers, to deepen the complexity of the query, confirming the holographic character of knowledge and the myth of value-free, neutral scholarship. . . . Like bell hooks [a professor, African-American leader, and prolific author] I am convinced that by positioning myself culturally/politically, I challenge the traditional ways of teaching that reinforce domination." *Assistant Professor of Education Ana Martinez Alemán, University of Massachusetts–Amherst* (1995, p. 74)

B. STRESSES AND VULNERABILITIES

6. "It is important to realize that the pipeline for minority doctorates *often empties into uninviting territory* where, as professors in this territory, they will experience social isolation, overt prejudice, a lack of mentors, and ambiguous expectations about what they should do to succeed. I believe this finding above, by Harvard researchers reporting in a September 2001 *New York Times* article, to be all too true. Furthermore, the academy is not immune to the politics of meanness. Here is a quote from a letter sent to me by a research assistant who left my laboratory. 'I hope you have forgiven me for leaving after investing your valuable time with me. But I was advised and convinced by other members of the department that it would be best that I leave. It's amazing to me how you're able to handle yourself in such a negative environment.' All of these are the types of experiences that underrepresented minorities, especially if they find themselves in majority institutions and as advocates of minorities, will likely experience. Given that we don't have a critical mass within the research institutions, I worry that we are not preparing our minority doctorates and new faculty to withstand these pressures." *Microbiology Professor John F. Alderete, University of Texas Health Science Center at San Antonio; he is also past president of the Society for the Advancement of Chicanos and Native Americans in Science* (personal correspondence, 2002)

7. "White supremacy creates in whites the expectation that issues of concern to them will be central in every discourse. . . . Because whiteness is the norm, it is easy to forget that it is not the only perspective. Thus, members of dominant groups assume that their perceptions are the pertinent ones, that their problems are the ones that need to be addressed, and that in discourse they should be the speaker rather than the listener. Part of being a member of a privileged group is being the center and the subject of all inquiry in which people of color or other non-privileged groups are the objects." *San Francisco State University Law Professor Trina Grillo and Santa Clara University Law Professor Stephanie Wildman (2000, pp. 650–651)*

8. "Certainly I knew many people who were not white, and I felt sorry for them—just as I pitied those born poor or with physical disabilities. On the other hand, it never occurred to me that I was white because my whiteness was coextensive with my membership in the human race. In the world in which I lived, human beings had no race—which is to say—they were white, just as they had no class—which is to say, they were all materially well off." *Philosophy and Women's Studies Professor Paula Rothenberg, William Paterson University of New Jersey (2000, p. 9)*

9. "Mine is the first generation of Latinas to be represented in colleges and universities in anything approaching significant numbers. . . . But, for the most part, we find ourselves isolated. Rarely has another Latina gone before us. Rarely is there another Latina whom we can watch and figure out all the little questions about subtextual meaning, about how dress or speech or makeup are interpreted in this particular environment." *University of New Mexico Law Professor Margaret Montoya (2000, p. 516)*

10. "Black and underrepresented minority faculty often must be better than the norm and able to navigate their way through the academic minefield twice as carefully as their non-black colleagues. I think the main important thing is performance. They [minority faculty] have to fight what the Jews used to. You had to be twice as good as any WASP [White Anglo-Saxon Protestant] around, in order to make your way." *Herman Feshback (European American) is Professor of Physics, M.I.T. (quoted in C. Williams, 2001, p. 43)*

11. "I overtip cabdrivers merely because they've stopped for me. I smile warmly just because a waitress hasn't seated me next to the kitchen door. I thank salespeople profusely when they don't throw my change on the counter. . . . These acts of kindness are simply my attempt to minimize the shame that I feel as a black person living at a time when the public sees us as thieves, as shoplifters, and a general threat to business." *Corporate lawyer and former college professor Lawrence Graham* (1995, p. 85)

12. "I think that it is important for me to recognize that I am also Dominican, not just a Latina. Initially I believed that calling myself Dominican was a less complicated matter, but I was wrong. I perpetuated many myths and pretended my Dominican identity was not a questionable issue at all. Like other Dominicans, I systematically denied my *mulatta* condition. Even right now as I write this it is difficult to acknowledge that indeed Dominicans are a mixture of Europeans (mainly Spaniards) and Africans. . . . Yet we look exclusively to the 'Madre Patria,' Spain, for our roots. Although there is a myriad of shades representing an extensive and rich process of contributions and cultural assimilations drawn from an extremely varied gamut of ethnic groups, we—I—insist on considering ourselves white or *mestizo* [a mixture of European and Indian]. We persist in using endless euphemisms to disguise the color of our skin and other traits of the African." *Virginia Commonwealth University English Professor Dulce Cruz* (1995, p. 95)

13. "Many Native American faculty express discomfort with the self-aggrandizing entrepreneurialism necessary to bring the value of their academic work to the attention of their peers. The informal unwritten rules impacting decision-making in higher education call for faculty to engage in self-promoting behavior that can be a source of cultural conflict for Native American faculty." *Ken Pepion (member of the Blackfeet Tribe) is Executive Director, Native American Program, Harvard University* (personal correspondence, 2002)

14. "Women and minorities, and minority women in particular, have a hard time in being accepted for what they can do. I know that. It's like that with me [an European-American woman], too. I have had the same problem to some extent. People don't think I can do many of the things that I actually do." *Mildred Dresselhaus, Professor of Physics, M.I.T.* (quoted in C. Williams, 2001, p. 371)

15. "Although my early work in academia reflected my own acceptance of the dominant culture, I have deliberately struggled to decolonize my own thinking, particularly by advancing the view of Chicano cultural capital. In addition, I have always been involved in the development and support of ethnic and culturally diverse students. . . . Ironically, when it comes time for my worthiness as an academic to be judged [at tenure and promotion time], it is done so by conservative and liberal white males who represent the heart of the status quo." *Professor of Education Herman Garcia, New Mexico State University* (1995, p. 153)

16. "Minority faculty can get into trouble when they focus on America's conduct toward its minorities and include facts which don't fit the history and social studies that students were taught as children. The students feel discomfort and complain. The complaint finally reaches trustees and legislators who say 'an un-American' curriculum is being taught the school, which will threaten the funding for the university. Consequently, the department chair is pressured to ask the minority teacher to rethink what he or she is teaching in the classroom. I have seen this scenario unfold many times. Tenure is a necessity for minority faculty members, since it offers some security that they can continue to teach and write the facts, as they really are and really happened, not what is most comfortable for their students and fellow majority faculty to hear and read." *Wayne Stein, Associate Professor and Chair of Native American Studies at Montana State University* (quoted in Moody, 2000, p. 31)

C. DIFFERENT VIEWS OF AFFIRMATIVE ACTION IN ACADEMIA

17. "Affirmative action is a violation of excellence. What I mean is that affirmative action requires you to bring in unqualified or not as well qualified faculty or students. Until women and minorities can do the same job and earn the same qualifications, they have no right to expect to be influential players in colleges and universities. It's as simple as that." *Anonymous*

18. "The white beneficiaries of racial practices assume that they reached their station in life on their merits and that minority communities advanced only through bending the rules. Critics of affirmative action have become convinced that higher scores [on standardized tests, such as the SAT, GRE, or LSAT] translate into more meritorious applications and that relying on an 'objective' set of measures would

constitute a fairer, race-neutral process. The evidence [offered] for this proposition is exceedingly thin; indeed, a substantial body of research literature and academic common practice refute this premise." *Michael Olivas, Professor of Law, University of Houston Law Center* (1993, pp. 19–20)

19. "I am proud to be a direct beneficiary of affirmative action, as a student [at Harvard College and then Stanford graduate school] and then as a professor [beginning as an assistant professor at UCLA]. I would not have been able to make my contributions to research, writing, and teaching without the opportunities provided by affirmative action programs." *University of Southern California History Professor George Sanchez, who is also Director of the USC Program in American Studies and Ethnicity and the first Haynes Foundation Fellow* (1993, p. ix)

20. "I get sick of all the complaints about affirmative action helping minorities who really don't need help. Well, I've never met a white person who says they would trade places with a minority person." *Anonymous*

21. "In my survey of 665 tenured engineering faculty at nineteen top-rated institutions [part of her doctoral dissertation at Harvard Graduate School of Education], I found very little difference in the self-reported productivity between White men, on the one hand, and White women, Blacks, Hispanics, and Asians on the other. Measuring the number of publications, size and number of research grants secured, teaching loads, or service activities, there was little or no material difference. It would appear that efforts to diversify engineering faculty do not dilute quality or productivity, as some anti–affirmative action leaders maintain." *Judy ("J.J.") Jackson, Vice Provost for Institutional Engagement, New York University* (personal correspondence, 2002)

D. BAD PRACTICES THAT MUST BE REPLACED

22. "How do we recruit new faculty members at law schools? Here is how it works. . . . whites have two chances of being hired—by meeting the formal criteria we start out with in September—that is, by being mythic figures—and also by meeting the second, informal, modified criteria we apply later to friends and acquaintances when we are in a pinch [in February]. Minorities have just one chance of being hired—the first." *Professor of Law Richard Delgado, University of Colorado* (1998, pp. 265–66)

23. "For universities . . . there must be culturally aware assessment at all stages of faculty recruitment and retention. The competitive, aggressive nature of some search processes is unnatural to Latino and other culturally diverse faculty who may value interdependence and who are more relational (rather than independent) in their social patterns of interacting. In a society where the majority group values independence and assertiveness, such relational styles may be evaluated as weaknesses. Deans, in other words, must recognize that the apparent over- or under-participation of culturally different faculty (my own Latino exuberance has at times been called to my attention) may be due to differing cultural styles of communication rather than to disinterest or lack of professionalism." *Assistant Professor of Education Robert Avilés, George Mason University* (1999, p. 6)

24. "For every [U.S.] minority student earning a doctorate, we [colleges and universities] award doctorates to nearly ten non-U.S. citizens, of whom about four will stay in the United States. . . . Some universities and faculty groups aggressively recruit foreign students. . . . Yet few make recruiting trips to institutions in their own backyards that graduate large numbers of minority students, let alone to high schools to encourage students to consider science early on. And many faculty members who are very comfortable requiring extra courses in English or undergraduate science for foreign graduate students are unwilling to do anything extra for minority students who are U.S. citizens. . . . Most of us [academic researchers] know very well—and even admit to each other privately—that the reason we import so many foreign graduate students is that they are a source of unquestioning, hard-working, intelligent, cheap labor who require little or no advising and who help us further our own careers. But graduate students should not be exploited as cheap labor. Training a smaller but more diverse population of graduate students would focus graduate education once more on its original goal: to educate and nurture the next generation of scholars. . . . Whatever our obligations to students from other countries, we cannot afford to turn our backs on another generation of promising American-born students." *David Burgess, Professor of Cell Biology at Boston College and former President of the Society for the Advancement of Chicanos and Native Americans in Science* (SACNAS Web site, 1998; also personal correspondence, 1999)

25. "With very few exceptions, a young teacher/scholar of color joins a largely male, largely white faculty. This does not mean, however, that the department has taken conscious steps to examine, assess, and ad-

just its culture in anticipation of diversity; more often than not, the thought has not even crossed the department's mind. Rather, it's business as usual: that is, the new faculty of color is expected to fit into the existing culture, in short, to assimilate, as other new faculty members before them have done." *Evelyn Hu-DeHart, Professor of History and Director of the Center for the Study of Race and Ethnicity, Brown University* (2000, pp. 29–30)

26. "First of all, let's acknowledge that few nonwhite scholars are being awarded grants to investigate and study all aspects of white culture from a standpoint of 'difference.' Doesn't this indicate just how tightly the colonizer/colonized [white/non-white] paradigm continues to frame the discourse on race and the 'Other'?" *English Professor bell hooks, City College of New York* (1990, p. 55)

E. NEW PRACTICES AND NEW VISIONS

27. "I see a critical part of my role as mentor being to persistently bolster the confidence of my mentees. This is particularly important in mentoring women and minorities as I have been struck by how often and to what extent they underestimate their intellectual abilities." *Professor Christopher Jones, formerly at Brown University and now Guthridge Professor and Chair of Mathematics at University of North Carolina–Chapel Hill* (personal correspondence, 2002)

28. "At Carnegie Mellon, we asked if it was really important for applicants to our computer science department to have had prior programming experience. Retrospective studies showed that less-experienced students could catch up by junior or senior year. We therefore eliminated experience as a key admissions preference, and adjusted the curriculum to provide appropriate entry points for less-experienced students. We immediately started enrolling far more women students, who proved they could do the work. As a result of this and other reforms, women now account for more than 40 percent of our computer science undergraduate enrollment. This is remarkable and suggests that academics may unwittingly construct unnecessary barriers that block diverse students from entering their programs." *Allan Fisher, President and CEO of Carnegie Technology Education and former Associate Dean of the School of Computer Science, Carnegie Mellon University; co-author of the book,* Unlocking the Clubhouse Door (personal correspondence, 2001)

29. "There is no doubt in my mind that higher education has inflicted great pain on students of color. To become academic success stories we must endure humiliation, reject old values and traditions, mistrust our experience, and disconnect with the past. Ironically, the academy preaches freedom of thought and expression but demands submission and loyalty. . . . It is my belief that institutions must consider [students'] past experience, language, and culture as strengths to be respected and woven into the fabric of knowledge production and dissemination, not as deficits that must be devalued, silenced, and overcome." *Laura Rendon, Professor of Education at Arizona State University; she also holds the Veffie Jones Endowed Chair at California State University–Long Beach* (1992, p. 62)

30. "The *Compact for Faculty Diversity* comprehensively helps graduate students of color anticipate and prepare for the complex challenges they will face as faculty on predominantly white campuses. No way is the *Compact* a portable fellowship program, dispensing merely a *check and a handshake*. The Compact helps to build a web of academic, psychological, financial, mentor, and peer support. Given the barriers and stresses that our students face, a comprehensive web of support is mandatory." *Ansley Abraham, Program Director, Southern Regional Education Board and Southern Director of the Compact for Faculty Diversity* (personal correspondence, 2002)

31. "One persistent feature of ethno-racial identities [is] that they risk becoming the obsessive focus, the be-all and end-all, of the lives of those who identify with them. They lead people to forget that their individual identities are complex and multifarious. . . . We are not simply black or white or yellow or brown, gay or straight or bisexual, Jewish, Christian, Moslem, Buddhist, or Confucian even as we struggle against racism . . . let us not let our racial identities subject us to new tyrannies. . . . So here are my positive proposals: live with fractured identities; engage in identity play; find solidarity [with your ethno-racial group or, more likely, with several groups] but recognize contingency, and above all, practice irony." *Anthony Appiah, Professor of Afro-American Studies and Philosophy, Princeton University* (Appiah and Gutmann, 1996, pp. 103–4)

32. "What do I mean by a society becoming more openly and interactively multicultural? A society is openly multicultural to the extent that all individuals—depending on their appreciations and talents—have effective access to many cultural possibilities, no single one of which comprehensively defines any person's identity and all of which are subject to change by the creative efforts of individuals. A society is interactively multicultural to the extent that individuals experience the creative effects of the mingling of different cultures." *Amy Gutmann, Professor of Philosophy and Dean of the Faculty, Princeton University* (Appiah and Gutmann, 1996, p. 175)

33. "If the Untouchables [in India] band together to *change* their caste condition, it is 'anti-casteist' even if they exclude the top castes [such as Brahmin] from their organization, and even if they are able to effectively make *one* of the criteria for selection to the practice of law [or another profession] their Untouchable caste status. . . . To argue that the behavior of the Untouchables to break down the structure of privilege for the Brahmins is 'casteism in reverse' makes no sociological (social structural) sense. . . . Sociologically and social structurally, it is [likewise] impossible to have 'reverse discrimination' [through the activation of affirmative action policies]." *New York University Sociology Professor Troy Duster* (1976, p. 78)

34. "My [Mexican] parents and I wanted to be regarded as white [Americans], just like Russian Jews, Germans, Italians, and Irish Catholics. I grew up wanting to be white. That is, to the extent of wanting to be colorless and to feel complete freedom of movement. . . . What I want for African-Americans is white freedom. The same as I wanted for myself." *Journalist Richard Rodriguez* (2002, p. 140)

CHAPTER 9

BAD PRACTICES

Scenarios for Discussion and Application
(with Discussion Guides)

THE FOLLOWING SCENARIOS (or mini–case studies) are offered to prompt reflection and problem-solving, not only in formal meetings but also in informal conversations among faculty and administrators. While the situations and dysfunction presented in the scenarios are exaggerated at times, I have found such scenarios to be important vehicles for engaging faculty and administrators in thoughtful discussions about their own campus problems.

As you read each scenario, ask yourself: *What's going wrong here? Going right? What bad practices and ineffective behavior—regarding recruiting, evaluating, mentoring, and retaining—are being illustrated? What Good Practices and strategies from chapters 4 through 6 should replace these? What steps should I or my colleagues take to help promote or institutionalize these Good Practices?* At the end of each scenario, I have provided a Discussion Guide that offers more formal assistance. Six scenarios are included in this chapter:

1. Deliberations of an Academic Search Committee
2. An Academic Search Committee Narrows the Field
3. Second Week as a New Assistant Professor of Mechanical Engineering
4. Preparing for the Tenure Review
5. Conversation between a Mentor and Mentee
6. Deliberations of a Tenure and Promotion Committee

SCENARIO 1: DELIBERATIONS OF AN ACADEMIC SEARCH COMMITTEE

This search committee is composed of three full professors of chemical engineering. Two (including the committee chair) are male, one is female; all are from European-American backgrounds and reared in the United States. Following is a glimpse of the committee members' conversation about the five finalists in their job search: Three job candidates are European-American males, one is an European-American female, and one is an African-American male.

Senior faculty #1 (woman): I trust we can try very hard to hire the black guy or the white woman. They both seem highly competent and would be assets for our department. We have to get serious about diversifying our faculty. Remember I told you that the other day the dean started breathing down my neck and lecturing me about how "we need diversity of thinking around here—we have too much standardization." That gave me pause.

Senior faculty #2: Well, I still say this committee of ours should have a minority on it from another engineering department. All of us were trained in the same conceptual box, and our thinking is still defined by that box. So how in the world are we going to be able to judge talent and competence and promise if it doesn't look and talk and act just like us?

Committee chair: Wait a minute, please. We're intelligent people here and we can think clearly and judge fairly. So let's proceed. Okay, someone summarize the black guy's qualifications so far.

Senior faculty #1 (woman): Well, Dewayne has already published five articles in solid journals. In his last year of graduate work, he won some sort of a teaching award from a national group of teaching assistants. And after graduating from Emory University three years ago with high honors, he's been working at Pfizer Central R&D for three years and doing very, very well. The recommendations from his research supervisors, both at Emory and at Pfizer, are very strong.

Senior faculty #2: Well, the doctorate from Emory makes me nervous. Let's remember that our three white male candidates are from Cal Tech or MIT. We can't be lowering our standards or even appearing to be lowering our standards. If that's the only way we can diversify, then I say it's not worth it.

Senior faculty #1 (Woman): Well, I thought almost a month ago that we had agreed to a ground rule: We wouldn't revisit the prestige of the home doctoral campus after we had made this final cut and narrowed the field to five super candidates.

Senior faculty #2: All I'm saying is that we expect white men to come from prestigious and tough places. Are you saying you don't think women and minorities can make it at Cal Tech and MIT?

Senior faculty #1 (woman): What I said a few weeks ago was this: It is much harder for women and minorities to get into the traditional and hallowed bastions of prestige, while it is much easier for white men because of their connections and the stereotypes that work in their favor. We can't assume that candidates from the "provinces" are, by definition, inferior.

Chair: Well, I'm getting tired of all this social-work talk. I worked like a dog at Cal Tech. No one gave me a blasted thing. I earned everything I got.

Senior faculty #1 (woman): Hey, we all worked like dogs, didn't we? So have both the woman and the minority candidate. Believe me, no one gave them anything. In fact, they probably had to work harder to get where they are and they had to deal day in and day out with stereotypes saying they didn't belong in chemical engineering.

Senior faculty #2: Okay, okay, I know, I know. My brilliant daughter is in middle management at Bank of America, after all. She is always talking to me about the stereotypes and stresses that she has to deal with in a white, male world. It's no picnic. Okay, let's get just on with our job here.

Chair: Listen, I think we should eyeball Dewayne's five articles, just in case some of our colleagues in the department question our judgment about his intellectual capabilities.

Senior faculty #1 (woman): If we take time to actually read his articles, that would be saying we are overriding the peer reviewers at the journals. We've never done more than superficially skim other candidates' articles, so I think it would be dangerous for us to start this with Dewayne.

Senior faculty #2: Look, we know that Dewayne would be a welcome addition to our department mainly because we are getting more and more non-traditional students. At least I think that's the way the dean's mind is working. But is that a good enough reason for us to hire him?

Chair: And to boot, wouldn't Dewayne stick out like a sore thumb as our one and only African American? After all, we are hiring a colleague here. Don't we need to feel comfortable having him around? This question is relevant, isn't it?

Senior faculty #2: Well, I'm totally confused about what we should be doing. First, we are told we should be gender-blind and race-blind. Then we're told that a "diverse" candidate ought to get brownie points for being different. Can anyone make sense of this?

Senior faculty #1 (woman): Well, I've been on a dozen search committees so here comes a wise-owl pronouncement. Is everyone ready? It is my humble opinion that search committees themselves can be beehives of subjectivity! If we want to cull out a candidate—white, black, or green—we can easily do it by putting up a pretext like "doctorate is from an inferior university" or "candidate makes me nervous" or "candidate didn't demonstrate enough energy and rigor in the job talk" or "candidate tries too hard" or "candidate couldn't handle the questions in Q&A." So are we looking for a pretext here or not?

Chair: No, we certainly are not! Let's compare how the five candidates would serve the current needs of our department. And also think about how they'd make us look to the outside world—and don't forget how we'd look in the *U.S. News & World Report* ratings war! So who wants to start? What do we see as our current needs? And let's drag out the job description again.

Discussion Guide: Issues for Analysis

1. Diversity on a Search Committee Diversifying the committee's membership is a Good Practice (see A-5 in chapter 4). But often only one women or one minority member is appointed to a search committee. It's hard to be a "solo" on such a committee and be the one who has to confront colleagues about issues of stereotyping and prejudice. It helps if the women/minorities appointed to a committee are senior and have other forms of "standing" (such as exemplary publication records, success in getting grants) that give them credibility with colleagues.

2. Inadequate Preparation for the Search Process Faculty search committees often do not dedicate time to laying out the steps of the search process or developing detailed programmatic needs of their departments before beginning to evaluate candidates. The result is pure *chaos*, as illustrated in this scenario. (To prevent such chaos, follow Good Practices A-3 and A-8 in chapter 4.) Moreover, committee members and the committee chair rarely get a chance to talk through with their dean and provost, before the search process begins, issues such as

- *Aren't we supposed to be race- and gender-blind? Then why are we making a special effort to hire women and minorities?*
- *The dean has been telling us to benchmark our department against the most prestigious institutions, but now wants us to hire someone from a less prestigious place. What gives?*
- *How are we going to look to our competitors when they learn that our new hire is from a state university rather than from the Ivy League?*
- *I thought affirmative action was over. Isn't that what all these new court decisions have been saying?*

These issues and confusions must be aired and dealt with, so that committee members are clear about their approach. (See Good Practices for Search Committees, A-20 to A-27 in chapter 4.)

Before beginning its work, a search committee should formulate a plan and ground rules. The ground rules may have to be revisited as the important tasks below are undertaken:

- Designing the job description
- Deciding how best to recruit potential candidates, particularly women and minorities
- Deciding what information to request from the candidates and their references
- Interpreting information in the candidates' files
- Comparing and contrasting candidates' files
- Interpreting a candidate's performance in a job interview or research presentation.

Committees and chairs who receive no coaching and monitoring from the provost and who have not formulated clear steps for their work tend to slip into bad practices. These are illustrated in the scenario and include

- Treating the files of minorities and women differently (for example, reevaluating their peer-reviewed publications but simply accepting the majority candidates' publications)

- Assuming that others should have to demonstrate what they themselves had to demonstrate—even when it's not relevant to the candidate's job
- Raising the bar for women and minorities— because the decision-makers are less confident about the veracity of the minority's accomplishments
- Making unwarranted assumptions (for instance, assuming that a graduate from Cal Tech or M.I.T. is automatically better than one from a less prestigious institution)
- Assuming that there is only one way for a candidate to demonstrate competence—the way that it has "always" been done (for more details, see A-8 and A-27 in chapter 4).

SCENARIO 2: AN ACADEMIC SEARCH COMMITTEE NARROWS THE FIELD

The Communications Department's search committee has finished interviewing ten candidates and has narrowed the field to four finalists: three European-American men and one African-American woman. The search committee itself is made up of four European-American men—all tenured, full professors. This is their conversation:

Professor A: Listen, I say we make an offer to Mary, our only minority. We need diversity in our department. You might have noticed that the dean and provost are breathing down our necks. I have no problem with Mary. Besides, she looks absolutely *great* compared to that guy we interviewed right before her.

Professor B: Hey, is that sloppy thinking, or what? She had the good luck to follow a guy totally asleep at the wheel—but is that a reason for us to hire her? I have reservations about her research and especially about her degree from Kansas. Pleeease! Does anyone even know where the University of Kansas is located?

Committee chair: Hey, watch your demeaning of the Midwest, fella. Some of my best friends are from the Midwest. There are some strong graduate departments out there, no matter what you fancy folks from Berkeley think.

Professor A: Look, I myself want to eliminate Jeffrey—the guy from NYU. I cannot *stand* pushy New Yorkers. I know he didn't seem aggressive in the interview but he's spent his whole life in the city. As soon as he gets here, he'll start interrupting everyone, finishing everyone's sentences, and promoting himself like there's no tomorrow.

Chair: Whoa, there, you're telling us more about yourself than about Jeffrey. Just because you're a smooth-talking Texan doesn't mean we have to hire everyone like you. Besides, we don't need another person in a Stetson hat!

Professor A: Well, some manners around this entire campus wouldn't hurt a thing, you know.

Chair: We know, we know. OK, let's get back to our candidates. What about Marvin? I know his Yale dissertation adviser, and he says Marvin's a very strong scholar and would be a good fit for this department.

Professor A: Well, I myself just can't see Marvin fitting in here. What I mean is that, well, he might be overwhelmed here. Hmm. I had to be pretty aggressive when I was starting out. Besides, he's not exactly middle class, you know. Sure, he's got the academic discourse down, but he's sort of rough and working class around the edges, don't you think?

Professor B: Look, about half of our students are from working-class backgrounds and are the first in their family to go to college. Marvin would be a terrific role model for them. Just because you don't want to have him over to your house for Brie and Chardonnay doesn't mean he wouldn't be effective with our students.

Professor A: Yeah, I guess I should be thinking about the students. Anyway, I want to talk some more about Mary. Why wouldn't she be good for our students? Sure, she'd be the first minority ever—so some of the students would question her authority and probably haze her. But we could help her get through all that. Besides, we already have three other women in the department, so Mary wouldn't have the hassle of also being the first and only woman.

Chair: I'm always bewildered when people talk about racial and gender hassles. I myself have never said an ugly or discouraging word to a woman or a minority. In fact, I thought everyone nowadays was trying to be gender-blind and color-blind. So if we do bring Mary on board, I see no reason to coddle her and assume she's going to have problems. This is the twenty-first century, you know!

Professor A: Yeah, well, maybe *you* haven't bumped into prejudice and the undervaluing of your credentials. But that doesn't mean that *other people*—who don't look like you—have it so easy. You can't assume that your experiences are the experiences that everyone else has. Some folks automatically enjoy advantages and others disadvantages. We have to tune in to this.

Chair: Oh, no, here goes the bleeding-heart speech again. Let me tell you, for the tenth time: I worked like a dog for everything I've gotten in life! No one gave me a thing. So don't start up with my having all sorts of advantages and head starts.

Professor B: Hey, time out. Listen now. Should we bring Mary and Marvin in to teach two classes? Wouldn't that make sense? I think they're our strongest candidates, and I'd like to keep the process moving. Is it a deal?

Discussion Guide: Issues for Analysis

1. Composition of the Committee To make the search committee in this scenario diverse, women (from the Communications Department) and senior minority faculty from other departments on campus could be added (see A-5 in chapter 4). It is important to have a search committee that reflects the pool in which you are searching. Why? The main reason revolves around the difficulties that people often have in evaluating people who are dissimilar to themselves:

- Majority committee members tend to feel more comfortable with candidates who are similar to them—as a result, they are likely to evaluate them more positively.
- Majority committee members almost certainly will bring stereotypes and prejudices to the table in evaluating women and minority candidates and may not even be aware that they are doing so.
- Majority committee members often find it harder to evaluate fairly the files of candidates who have been involved with doctoral campuses, scholarly activities and projects, and publication outlets either unknown or little understood by them (see chapter 1).

2. Inadequate Preparation for the Committee before It Begins Its Work A search committee and its chair should receive coaching from the provost or designated official before it begins its work (A-3, chapter 4). Committee members should be helped to anticipate and overcome stereotypes and predictable errors that occur as they interpret and judge candidates' performance or promise. Such coaching is especially important when the candidates differ from the committee in background or gender. Moreover, the chair in particular should be prepped so that she/he can keep the committee's discussion on relevant matters and promote careful decision-making.

3. Sloppy and Stereotypical Thinking by Search Committees Search committees should receive coaching and reminders about typical violations of critical thinking that are likely to occur in the hiring process. Committee members and chairs should be equipped to recognize and then self-correct these errors in their own thinking and in the group's thinking (see A-27 in chapter 4).

Examples of sloppy thinking in the above discussion scenario include

- Relying on negative stereotypes (about New Yorkers as well as Midwesterners)
- Failing to suspend judgment about a particular candidate until all the evidence is in and properly evaluated
- Including in committee deliberations random information about candidates that is irrelevant to job performance
- Failing to understand the limitations and biases involved in face-to-face interviews
- Failing to recognize that an interviewee who follows an unimpressive candidate may enjoy unfair advantage over all others (called a "halo effect")—and conversely a "horn effect" when the luster of one candidate's performance dramatically fades, because it closely follows the impressive performance of another candidate
- Rushing to a decision to hire without careful consideration of all the evidence
- Denying evidence that non-majorities face racial and gender hassles.

4. Elitism Academia can be rife with elitism that prevents fair decision-making. Elitism in this scenario revolves around

- Social class
- Academic pedigree (where the doctorate was earned)
- Academic qualifications.

5. Lack of Self-Awareness and Awareness about Others' Experience

- Although a committee member may never have expressed, blatantly or subtly, either white-supremacist or male-supremacist sentiments, the committee member may, nevertheless, unwittingly hold some of these notions.

• The search committee could have benefited from consulting with (or reading about) white women and minority faculty, to learn about their experiences in majority departments. Such reaching out is necessary so that the committee members thoroughly understand how the reception of minorities in academia can differ dramatically from that of majorities (see chapters 1–3).

SCENARIO 3: SECOND WEEK AS A NEW ASSISTANT PROFESSOR OF MECHANICAL ENGINEERING

Here is a conversation between Christian Miller (a brand new assistant professor of mechanical engineering at Comprehensive University in Seattle) and Wade Smith (the chair of the department for the past two years). Dr. Miller has African-American ancestry; he grew up in Virginia. Dr. Smith is of European-American ancestry and was raised in Massachusetts. The other eight members of the department also have European-American heritages and were reared in the Northwest and Midwest. A visiting professor, of Russian ancestry, has just arrived and will be in the department for two years.

Wade: Good to see you, Chris. Sit down, please. How are things going during this second week? I've had you on my mind but I've just been overwhelmed, what with the departmental secretary ill now for a month and I myself trying to resolve all the room mix-ups, delays in book deliveries, and a dozen other things—plus help the new dean set up some committees. Here, relax. Please have some coffee.

Chris: Oh, thanks. Well, I'm very busy, of course, with my new courses and new students—who are really great. A few colleagues have dropped by to say a quick hi, and sometime soon I hope I'll be going to lunch with some of them. I do have one technical problem. I hate to mention it, given that you're so overloaded in this busiest season of the year.

Wade: No, please tell me. I want to be truly supportive and help you adjust. Please tell me.

Chris: Well, I am wondering when the new computer for my office will be installed. Not having it up and running is a pain. And I really need my e-mail connection here in the office. Should I be getting paranoid about this?

Wade: Oh, my gosh. I was told your computer was all taken care of. I apologize. I promise that by the end of the week the computer center will have it ready for you. Now, tell me how the students are taking to you. How do you feel in the classroom here?

Chris: Well, I'm intense about teaching, as you know. Some of my students are a bit disgruntled because I seem to be assigning more homework assignments than other faculty. Or at least that's what the students are trying to tell me. Maybe I could have you look at my course syllabi and give me your reaction.

Wade: Yes, certainly. I'd be glad to. I probably should have looked at your syllabi last summer so I could have been of more help. Listen, Chris, I just want to say. Huh, well, I want to say that you should let me know if any students or faculty around here give you a bit of a hard time. Like, well, maybe they mumble something about your being an "affirmative action" hire and not fully qualified. In any organization, there are always small-minded people, unfortunately. So ignore such people if you run into them. All this will pass.

Chris: Oh no. I'm sorry to hear about this. How do you advise me to handle it?

Wade: Well, let's not worry about it. Probably nothing like this will happen. Let's move on to something more pleasant. Have you found a colleague to collaborate with on a research or consulting project? I know I said that would be an easy thing to arrange on this campus.

Chris: So far no one has expressed much interest in the subject of my dissertation. That's understandable, since the faculty in this department specialize in quite different areas. But I really want to get into a collaborative project with one or more senior folks, because my dissertation adviser said that all new faculty can learn so much from experienced researchers. But I, of course, don't know any senior people in the Seattle area. Not yet, anyway. Can you help me meet a few? What advice do you have?

Wade: Oh, my gosh. You're right, of course, that this area is rich with experts and enthusiasts in every field imaginable. I'll do some thinking about how I might help you with some introductions. If I can't find time this semester, then I will do it next semester. OK?

Chris: Yes. That would be great. And remember you said during my job interview that I could have a mentoring committee, with at least two faculty from outside my department. This, too, is something that would really get me connected to this campus and help me thrive. When do you think that committee will be set up?

Wade: Well, didn't you think the campus's orientation for all new faculty was helpful?

Chris: Yes. It was short and sweet. I certainly do better under-stand the intricacies of the pension fund. But what I really feel I need is coaching in professional development. A friend of mine in Los Angeles says his mentoring committee is great—they don't shy away from tough issues and they give him handy pointers about the tenure process. I guess the committee meets with him once a month for lunch. Oh yeah, then twice a year, all the mentoring committees and their mentees get together. That's what I had in mind.

Wade: I think it's a great idea, as I said before. But when I talked to our dean about it, he said that the smallness of this campus prohibits our having a sufficient number of interested senior faculty who would serve as mentors to new faculty. I guess this would be a lot easier at a huge university.

Chris: Yeah—I suppose—but I don't want to set myself up for failure here. All this is new and bewildering at times for me, es-pecially because I've never been any place where there were so few minorities. It would be nice to have some senior people to talk with.

Wade: Well, Chris, I feel the same about being a department chair. I could use some mentors myself. Let's have some more coffee.

Discussion Guide: Issues for Analysis

1. Department Chairs Often Are Not Trained to Provide Support In many institutions, department chairs hold their positions only for two or three years. Then the position is rotated to another member of the department. As a result, many department chairs are woefully unpre-pared to deal with the issues they confront. If the chair is to be a major source of support for the new hire, the dean or provost must accept responsibility for continuously training department chairs (see chapter 5, section B-7).

In actual practice, some of the support that new hires receive is provided by the departmental secretary. It might be wise for departments to acknowledge this fact by actively integrating secretaries into the support system for new hires and providing them the resources they require to do a good job.

2. When to Help the New Hire A new hire usually receives a lot of attention during the search process, but then the newcomer is "abandoned" during the three or four months leading up to his/her first academic year. During the summer, faculty (and the department chair) are busy with their own research and writing, are out of town on vacation, or are just trying to stay away from the campus. This annual summer disappearance has nothing directly to do with the new hire, but it can be perceived by that person as insulting or showing a lack of interest in his/her welfare.

If a department is to help a new hire prepare for his/her teaching responsibilities, this needs to be done months before the new colleagues's first classes begin (see Good Practices B-15 in chapter 4). The new hire would benefit from knowing such things as

- Regulations: syllabus form and content, the academic calendar, grading systems, academic honesty codes, copyright permissions systems, ordering books, and so forth
- Profile of students and their needs
- Usual practices in the department regarding pedagogy and grading
- Common student complaints
- Physical facilities and equipment and how to get access to them.

At the beginning of the new academic year, the department chair, faculty, and staff have a lot of extra pressures on them. It's hard to find the time and energy to reach out to a new hire—just at the moment when that person needs help the most. Unless it is someone's particular responsibility to support the new hire, it's unlikely that anyone will do it (see B-21 in chapter 5).

3. Coordination of Administrative Offices That Provide Support to the New Hire Departments depend on other administrative offices to provide a variety of services to new hires. These include such things as an office, office furniture, keys, computer equipment, lab equipment, Internet and e-mail connections, phone and voice mail, business cards, stationery, and forms. It is extremely rare for a college or university to have an office that coordinates this process for all new hires. Thus, responsibility for anticipating these needs, making the necessary requests, and following up to make sure everything gets done usually falls to the department chair and departmental staff. Much aggravation can be avoided if the chair takes this responsibility seriously and begins early in the summer.

4. Providing Mentors and Collaborators New hires need help right away understanding the tenure process and how one builds a successful tenure file. New hires should be advised in these matters by their department chair and/or professional-review committee (see B-20 in chapter 5). This, however, is not sufficient. They will get a better sense of policy versus practice, the history of the department in tenure matters, and departmental politics if they hear from "wise owl" mentors inside and outside the department. (See B-1, B-7, and B-21 in chapter 5 and Good Practices for Senior Mentors in chapter 6.)

To build a successful tenure file, new hires need advice about such departmental and collegiate matters as which courses to teach and avoid, how to improve student evaluations of their courses, which committee responsibilities to seek and avoid, and where the political minefields are located. Such advice requires active involvement with senior and junior faculty inside and *outside* the department.

With regard to research, it is sometimes hard for a new hire to collaborate with departmental colleagues because there tends to be only one person per field within a small department. In other words, the new hire is the only person in his/her field. New hires can benefit enormously from help given by the chair in reaching out to faculty in other institutions who might become collaborators or mentors (B-19 in chapter 5). In addition, the newcomer could follow some of the self-help pointers provided in chapter 6.

5. Lack of Support Is Doubly Debilitating for Women and Minorities Wanting to be perceived as competent and feeling like outsiders, women and minorities—as new hires in a largely majority institution—may be reluctant to ask for assistance and advice. This makes it all the more important for departments to be proactive until the new hire feels more comfortable requesting help.

Also, lack of support is likely to be perceived more negatively by new hires who are women and minorities than by new majority hires. Having been excluded and demoralized at times because of their gender or ethnic background, women and minorities may interpret even unintentional slights as negative messages sent specifically to them. (See mentoring Good Practice C-3 in chapter 6.)

6. Being Labeled an "Affirmative Action Hire"   Not only do new hires who are women and minorities face all the difficulties described above, they may also need proactive support in dealing with suspicion from students and colleagues. Particularly if the new hire is the department's first woman or minority, some students and faculty are likely to see the person as unqualified–as having been hired only to fill some "affirmative action quota" (see no. 9 in chapter 1). The department chair and senior faculty must anticipate this issue, discuss it frankly with the new hire *before* it happens, and be prepared with ideas about helping the new hire on this issue. Further, the chair should hold one or more departmental meetings before new hires arrive, to anticipate and head off problems by having candid talks with colleagues (see chapter 5, Good Practices B-14 and B-13).

Because the new hire is likely to be the first woman or minority in the department, the chair may be very uncomfortable dealing with this issue and may need help from the dean, another senior academic officer, or an external expert.

Scenario 4: Preparing for the Tenure Review

Sandra Garcia is an assistant professor of history at a large research university. Puerto Rican American, she is the first and only U.S. minority and female in the department of ten men. (Nine have European-American ancestry and were reared in the United States, while one is Japanese and a visiting professor for another two years.) Dr. Garcia is in the process of assembling the documents that will make up her tenure case file. She is talking to a friend who is a faculty member in the English department at the same university.

Sandra: I now realize how little feedback I have gotten about my job performance. What I really needed were regular job reviews every year, like my friend in Berkeley got. I just gave up because I knew these kind of reviews were not part of the scene here. No one has ever given me even a hint, a clue. And I've been uneasy all along about this.

Friend: Say, remember that terrific response you got to your convocation speech—from Provost Smith a few years ago? Did he ever write you a note for your tenure file?

Sandra: Well, no, I never figured out how to get it. Really, the speech wasn't that big a deal. I felt embarrassed about asking him, to tell you the truth. And now, you know, he's not even provost any more. Oh well.

Friend: You should feel really good about that publication record of yours. You've really done well on that front. And I bet those articles have brought you connections to VIPs in your field, right?

Sandra: Well, not exactly. My friend in Albuquerque keeps telling me to build "champions" for myself. I keep telling him he sounds like a cereal commercial. He said I could use my articles as entrée to influential people in my specialty. I kept telling him the whole process sounds goofy to me. If someone is impressed with my publications, they'll contact me. But no one has yet. That's a bit puzzling.

Friend: Yeah, I know. And I bet the whole process of finding champions for yourself is complicated. Who has the time?

Sandra: Besides, it's got to be far more important for me to build positive relations with senior colleagues in my own department. They're the ones who will be making the tenure decision. So I've always tried to be pleasant and agreeable with every one of them. And I've never said no to the dean or chair when they asked me to serve on all those departmental and campus-wide committees. That ought to count for something, being the token for diversity.

Friend: Well, I'm not sure. All I know is that my chair keeps saying to me that I'm not doing enough "self-promotion." Self-promoting must be some kind of weird game that white men play! I tell you this: I wasn't raised that way. It feels very creepy.

Sandra: There's some game-playing going on, that's for sure. I wouldn't mind self-promoting, I guess, if I had some idea of what would work for me. But I think with my tenure case, I will just have to trust in the inherent fairness of the system. It's supposed to be a meritocracy, after all!

Discussion Guide: Issues for Analysis
1. Is the Tenure Process a Meritocracy?

- The performance of any given tenure committee depends in part on how experienced and knowledgeable the membership is. Some faculty work hard at knowing the institution's rules and procedures and carefully adhering to them, while others tend to "wing it" and bring their own preferences and practices to the table. Deans and department chairs need to make sure through education and training that the committee knows what to do (and what not to do); appointing a knowledgeable committee chair can help.

- Majority committee members almost certainly will bring stereotypes and prejudices to the table in evaluating women and minority candidates and may not even be aware that they are doing so. Deans must make sure that committee members are aware of this tendency and that they actively work to monitor their own and their peers' behavior. (See nos. 1 and 8 in chapter 1; chapter 3; A-27 in chapter 4; and B-6 in chapter 5.)
- Majority committee members often tend to feel more comfortable with candidates who are similar and, as a result, like them better and evaluate them more positively than women and minorities—*regardless* of what is in the candidate's file. It helps if the chair leads the effort to evaluate only what is in the file and to do so in terms of the institution's specified standards and criteria for tenure.

2. Candidate for Tenure Is Uncertain about What Is Expected Beginning during the hiring process and continuing throughout the pretenure period, new faculty should be told what is expected of them as they work toward tenure. Sandra, the junior faculty member in this scenario, lacks such information and is terribly vulnerable. Factors such as the following should be thoroughly discussed:

- What is the relative emphasis on teaching, research, and community and professional service? How has this changed in the department over the years?
- Are there any minimum standards that must be met within each area, such as teaching both undergraduate and graduate courses, teaching at least five different preparations, publishing at least two articles in top-tier journals, having a book accepted for publication, giving at least one national-association presentation per year, demonstrating leadership on *particular* college or university committees, or serving as a committee chair in the candidate's relevant professional association?
- If there are no specific written standards, what have recent committees looked for as they evaluate a candidate's files?

- How many outside reviewers of the candidate's research will be used? Who chooses them? What credentials should these reviewers have?

3. Candidates for Tenure Should Receive Periodic Evaluations during the Pre-tenure Process as Well as Mentoring by Senior Faculty inside or outside the Department   Although candidates find it helpful to receive detailed instructions about the requirements for tenure, there is no substitute for periodic, written evaluation of the candidate's file during the pre-tenure period. These evaluations should be done by faculty, chairs, and deans in order for a candidate to have confidence that their advice is trustworthy (B-20 in chapter 5).

Also, deans and department chairs tend to change rapidly in academic institutions. As these administrators change, what is expected for tenure may also change. A candidate for tenure is protected a bit if he/she has formal letters in the file from previous review committees and administrators that comment positively on the candidate's performance and lay out what is expected of the candidate in the remainder of the pre-tenure period. In this scenario, Sandra's vulnerability is compounded because she lacks one or more faculty mentors either within or outside her department. While she herself should have been cultivating such allies (see D-1 and D-19 in chapter 6), the department for its part should have formally or informally ensured that she had mentors or a professional review committee to coach her in her teaching, publications, self-promotion, keeping records for her tenure case, and building collegiality with her associates (see Good Practices for Departments in chapter 5). Her isolation is sad. And it is obvious that she has been overloaded with committee assignments because, as a minority, she "represents" diversity (see B-18 in chapter 5 and no. 5 in chapter 1).

4. Candidates for Tenure Need to Find Their Own Champions, inside and outside the Department, College, and Institution   Academic institutions differ substantially in who reviews a candidate's file at tenure time. Some institutions rely largely on senior faculty from the candidate's department; others have complex multilevel review systems involving faculty and administrators from the department, college, and university. In both systems, outside experts in the candidate's field are invited to comment on the quality of the candidate's scholarship. Thus, a candidate for tenure needs to be concerned about how his/her file will be perceived by a variety of people *inside* and *outside* the institution.

Some candidates make the mistake of focusing solely on their scholarship and how it is seen by experts outside the institution. A candidate for tenure should never forget that a tenure committee is, in part, making a decision about whether a candidate will make a compatible long-term departmental colleague. If a committee doesn't like a particular candidate and doesn't want him/her as a colleague, the tenure process has enough ambiguity that it is quite easy to find a pretext for rejecting that person. Women and minorities who are solos and pioneers in their departments need to be especially concerned about this matter and seek advice about ways to build collegial relations, since many departmental and collegiate faculty will start out feeling uncomfortable with them.

Other candidates make the mistake of focusing solely on being accepted by their departmental colleagues. They have the tendency to never say no to any request made of them—teaching the courses with the biggest enrollments, advising all the women and minority students, sitting on too many committees. But these pre-tenure faculty need to remember that they need to cultivate champions outside the department in their special field of study. Throughout the pre-tenure process, the candidate should be preparing his/her tenure file. This includes building professional relationships with external experts in the field who will be ready to vouch for the excellence of the candidate's scholarship at tenure time. (See Pointers and Strategies for Pre-tenure Faculty Mentees, in chapter 6.)

5. Candidates Need to Self-Promote and Actively Work to Find Champions inside and outside the Institution

- Majority males are taught that they should aggressively self-promote and usually have abundant practice doing so. But women and minorities (like Sandra in the scenario) often have not practiced these skills and may need prompting; they may concomitantly lack the general network of contacts that majority men enjoy. For these reasons, the self-help strategies set forth in chapter 6 should be brought to the attention of all new faculty hires, especially women and minorities. These self-help strategies should also be reviewed in any mentoring programs for pre-tenure faculty.
- Proactively reaching out to find champions and promoting one's own interest are extremely difficult for some faculty members who come from family backgrounds and cultures that penalize an individual for standing out from the group (such as some Native American tribes and certain religious cultures). Many women, too, have been taught to keep low profiles and be self-effacing; they are afraid someone will

think they are being unfeminine and too pushy for the status ascribed to them.

- Personality, of course, plays a role in self-promotion. Proactively reaching out to find champions and promoting one's own interest can be extremely difficult for those who are shy and introverted in temperament. Mentors and mentoring programs should be alert to these differences in personality, cultural context, and gender expectations—and ensure that all new faculty hires are finding their own effective ways to promote their work and garner the recognition they deserve (see Good Practices for Senior Mentors, chapter 6).

SCENARIO 5: CONVERSATION BETWEEN A MENTOR AND MENTEE

Jaree Jackson is the first and only U.S. minority in an English department at a liberal arts college. She is also the department's first new hire in a decade. Her assigned mentor is Greg Jarrell, a full professor of English who is European-American in background; Jaree Jackson is African American. The other faculty in the department—three women and three men—all are of European-American heritage. What follows is a conversation between the mentor and mentee.

Greg: Jaree, I'm so glad you waved to me yesterday and arranged for us to meet today. How are things going, in your second month here? I hope you're enjoying the department and your new life here.

Jaree: Yes, I'm doing just fine. But I do have one matter to discuss with you, if you have the time. Or if you'd have more time later in the week, we can reschedule. I don't want to bother you.

Greg: Jaree, no bother. Please, sit down. We have a full thirty minutes before I run to see the provost. As I told you on your first day in the department, I really want to be a solid mentor to you. Sorry I have been so busy—well, we all were—during September and October. That's our high season, of course, and my wife's illness has really overloaded me with a stack of tasks. I've barely been able to keep my head above water, and the dean refused to send in any reinforcements. But, hey, we're here to talk about you. What's on your mind?

Jaree: Well, you know how much I love teaching. But lately, I get the sense that several students in my introductory course are feeling uncomfortable or maybe even resentful about my being the instructor. As you know, at Michigan in my doctoral department, I had so many colleagues from diverse backgrounds, but here is very different. A few students, at least, seem to think I'm not qualified to be their professor.

Greg: Well, I'm guessing that you've just got the first-year jitters. It takes a while to earn students' deference and to actually feel comfortable as a new teacher in the classroom. I remember that I was a bundle of nerves in my first year of teaching.

Jaree: You were? How did you handle it?

Greg: Well, my experiences happened so long ago that they would just bore you. And they would tarnish my halo if I disclosed them to you. Just kidding! Listen, why don't I call up the head of our Teaching and Learning center and see if you two can have a heart-to-heart talk. And I would recommend that the center videotape you as you teach in a simulated classroom setting, so you can see if you're doing anything that is making the students uncomfortable.

Jaree: I won't deny that I feel the first-year jitters. And I would be open to getting some coaching about teaching—for example, in how to stop overpreparing for class, if there's such a thing. But Greg, what I feel is that there are maybe three students who challenge me on a regular basis.

Greg: Challenge you how?

Jaree: Well, one will say that she doesn't agree with the "simplistic" interpretation I'm offering about something. Another will say something vaguely sarcastic about "so what else is new—we went over that in my high school class." Yet another will say, at least once a week, that he wonders why the class is required to read so many minority authors in a traditional American literature course.

Greg: This does seem strange. Remember that you and I together with the department chair discussed your readings for all your courses, during the summer. He and I thought you had made terrific choices. I must say that I have never heard about any other instructor being talked to quite like this!

Jaree: Well, a friend of mine at Vanderbilt says that I should stop the class when this happens and have a "meta-talk" involving all the students in the class.

Greg: Oh, I certainly wouldn't do that. That could just escalate the tension or whatever. I'm trying to think back. Two years ago, we had a visiting professor from Nigeria with us. And before that, a visiting professor from Japan. Neither of them reported any problems like this. Of course, both were men and quite a bit older and more experienced than you.

Jaree: Well, I get the sense that my credentials and my authority are being slowly undermined, and I don't know what to do. I love classroom teaching—it's a passion with me. So I know I must do something to address the problem facing me.

Greg: Well, maybe I could arrange a conversation between you and the chair of our math department. He's from India and maybe could give you some advice about how he deals with our white students. Maybe some of them in the past have tried to undermine him. I just don't know.

Jaree: Hmm, I really don't want to bother him, Greg. It's hard enough bringing this matter to you even though you're my mentor. I feel embarrassed that I have to involve you in this problem.

Greg: Look, we're faculty, and we all think we're self-sufficient. Of course, that's the ideal. But you did the right thing coming to me with this. I just wish I knew what more to do that would help you. Let me think.

Discussion Guide: Issues for Analysis

1. Duties of the Mentor

- To ensure a strong start and smooth transition for faculty hires, the mentor should schedule one or more monthly check-in meetings with each new mentee during the first semester. Unfortunately, Greg in this scenario has succumbed to "busyness" and has failed to monitor Jaree, the new faculty member, during a critically important time of her career. In addition, Greg has relied on the new hire's initiative to seek him out for advice, whereas the protocol should be the reverse: He should routinely and proactively offer warm encouragement and problem-solving assistance.
- Following Good Practice B-15 in chapter 5, the department chair and Greg did review Jaree's reading lists for her courses during the summer before she began as a new assistant professor. Other transition materials—sample syllabi, grading policy

handbook, faculty handbook, and so forth—should also be distributed to new hires in the summer. Anticipating predictable misunderstandings and problems and preventing them before they occur are essential duties of the chair and the mentor.

- Departmental Good Practice B-16 from chapter 5, if followed, might have disarmed the three students: On the first day of the semester, the chair could have visited the new hire's classes to underscore how fortunate the department was to have secured such an accomplished new colleague. The chair's brief and enthusiastic introduction could frame the first classroom experiences in an important and positive way for the students, the department, and the new hire.

2. Active Listening and Problem-Solving by the Department Chair

- Using active listening techniques, Greg could have gathered more information about Jaree's "critical incident" and also shown more solidarity with her (see Good Practices for Senior Mentors, in chapter 6). Greg might have used such lines as "Tell me more" or "This situation must be hard for you." In sympathetic ways, he could have tried to understand whether Jaree had ever before faced before this particular problem: students' questioning her authority. If she had, how did she deal with the previous critical incident? What does this current incident mean to her personally and professionally?
- Instead of active listening, Greg quickly begins diagnosing the problem and sending Jaree off to the Teaching Center for help. In his haste, he is compounding the bewilderment and isolation that Jaree is trying to be cope with.
- Greg should gather more information from Jaree and then help her plan ways to transform the negative situation into a positive one. For instance, he might suggest that Jaree meet individually with each of the troublesome students, since each of them is likely to be "coming from a different place." He could then coach her on how to handle the meetings: First, for example, she could remind the student of his/her comments and tell the student what concerns those remarks raised for her, the professor; next, she could ask a few questions to learn more about the reasons for the student's actions; third, she might find a way to address the student's concerns (perhaps by giving a student who feels insufficiently challenged more demanding work); and fourth, she might ask the student in the

future to express his/her concerns in a way that is more appropriate (perhaps by coming to see her during her office hours).

3. Confusion between Immigrant and Colonized Minorities   International scholars from India, Nigeria, or wherever do not usually have to deal with the painful history and cultural tension in this country that colonized U.S. minorities like Jaree usually experience. The cultural contexts can dramatically differ between immigrant minorities and colonized minorities (such as Native Americans, African Americans, Puerto Rican Americans, Mexican Americans, and Native Hawaiians). Greg does not realize the differences in cultural contexts and histories, so he mistakenly assumes that an international scholar from India or Nigeria would have the same or similar experiences as Jaree, a member of a U.S. castelike minority group. As chapter 3 shows, colonized minorities often have to cope with extra burdens and taxes. Mentors should be savvy about this.

4. Other Mentor-Mentee Issues

- Greg could have candidly disclosed a confusing situation or failure related to classroom teaching from his own past. Jaree needs to know that she is not the only one who has ever had a troubling classroom dynamic. Also, Greg could be more supportive of Jaree, by saying, "Listen, we are so lucky to have you in this department. I have every confidence that you and I will figure out how to sweeten the interaction between you and these three students."
- As a mentee, Jaree is giving typical signals that she may not feel entitled to mentoring by Greg. She wonders if she is bothering him; she feels "embarrassed" to bring her problem to him. A mentor (as well as a campus-wide mentoring program) must be aware that some new hires will indeed be sheepish about seeking help and encouragement. That is why the senior colleagues and the mentoring coordinators must be alert and help mentees move beyond this stage of hesitancy (see Good Practices for Senior Mentors, in chapter 6).

SCENARIO 6: DELIBERATIONS OF A TENURE AND PROMOTION COMMITTEE

This tenure and promotion committee at a comprehensive university includes four European-American, tenured, male professors of chemistry. In their department are a few other colleagues: one European-American female assistant professor; one visiting Chinese professor;

and Walter Bigfoot, the assistant professor being considered for tenure and promotion. Dr. Bigfoot is the first and only U.S. minority in the department.

Professor A: I hope we can reach our final decision this afternoon. This is our fourth deliberation. I'm close to the end of my patience and figure everyone else is, too.

Professor B: To start, I want to repeat what I said at our last meeting: Walter is a lovely and quiet guy and brings diversity to our department because of his Mohawk heritage. But I think he would be better suited at a small liberal arts college or a community college. Because we're a comprehensive university trying to improve our standing and rating within the larger higher education community, we have to hold Walter to the ten articles that must be produced over six years. Otherwise, we'll never be able to move up to being a doctoral department.

Professor C: Wait a minute—isn't that overstating the case a bit? I don't think *Walter* is blocking our progression. Listen, did any of you actually look at Walter's eight articles? Well, I did. In my view, they're simply outstanding. I say it's time to stop superficially counting articles and instead ponder the intellectual quality of them. We've boxed ourselves into a rigid corner—this makes no sense. Shouldn't we be looking at his overall research program and also be giving him credit for the two new articles he has under consideration by top journals? And remember, too, that Walter has gotten very strong scores in every one of his annual job-performance reviews.

Professor A: Well, I don't think we have to give much weight to those annual reviews, do we? For sure, we shouldn't change our ten-article rule in midstream. That would be unfair. We'd have to change the policy prior to coming to the evaluation table, wouldn't we?

Professor C: Look, yesterday I checked on some tenure decisions in the recent past. Over the last few years, our department's committees have bent the rules a bit. There's precedence for weighing judiciously—rather than just counting mechanically on our fingers *like a first-grader, for Pete's sake.* Listen, Walter has plenty of points to offset the lack of two more articles. First, he has published four times in the top three journals in his field—that's better than most of us did at his stage. Next, he represents our department and campus in an admirable manner.

None of us has ever been called on to appear on television interview programs or meet with trustees to talk about scientific curriculum. And one time, I think Walter was invited in to see the trustees and give his opinion about the ethnic studies department being proposed by a group of faculty.

Professor B: Well, that's my point. Walter should have a categorical no ready when the president or the provost asks for his leadership and appearance at these things. His sole commitment must be to his scientific discipline. I myself could care less about an ethnic studies department.

Committee chair: Wait a minute. Hold it. We all know that Walter is highly committed to the advancement of chemistry. Isn't he already an officer in the regional professional society? Yeah, I know he is. And through his grant awards, he's been able to bring in some very expensive equipment to our department, which most of us have had occasion to use. And what about his very high ratings on teaching evaluations by students? His only problem was in the first year when some students tried to haze him and get under his skin. I guess they thought a Native American couldn't be sufficiently competent or qualified to be an instructor to them. Well, he and the chair worked through all this. I know that no majority assistant professor ever had to deal with such a taxing situation. Walter did deal with it and refused to become bitter about the experience.

Professor B: Well, can *I* prevent students from acting silly? Can I control them? It's not my fault that Walter was drug around on the carpet. I don't know—maybe, just maybe, he didn't come across to the students as authoritative and worthy of their respect.

Professor C: That's baloney! Let's not be blaming the victim. Walter did not deserve that hazing.

Professor B: Okay, okay. I do admit that Walter's teaching seems very strong. But I do want to look at his grades over the past six years to see if he gives higher marks, on average, than the rest of us. I should do that. It would be important for all of us to know where he comes out.

Professor C: Hold it. We're not willing to read Walter's articles to verify their intellectual caliber because that might give him a few more points. But we are willing to suspect his teaching ratings and see if we can find a way to subtract some points? Hold on.

Chair: I want to change the subject. I believe Walter has had to put up with a lot in this department. Some of us were uncomfortable around him for a while. Remember? At first, we just held back and didn't offer any inside tips or personal pep talks or friendship. And in fact, a few of us—who will go unnamed—remain uncomfortable in his presence and still try to avoid him whenever possible.

Professor C: I agree that Walter has had extra weight to carry, in dealing with our white students and faculty. Being a pioneer can't be easy. But through these trials and stresses, he has continued to be an inspiring teacher and a decent colleague. Even though he is different from the typical assistant professors we hire, he has proven to be an asset to this department and campus. I think the fit is good and we should keep him around, as an associate and tenured professor. I say we should keep him.

Professor B: Not so fast. Not so fast. I'm not willing to give Walter extra points for his courage in being here. That's silly. He could have gone to a tribal college or a community college to begin his career. But he chose to come here. He had to know what he was getting into.

Professor C: I think I'm hearing an argument that we want only clones here and that we don't want to become a multicultural campus. And we're not willing to try and understand what kind of special challenges and burdens a minority pioneer would have to face.

Professor B: This stuff is irrelevant—totally, totally irrelevant. I'm not willing to go forward with this topic. I want to return to the eight articles: Walter is close—I admit— but still short of the requirement. I'm sorry, but that's where our hurdle is set.

Professor C: Let me ask you something. If Walter had gotten his Ph.D. at Harvard, would you be so uneasy about his eight articles?

Professor B: Look. The fact is that Walter started at a community college and then went to the University of Washington for his undergrad and grad degrees. I have to admit that the community college credential really sticks in my craw. Yes, I do admit that going to a private prep school and a competitive undergrad institution would look better for him. Of course it would!

Professor C: Oh, fine. Now we're really getting into irrelevant matters and into elitism. Listen. Walter, like many first-generation-to-college and low-income folks, started where he could start. It's how far he has come that shows his mettle, for goodness sake. How many of *us* could have done what he has done?

Professor B: I can't abide this bleeding-heart talk. Please, please, spare me. It's time for a vote.

Discussion Guide: Issues for Analysis

1. Inadequate Coaching for This Tenure and Promotion Committee
Before the review committee began its deliberations, the provost, dean, department chair, and/or an outside consultant should have led discussion with committee members and the committee chair on important matters such as

- How much should annual job-performance reviews count during a tenure review?
- Can the committee use any discretion in departing from the ten-article rule of the department? What is the goal of that rule? Can the goal be met in any other ways? Should the quality and rigor of the tenure candidate's overall research program be considered?
- How can the committee stay focused on those items that should be considered during the tenure review of a candidate? How can the committee distinguish irrelevant from relevant matters?
- Is it fair to continue ratcheting up the requirements for a single tenure candidate, with the assumption that this ratcheting up will somehow help the department reach its lofty ambitions (to become a doctoral department or whatever)?
- What does "raising the bar" mean? How can a committee be on guard against this, especially when it is considering non-majority candidates?
- What instances of sloppy thinking and decision-making predictably arise during evaluation processes? How can these mistakes be overcome? (See A-3 and A-27 in chapter 4; B-6 in chapter 5; and no. 12 in chapter 1.)

2. Examples of Slopping Thinking in the Scenario

- The conversation in the scenario jumps from topic to topic and is scattered. A well-coached committee chair could keep grounded the members' conversation and thought processes and could prevent or challenge superficial actions, such as Professor A's breezy dismissal of Walter's annual performance reviews.

- Cloning. Professor B seems to think that Walter doesn't belong at a comprehensive university and should be at a tribal college or liberal arts college. It doesn't seem to matter that Walter's publications, research grants, and teaching record are strong and that he is highly regarded by other colleagues. (See A-27 in chapter 4.)

- Elitism. Professor B is also bothered that Walter began his postsecondary education at a community college even though he received his doctorate from a Research I university and has done very well as an assistant professor. (See A-27 in chapter 4 and no. 4 in chapter 2.)

3. Discomfort and Standoffish Behavior toward a Minority Colleague

The scenario is suggesting that Professor B is suffering from *aversive racism*, because he tries to avoid associating with Walter. When Walter first arrived in the department, the other members of the department also were standoffish—but they fortunately moved beyond their initial unease and became supportive colleagues who disclosed inside information and pointers to Walter. (See no. 3 in chapter 1 as well as A-27 in chapter 4.)

4. Trying to Become a Multicultural Department

Because this chemistry department has hired only one U.S. minority and one European-American woman, it is still merely adding token representation of diversity. (See B-12 in chapter 5 for discussion of the stages of evolution toward a multicultural organization.) Nevertheless, in the scenario we hear some empathetic concern for the extra taxes and challenges imposed by students and colleagues that Walter, as a member of a colonized minority group, has had to deal with (see section 1 in chapter 3). And clearly, three of the four members of the tenure-review committee not only appreciate the strengths and collegiality that Walter brings to the department and campus, but also are attempting to protect him from the toxicity of Professor B. (See B-12 in chapter 5.)

5. Presumption of Incompetence

A few students during the first year of Dr. Bigfoot's teaching questioned his authority. This questioning can be a typical stressor, particularly for members of colonized minorities at predominantly majority campuses and departments (as I discussed in nos. 1, 6, and 8 of chapter 1). While majority male professors will usually not have this problem, majority females will if they are regarded negatively as overreaching their conventional lower "place" in society. In Walter's case, his department chair exerted wise leadership by helping to resolve the problem with the resistant students. (See B-14, B-15, and B-16 in chapter 5.)

CONCLUSION

To DIVERSIFY AMERICA'S COLLEGES AND universities will not be easy. Because many majority power-holders express genuine bewilderment and frustration with their efforts at faculty diversity, I have presented in this book comprehensive answers to the key question: What works?

Many of the good practices and guidelines offered here are nuts-and-bolts specific, ranging from how to organize training sessions for academic search committees, mentors, and minority pre-tenure faculty to how to coach provosts, deans, and chairs for the courageous leadership they must exert if faculty diversity is to be achieved on their campuses.

But behind all the concrete practices and pointers must be the larger conceptual realization that academe, like the political and economic spheres of this society, is still structured to favor the success of some groups and disfavor others. Members of the dominant majority group, especially if they are male, enjoy the presumption of competence and a number of other unspoken advantages and hidden profits. Immigrant minorities benefit from higher status and several unspoken advantages relative to the lower status and myriad hidden penalties imposed on colonized minorities.

For power-holders at our colleges and universities to see this complex state of affairs will require exceptional honesty and clarity of thought. Then to take remedial steps and encourage the adoption of new practices, both cognitive and institutional, will take even more moral courage and intellectual fortitude. But to give new breath to our democracy's uplifting political rhetoric and to the extravagance of the American dream—this is a strenuous and worthy task for majority administrators and faculty and indeed all of us.

BIBLIOGRAPHY

Acuna, R. 2000. *Occupied America: A History of Chicanos*. Reading, MA: Addison Wesley Longman.

Adams, M., ed. 1992. *Promoting Diversity in College Classrooms: Innovative Responses for the Curriculum, Faculty, and Institutions*. San Francisco: Jossey-Bass.

Aguirre, A., Jr. 2000. *Women and Minority Faculty in the Academic Workplace*. San Francisco: Jossey-Bass.

Aguirre, A., Jr., and R. Martinez. 1993. *Chicanos in Higher Education: Issues and Dilemmas for the Twenty-First Century*. ASHE-ERIC Higher Education Report, no. 3. Washington, DC: George Washington University.

Alberts, B. 1997. A Scientist Assaults the Science of Testing. *Business Week*, October 6. http://www.businessweek.com.

Alemán, A. 1995. *Actuando*. In *The Learning Ivory Tower: Latino Professors in American Universities*, ed. R. Padilla and R. Chavez. Albany: State University of New York Press.

Alvarez, R. 1973. The Psycho-Historical Socioeconomic Development of the Chicano Community in the United States. *Social Science Quarterly* 53 (March): 920–42.

Alicea, I. 2001. Latino Perspectives on Paige, New Secretary of Education. *Hispanic Outlook*, February 26, 7–10.

Anzaldúa, G. 1987. *Borderlands: The New Mestiza*. San Francisco: Aunt Lute Books.

Appiah, K., and A. Gutmann. 1996. *Color Conscious: The Political Morality of Race*. Princeton, NJ: Princeton University Press.

Astin, H., A. Antonio, C. Cress, and A. Astin. 1997. *Race and Ethnicity in the American Professoriate, 1995–96*. Los Angeles: Higher Education Research Institute, University of California–Los Angeles.

Avilés, R. 1999. How to Recruit and Retain Latino Faculty. *Hispanic Outlook*, February 12, 64.

Ayers, W. 2000. The Standards Fraud. In *Will Standards Save Public Education?* ed. D. Meier and Associates. Boston: Beacon Press.

Banks, J., and C. Banks, eds. 1989. *Multicultural Education: Issues and Perspectives*. Boston: Allyn and Bacon.

Bell, D. 1992. *Faces at the Bottom of the Well*. New York: Basic Books.

Bell, E., and S. Nkomo. 2001. *Our Separate Ways: Black and White Women and the Struggle for Professional Identity*. Boston: Harvard Business School Press.

Benjamin, L. 1998. *The Black Elite: Facing the Color Line in the Twilight of the Twentieth Century*. Chicago: Nelson-Hall.

Bensimon, E., K. Ward, and K. Sanders. 2000. *The Department Chair's Role in Developing New Faculty into Teachers and Scholars.* Bolton, MA: Anker.

Berliner, D. and B. Normally. 1995. *The Manufactured Crisis: Myths, Fraud and the Attack on America's Public Schools.* Boston: Addison-Wesley.

Berreman, G. 1960. Caste in India and the United States. *American Journal of Sociology* 66: 120–27.

———. 1967. Stratification, Pluralism and Interaction: A Comparative Analysis of Caste. In *Caste and Race: Comparative Approaches*, ed. A. DeReuck and J. Knight. London: J. and A. Churchill.

Blackshire-Belay, C. 1998. The Status of Minority Faculty Members in the Academy. *Academe*, July–August, 1998, 30–36.

Blackwell, J. 1981. *Mainstreaming Outsiders: The Production of Black Professionals.* Bayside, NY: General Hall.

———. 1989. Mentoring: An Action Strategy for Increasing Minority Faculty. *Academe*, September–October, 8–14.

———. 1991. Graduate and Professional Education for Blacks. In *The Education of African-Americans*, ed. C. Willie, A. Garibaldi, and W. Reed. Boston: Trotter Institute, University of Massachusetts–Boston.

Blauner, R. 1972. *Racial Oppression in America.* New York: Harper and Row. [Chapter 2 of this book, "Colonized and Immigrant Minorities," has been widely anthologized and has been republished with slight revisions in R. Blauner, *Still the Big News: Racial Oppression in America* (Philadelphia: Temple University Press, 2001).]

Blue-Eyed. 1995. Videotape. San Francisco: California Newsreel.

Boice, R. 1992a. "Lessons Learned about Mentoring." In *Developing New and Junior Faculty*, ed. M. Sorcinelli and A. Austin. San Francisco: Jossey-Bass.

———. 1992b. *The New Faculty Member: Supporting and Fostering Professional Development.* San Francisco: Jossey-Bass.

———. 1993a. Early Turning Points in Professional Careers of Women and Minorities." In *Building a Diverse Faculty*, ed. J. Gainen and R. Boice. San Francisco: Jossey-Bass.

———. 1993b. New Faculty Involvement for Women and Minorities. *Research in Higher Education* 34(3): 291–341.

———. 2000. *Advice for New Faculty Members.* Boston: Allyn and Bacon.

Boissevain, J. 1974. *Friends of Friends: Networks, Manipulators, and Coalitions.* Oxford: Basil Blackwell.

Bonilla, J., C. Pickeron, and T. Tatum. 1994. Peer Mentoring among Graduate Students of Color: Expanding the Mentoring Relationship. In *Mentoring Revisited: Making an Impact on Individuals and Institutions*, ed. M. Wunsch. San Francisco: Jossey-Bass.

Bourdieu, P. 1977. Cultural Reproduction and Social Reproduction. In *Power and Ideology in Education*, ed. J. Karabel and A. Halsey. New York: Oxford University Press.

———. 1998. *Practical Reason: On the Theory of Action.* Palo Alto, CA: Stanford University Press.

Bourdieu, P., and J. Passeron. 1977. *Reproduction in Education, Society, and Culture.* London: Sage.

Bowen, W., and D. Bok. 1998. *The Shape of the River: Long-Term Consequences of Considering Race in College and University Admissions.* Princeton, NJ: Princeton University Press.

Bowser, B., T. Jones, and G. Young, eds. 1995. *Toward the Multicultural Campus.* Westport, CT: Praeger.

Breiger, R. 1988. *Social Resources and Social Mobility: A Structural Theory of Status Attainment.* Cambridge: Cambridge University Press.

Brender, A. 2001. In Japan, Education for Koreans Stays Separate and Unequal. *Chronicle of Higher Education*, February 9, A40–41.

Bronstein, P., E. Rothblum, and S. Solomon. 1993. Ivy Halls and Glass Walls: Barriers to Academic Careers for Women and Ethnic Minorities. In *Building a Diverse Faculty*, ed. J. Gainen and R. Boice. San Francisco: Jossey-Bass.

Brown, K. 1993. African-American Immersion Schools: Paradoxes of Race and Public Education." In *Critical Race Theory*, ed. R. Delgado and F. Stefancic. Philadelphia: Temple University Press.

Bruner, J. 1996. *The Culture of Education*. Cambridge, MA: Harvard University Press.

Burgess, D. 1998. The President's Comments on Diversity Issues: Barriers to Graduate School for Minority-Group Students. SACNAS (Society for the Advancement of Chicanos and Native Americans in Science). http://www.sacnas.org.

Butterfield, F. 2000. Racial Disparities Seen as Pervasive in Juvenile Justice. *New York Times*, April 26, A1, A18.

Caplan, N., J. Whitmore, and M. Choy. 1989. *The Boat People and Achievement in America: A Study of Family Life, Hard Work, and Cultural Values*. Ann Arbor: University of Michigan Press.

Carter, T. 1970. *Mexican Americans in School: A History of Educational Neglect*. Princeton, NJ: College Entrance Examination Board.

Carter, T., and R. Segura. 1979. *Mexican Americans in School: A Decade of Change*. Princeton, NJ: College Entrance Examination Board.

Chavez, J. 1984. *The Lost Land: The Chicano Image of the Southwest*. Albuquerque: University of New Mexico Press.

Christensen, C., D. Garvin, and A. Sweet, eds. 1991. *Education for Judgment: The Artistry of Discussion Leadership*. Cambridge, MA: Harvard Business School Press.

Chang, R. 1993. Toward an Asian American Legal Scholarship. In *Critical Race Theory*, ed. R. Delgado and J. Stefancic. Philadelphia: Temple University Press.

Clance, P. 1985. *The Imposter Phenomenon: When Success Makes You Feel Like a Fraud*. New York: Bantam Books.

Clark, S., and M. Corcoran. 1986. Perspectives on the Professional Socialization of Women Faculty: A Case of Accumulative Disadvantage? *Journal of Higher Education* 57: 20–43.

Cole, J. 1979. *Fair Science: Women in the Scientific Community*. New York: Free Press.

Cole, J., and S. Cole. 1973. *Social Stratification in Science*. Chicago: University of Chicago Press.

Coleman, A. 2001. *Affirmative Action* through a Different Looking Glass. *Diversity Digest*, Spring, 1, 2, 12.

Conley, F. 1998. *Walking Out on the Boys*. New York: Farrar, Straus and Giroux.

Connor, K., and E. Vargyas. 1992. The Legal Implications of Gender Bias in Standardized Testing. *Berkeley Women's Law Journal* 7: 13–89.

Cooper, J., and D. Stevens, eds. 2002. *Tenure in the Sacred Grove: Issues and Strategies for Women and Minority Faculty*. Albany: State University of New York Press.

Corcoran, M., and S. Clark. 1984. Professional Socialization and Contemporary Career Attitudes of Three Faculty Generations. *Research in Higher Education* 20: 131–53.

Correspondents of *The New York Times*. 2001. *How Race Is Lived in America*. New York: Holt.

Cose, E. 1993. *Rage of a Privileged Class: Why Are Middle Class Blacks Angry? Why Should Americans Care?* New York: HarperCollins.

———. 1997. *Color-Blind: Seeing beyond Race in a Race-Obsessed World*. New York: HarperCollins.

Creighton, J. 1997. The SAT Solution: None of the Above. *Boston Globe*, September 29, A15.

Creswell, J. 1985. *Faculty Research Performance: Lessons from the Sciences and the Social Sciences*. ASHE-ERIC Higher Education Report, no. 4. Washington, DC: Association for the Study of Higher Education.

Cruz, D. 1995. Struggling with the Labels That Mark My Ethnic Identity. In *The Leaning Ivory Tower: Latino Professors in American Universities*, ed. R. Padilla and R. Chavez. Albany: State University of New York Press.

Cummins, J. 1986. Empowering Minority Students: A Framework for Intervention. *Harvard Educational Review* 56: 18–36.

Dahl, R. 2001. *How Democratic Is the American Constitution?* New Haven, CT: Yale University Press.

Darling-Hammond, L. 1998. Unequal Opportunity: Race and Education. *Brookings Review.* Spring, 28–32.

Davis, J. 1994. *Coloring the Halls of Ivy: Leadership and Diversity in the Academy.* Bolton, MA: Anker.

Davis, P. 1993. Law as Microaggression. In *Critical Race Theory,* ed. R. Delgado and J. Stefancic. Philadelphia: Temple University Press.

Delgado, R. 1998a. Mexican Americans as a Legally Cognizable Class. In *The Latino/a Condition,* ed. R. Delgado and J. Stefancic. New York: New York University Press.

———. 1998b. Storytelling for Oppositionists and Others. In *The Latino/a Condition,* ed. R. Delgado and J. Stefancic. New York: New York University Press.

Deloria, V., Jr. 1987. Identity and Culture. In *From Different Shores: Perspectives on Race and Ethnicity in America,* ed. R. Takaki. New York: Oxford University Press.

Denton, D. 2002. Successful Strategies for Increasing Faculty Diversity in Engineering. At the session "Gender Bias in Faculty Hiring, Retention, and Promotion?" held on Feb. 18, 2002 at the American Association for the Advancement of Science conference, Boston.

Departmental Change Workshops. 1996–97. Led by JoAnn Moody, at the Compact for Faculty Diversity's Institute on Teaching and Mentoring (Boston, 1996, and New Orleans, 1997).

DeVos, G. 1967a. Essential Elements of Caste: Psychological Determinants in Structural Theory. In *Japan's Invisible Race,* ed. G. DeVos and H. Wagatsuma. Berkeley: University of California Press.

———. 1967b. Minority Status and Attitude toward Authority. In *Japan's Invisible Race,* ed. G. DeVos and H. Wagatsuma. Berkeley: University of California Press.

———. 1967c. Psychology of Purity and Pollution as Related to Social Self-Identity and Caste. In *Caste and Race: Comparative Approaches,* ed. A. DeReuck and J. Knight. London: J. and A. Churchill.

———. 1992. *Social Cohesion and Alienation: Minorities in the United States and Japan.* Boulder, CO: Westview Press.

DeVos, G., and C. Lee. 1981. *Koreans in Japan.* Berkeley: University of California Press.

DeVos, G., and M. Suarez-Orozco. 1990. *Status Inequality: The Self in Culture.* Newbury Park, CA: Sage.

Directory (1995–96) of Advisors for NEBHE's Science and Engineering Academic Support Network. 1995. Boston: New England Board of Higher Education.

DiTomaso, N., G. Farris, and R. Cordero. 1993. Diversity in the Technical Work Force: Rethinking the Management of Scientists and Engineers. *Journal of Engineering and Technology Management* 10 (January–February): 101–27.

Doane, A. 1999. Dominant Group Ethnic Identity in the United States: The Role of "Hidden" Ethnicity in Intergroup Relations. In *Majority and Minority: The Dynamics of Race and Ethnicity in American Life,* ed. N. Yetman. Needham Heights, MA: Allyn and Bacon.

Duster, T. 1976. The Structure of Privilege and Its Universe of Discourse. *American Sociologist* 11: 73–78.

Dyson, M. 1996. *Race Rules: Navigating the Color Line.* Reading, MA: Addison-Wesley.

Epps, E. 1989. Academic Culture and the Minority Professor. *Academe* 36: 23–26.

Exum, W., R. Menges, B. Watkins, and P. Berhind. 1984. Making It at the Top: Women and Minority Faculty in the Academic Labor Market. *American Behavioral Scientist* 27: 301–24.

Fair, B. 1997. *Notes of a Racial Caste Baby: Color Blindness and the End of Affirmative Action.* New York: New York University Press.

Farquhar, R. 2001. Faculty Renewal and Institutional Revitalization in Canadian Universities. *Change* (July–August): 13–20.

Feagin, J., and M. Sikes. 1994. *Living with Racism: The Black Middle-Class Experience.* Boston: Beacon Press.

Feagin, J., and H. Vera. 1995. *White Racism: The Basics.* New York: Routledge.

Federal Glass Ceiling Commission. 1995. *Good for Business: Making Full Use of the Nation's Human Capital.* Washington, D.C.: U.S. Department of Labor.

Fine, M., L. Weis, L. Powell, and L. Wong, eds. 1997. *Off White: Readings on Race, Power, and Society.* New York: Routledge.

Fink, D. 1984. *The First Year of College Teaching.* San Francisco: Jossey-Bass.

Fischer, C., M. Jankowski, S. Lucas, A. Swidler, and K. Vos. 1996. *Inequality by Design: Cracking the Bell Curve Myth.* Princeton, NJ: Princeton University Press.

Fiske, P. 1996. *To Boldly Go: A Practical Career Guide for Scientists.* Washington, DC: American Geophysical Union.

Fitzgerald, T. 2001. Held Back by the Glass Border. *Boston Globe*, February 4, B4.

Frank, F. 1999. Taking Up a Professorial Line at Florida A&M University. In *Affirmed Action: Essays on the Academic and Social Lives of White Faculty Members at HBCUs*, ed. L. Foster, J. Guydes, and A. Miller. Lanham, MD: Rowman and Littlefield.

Frankenberg, R. 1993. *White Women, Race Matters: The Social Construction of Whiteness.* Minneapolis: University of Minnesota Press.

Franklin, R. 1991. *Shadows of Race and Class.* Minneapolis: University of Minnesota Press.

Fried, L., C. Francomano, S. MacDonald, E. Wagner, E. Stokes, K. Carbone, W. Bias, M. Newman, J. Stobo. 1996. Career Development for Women in Academic Medicine: Multiple Interventions in a Department of Medicine. *Journal of the American Medical Association* 276 (September 18): 898–905.

Gaertner, S., and Dovidio, S. 1986. The Aversive Form of Racism. In *Prejudice, Discrimination, and Racism*, ed. S. Gaertner and J. Dovidio. Orlando, FL: Academic Press.

Gainen, J. and R. Boice (eds.) 1993. *Building a Diverse Faculty.* San Francisco: Jossey Bass.

Gallos, J., and J. Ramsey. 1997. *Teaching Diversity.* San Francisco: Jossey-Bass.

Gamson, Z. 1995. The Seven Principles for Good Practice in Undergraduate Education: A Historical Perspective. In *The Seven Principles in Action*, ed. S. Hatfield. Bolton, MA: Anker.

Gappa, J., and D. Leslie. 1993. *The Invisible Faculty: Improving the Status of Part-Timers in Higher Education.* San Francisco: Jossey-Bass.

Garcia, E. 1991. Where's the Merit in the S.A.T.? *New York Times*, December 26, 28.

Garcia, H. 1995. Toward a Postview of the Chicano Community in Higher Education. In *The Leaning Ivory Tower: Latino Professors in American Universities*, ed. R. Padilla and R. Chavez. Albany: State University of New York Press.

Garcia, M. 2000. "Introduction." In *Succeeding in an Academic Career: A Guide for Faculty of Color*, ed. M. Garcia. Westport, CT: Greenwood Press.

Garvey, J., and N. Ignatiev. 1997. Toward a New Abolitionism—A Race Traitor Manifesto. In *Whiteness: A Critical Reader*, ed. M. Hill. New York: New York University Press.

Garza, H. 1993. Second-Class Academics: Chicano/Latino Faculty in U.S. Universities. In *Building a Diverse Faculty*, ed. J. Gainen and R. Boice. San Francisco: Jossey-Bass.

Gibson, M. 1987. The School Performance of Immigrant Minorities: A Comparative View. *Anthropology and Education Quarterly* 13: 3–27.

———. 1988. *Accommodation without Assimilation: Sikh Immigrants in an American High School.* New York: Cornell University Press.

———. 1991. Minorities and Schooling: Some Implications. In *Minority Status and Schooling: A Comparative Study of Immigrant and Involuntary Minorities*, ed. J. Ogbu and M. Gibson. New York: Garland.

Ginorio, A. 1995. *Warming the Climate for Women in Academic Science.* Washington, DC: Association of American Colleges and Universities.

Giroux, H. 1992. *Border Crossings: Cultural Workers and the Politics of Education.* New York: Routledge.

———. 1997. Racial Politics and the Pedagogy of Whiteness. In *Whiteness: A Critical Reader,* ed. by M. Hill. New York: New York University Press.

Gladwell, M. 2000. The Art of Failure. *New Yorker,* August 21–28, 92.

Glazer-Raymo, J. 1999. *Shattering the Myths: Women in Academe.* Baltimore: Johns Hopkins University Press.

Goodman, D. 2001. *Promoting Diversity and Social Justice: Educating People from Privileged Groups.* San Francisco: Sage.

Graham, L. 1995. *Member of the Club: Reflection on Life in a Racially Polarized World.* New York: Harper.

Gray, H. 1999. *We Can't Teach What We Don't Know.* New York: Teachers College, Columbia University.

Green, M. 1989. *Minorities on Campus: A Handbook for Enhancing Diversity.* Washington, DC: American Council on Education.

Gregory, S. 1995. *Black Women in the Academy.* Lanham, MD: University Press of America.

Grillo, T., and S. Wildman. 2000. Obscuring the Importance of Race. In *Critical Race Theory,* ed. R. Delgado and F. Stefancic. Philadelphia: Temple University Press.

Grosfoguel, R., and C. Georas. 2000. *Coloniality of Power* and Racial Dynamics: Notes toward a Reinterpretation of Latino Caribbeans in New York City. *Identities* 7: 85–125.

Guinier, L., and S. Sturm, eds. 2001. *Who's Qualified?* Boston: Beacon Press.

Guinier, L., and G. Torres. 2002. *The Miner's Canary: Enlisting Race, Resisting Power, Transforming Democracy.* Cambridge, MA: Harvard University Press.

Gustafson, M., ed. 1991. *Becoming a Historian: A Survival Manual for Women and Men.* Washington, DC: American Historical Association.

Harleston, B., and M. Knowles. 1997. *Achieving Diversity in the Professoriate: Challenges and Opportunities.* Washington, DC: American Council on Education.

Haro, R. 2001. The Dearth of Latinos in Campus Administration. *Chronicle of Higher Education,* December 16, 48.

Harris, C. 1993. Whiteness as Property. In *Black on White: Black Writers on What It Means to Be White,* ed. D. Roediger. New York: Schocken. [Harris's original article appeared in the 1993 *Harvard Law Review.*]

Harvey, W. 1994. African American Faculty in Community Colleges. In *Creating and Maintaining a Diverse Faculty,* ed. W. Harvey and J. Valadez. San Francisco: Jossey-Bass.

———. ed. 1999. *Grass Roots and Glass Ceilings: African-American Administrators on Predominantly White Colleges and Universities.* Albany: State University of New York Press.

Haynes, B. 2001. *Red Lines, Black Spaces.* New Haven: Yale University Press.

Hill, H. 1989. Black Labor and Affirmative Action. In *The Question of Discrimination: Racial Inequality in the U.S. Labor Market,* ed. S. Shulman and W. Darity Jr. Middletown, CT: Wesleyan University Press.

Hochschild, J. 1995. *Facing Up to the American Dream: Race, Class, and the Soul of the Nation.* Princeton, NJ: Princeton University Press.

hooks, b. 1990. *Yearning: Race, Gender, and Cultural Politics.* Boston: South End Press.

Howard, G. 1999. *You Can't Teach What You Don't Know.* New York: Teachers College.

How Not to Pick a Physicist. 1996. *Science* 274: 710–13.

Hu-DeHart, E. 1999. Introduction: Asian American Formations in the Age of Globalization. In *Across the Pacific: Asian Americans and Globalization,* ed. E. Hu-DeHart. Philadelphia: Temple University Press.

———. 2000. Office Politics and Departmental Culture. In *Succeeding in an Academic Career: A Guide for Faculty of Color,* ed. M. Garcia. Westport, CT: Greenwood Press.

Ibarra, R. 1996. *Latino Experiences in Graduate Education: Implications for Change.* Washington, DC: Council of Graduate Schools.

Ignatiev, N. 1995. *How the Irish Became White.* New York: Routledge.

Impact of Census' Race Data. 2001. *USA Today,* March 13, 1A–2A.

Jackson, B., and R. Hardiman. 2003. Stages in the Development of a Multicultural Organization. Distributed at B. Jackson and L. Marchesani's Institute on Multicultural Organizational Development, held at the National Conference on Race and Ethnicity, San Francisco.

Jackson, K. 1986. *Crabgrass Frontier: The Suburbanization of the United States.* New York: Oxford University Press.

Jacobs, J. 1989. *Revolving Doors: Sex Segregation and Women's Careers.* Palo Alto, CA: Stanford University Press.

Jacobson, M. 1998. *Whiteness of a Different Color: European Immigrants and the Alchemy of Race.* Cambridge, MA: Harvard University Press.

Jarvis, D. 1991. *Junior Faculty Development: A Handbook.* New York: Modern Language Association.

Johnson, B., and W. Harvey. 2002. The Socialization of Black College Faculty: Implications for Policy and Practice. *Review of Higher Education* 25: 297–314.

Johnsrud, L. 1993. Women and Minority Faculty Experiences: Defining and Responding to Diverse Realities. In *Building a Diverse Faculty,* ed. J. Gainen and R. Boice. San Francisco: Jossey-Bass.

Jones, L., ed. 2001. *Retaining African-Americans in Higher Education: Challenging Paradigms for Retaining Students, Faculty and Administrators.* Sterling, VA: Stylus.

Kain, J. 1969. *Race and Poverty: The Economics of Discrimination.* Englewood Cliffs, NJ: Prentice-Hall.

Kanter, R. 1997. *Men and Women of the Corporation.* New York: Basic Books.

Karabel, J. 1986. Community Colleges and Social Stratification in the 1980s. In *The Community College and Its Critics,* ed. S. Zwerling. San Francisco: Jossey-Bass.

Kiang, P. 1992. Issues of Curriculum and Community for First-Generation Asian Americans in College. In *First-Generation Students: Confronting the Cultural Issues,* ed. S. Zwerling and H. London. San Francisco: Jossey-Bass.

Kozol, J. 1991. *Savage Inequalities: Children in America's Schools.* New York: Harper.

Kramer, B. 1991. Education and American Indians: The Experiences of the Ute Indian Tribe. In *Minority Status and Schooling: A Comparative Study of Immigrant and Involuntary Minorities,* ed. J. Ogbu and M. Gibson. New York: Garland.

Kushnick, L. 1981. Racism and Class Consciousness in Modern Capitalism. In *Impacts of Racism on White Americans,* ed. B. Bowser and R. Hunt. Beverly Hills, CA: Sage.

Lambert, C. 2001. French Women in Politics: The Long Road to Parity. Brookings Institution. http://www.brook.edu/fp/cusf/analysis/women.htm.

Lee, Y. 1991. Koreans in Japan and the United States. In *Minority Status and Schooling: A Comparative Study of Immigrant and Involuntary Minorities,* ed. J. Ogbu and M. Gibson. New York: Garland.

Lemann, N. 1999. *The Big Test: The Secret History of the American Meritocracy.* New York: Farrar, Straus and Giroux.

Light, I. 1987. Ethnic Enterprise in America: Japanese, Chinese, and Black. In *From Different Shores: Perspectives on Race and Ethnicity in America,* ed. R. Takaki. New York: Oxford University Press.

Lipsitz, G. 1998. *The Possessive Investment in Whiteness: How White People Profit from Identity Politics.* Philadelphia: Temple University Press.

Littlefield, D., Jr. and L. Underhill. 1973. Black Dreams and Free Homes: The Oklahoma Territory, 1891–1894. *Phylon.* 34, 4: 342–57.

Loo, C., and G. Rolison. 1986. Alienation of Ethnic Minority Students at a Predominantly White University. *Journal of Higher Education* 57 (January–February): 65–75.

Lutz, F. 1979. The Deanship: Search and Screening Process. *Educational Record* 60 (Summer): 261–71.

MacQuarrie, B. 1999. Black Drivers Describe Harassment by Police. *Boston Globe*, April 13, A1, A9.

Marabel, M. 1995. *Beyond Black and White: Transforming African-American Politics.* New York: Verso.

Markus, H., C. Steele, and D. Steele. 2000. Colorblindness as a Barrier to Inclusion: Assimilation and Nonimmigrant Minorities. *Daedalus.* 129, no. 4: 233–59.

Margolis, E., and M. Romero. 1998. "The Department Is Very Male, Very White, Very Old, and Very Conservative": The Functioning of the Hidden Curriculum in Graduate Sociology Departments. *Harvard Educational Review*, 68 (Spring): 1–32.

Martinez, O. 2001. *Mexican-Origin People in the United States.* Tucson: University of Arizona Press.

Massey, D., and N. Denton. 1993. *American Apartheid: Segregation and the Making of the Underclass.* Cambridge, MA: Harvard University Press.

Matute-Bianchi, M. 1989. Ethnic Identities and Patterns of School Success and Failure among Mexican-Descent and Japanese-American Students in a California School. *American Journal of Education* 95: 233–55.

Matute-Bianchi, M. 1991. Situational Ethnicity and Patterns of School Performance among Immigrant and Nonimmigrant Mexican-Descent Students. In *Minority Status and Schooling: A Comparative Study of Immigrant and Involuntary Minorities*, ed. J. Ogbu and M. Gibson. New York: Garland.

McCarthy, R. 2001. Negative Stereotypes: A Personal View. *Monitor on Psychology*, April, 31.

McIntosh, P. 1988. *White Privilege and Male Privilege.* Working Paper no. 189. Wellesley, MA: Wellesley College Center for Research on Women.

———. 1989. White Privilege: Unpacking the Invisible Knapsack. *Peace and Freedom* (July–August): 10–14.

McKay, N. 1995. Minority Faculty in [Mainstream White] Academia. In *The Academic's Handbook*, ed. A. DeNeef and C. Goodwin. Durham, NC: Duke University Press.

McWhorter, J. 2000. *Losing the Race: Self-Sabotage in Black America.* New York: Free Press.

Meier, D. 1995. *The Power of Their Ideas: Lessons for America from a Small School in Harlem.* Boston: Beacon Press.

———. 1999. A Conversation about Schools with Deborah Meier. *Connection*, Fall–Winter. Boston: New England Board of Higher Education.

Menchaca, M. 1998. Chicano Indianism. In *The Latino/a Condition*, ed. R. Delgado and J. Stefancic. New York: New York University Press.

Menges, R., and W. Exum. 1983. Barriers to the Progress of Women and Minority Faculty. *Journal of Higher Education* 54: 123–43.

Merton, R. 1988. The Matthew Effect in Science. *Isis* 79: 606–23.

Mervis, J. 2001. New Data in Chemistry Show "Zero" Diversity. *Science* 292: 1291.

Michigan State University. 2001. Best Practices for a Successful Academic Search. http://www.msu.edu/~aacm

MIT Faculty Newsletter, March 1999. http://web.mit.edu/fnl/women/women.html. [Updates on gender equity at MIT appear periodically at this Web site.]

Montero-Sieburth, M. 2001. An Overview of the Educational Models Used to Explain the Academic Achievement for Latino Students. In *Effective Programs for Latino Students*, ed. R. Slavin and M. Calderon. Mahwah, NJ: Lawrence Erlbaum Associates.

Montoya, M. 2000. *Máscaras, Trenzas, y Greñas:* Un/Masking the Self While Unbraiding Latina Stories and Legal Discourse. In *Critical Race Theory*, ed. R. Delgado and J. Stefancic. Philadelphia: Temple University Press.

Moody, J. 1996. *Vital Information for Graduate Students of Color.* New Haven, CT: University of New Haven Press.

———. 1999. Retaining Non-majority Faculty—What Senior Faculty Must Do. *Department Chair*, Summer, 1, 19–20.

———. 2000. Tenure and Diversity: Some Different Voices. *Academe*, May–June, 30–33.

———. 2001. *Demystifying the Profession: Helping Junior Faculty Succeed.* New Haven, CT: University of New Haven Press.

Moore, W., and L. Wagstaff. 1974. *Black Educators in White Colleges.* San Francisco: Jossey-Bass.

Morey, A., and M. Kitano, eds. 1997. *Multicultural Course Transformation in Higher Education.* Boston: Allyn and Bacon.

Morrison, A., R. White, and E. Van Velsor. 1992. *Breaking the Glass Ceiling: Why Women Don't Reach the Top of Large Corporations.* Reading, MA: Addison-Wesley.

Morrison, T. 1992. *Playing in the Dark: Whiteness and the Literary Imagination.* New York: Random House.

Nahavandi, A., and A. Malekzadeh. 1999. *Organizational Behavior: The Person-Organization Fit.* Upper Saddle River, NJ: Prentice Hall.

Neimann, Y. 1999. The Making of a Token: A Case Study of Stereotypical Threat, Racism, and Tokenism in Academe. *Frontiers.* 20, no. 1: 111–34.

Nieto, O. 2000. *Puerto Rican Students in U.S. Schools.* Mahwah, NJ: Lawrence Erlbaum Associates.

Nieves-Squires, S. 1991. *Hispanic Women: Making Their Presence on Campus Less Tenuous.* Washington, DC: Association of American Colleges.

Oakes, J. 1985. *Keeping Track: How Schools Structure Inequality.* New Haven, CT: Yale University Press.

O'Brien, E. 2001. *Whites Confront Racism: Antiracists and Their Paths to Action.* Lanham, MD: Rowman and Littlefield.

Ogbu, J. 1978. *Minority Education and Caste: The American System in Cross-Cultural Perspective.* New York: Academic Press.

———. 1991. Immigrant and Involuntary Minorities in Comparative Perspective. In *Minority Status and Schooling: A Comparative Study of Immigrant and Involuntary Minorities,* ed. J. Ogbu and M. Gibson. New York: Garland.

———. 1992. Understanding Cultural Diversity and Learning. *Educational Researcher* 21 (November): 413–23.

Ogbu, J., and M. Matute-Bianchi. 1986. Understanding Sociocultural Factors: Knowledge, Identity, and School Adjustment. In *Beyond Language: Social and Cultural Factors in Schooling Language Minority Students.* Sacramento: Bilingual Education Office, California State Department of Education.

Ogbu, J., and H. Simons. 1998. Voluntary and Involuntary Minorities: A Cultural-Ecological Theory of School Performance with Some Implications for Education. *Anthropology and Education Quarterly* 29: 155–88.

Olivas, M. 1993. The Attack on Affirmative Action. *Change*, March–April, 16–20.

Oliver, M., and T. Shapiro. 1995. *Black Wealth/White Wealth: A New Perspective on Racial Inequality.* New York: Routledge.

Olsen, D., S. Maple, and F. Stage. 1994. Women and Minority Job Satisfaction: Professional Role Interests, Professional Satisfactions, and Institutional Fit. *Journal of Higher Education* 66: 267–93.

Oquendo, A. 1998. Re-Imagining the Latino/a Race. In *The Latino/a Condition,* ed. R. Delgado and J. Stefancic. New York: New York University Press.

Padilla, R., and R. Chavez, eds. 1995. *The Leaning Ivory Tower: Latino Professors in American Universities.* Albany: State University of New York Press.

Patterson, O. 1998a. Affirmative Action: Opening Up Workplace Networks to Afro-Americans. *Brookings Review.* Spring, 17–23.

———. 1998b. *Rituals of Blood: Consequences of Slavery in Two American Centuries.* New York: Perseus.

Peterson-Hickey, M., and W. Stein. 1998. Minority Faculty in Academe: Documenting the Unique American Indian Experience. In *Keeping Our Faculties* conference papers. Minneapolis: University of Minnesota.

Pigford, A. 1988. Being a Black Faculty Member on a White Campus: My Reality. *Black Issues in Higher Education*, October 24, 76.

———. 1996. Scaling the Ivory Tower to Tenure and Promotion: One Black Professor's Perspective Revisited. Paper distributed at the Compact for Faculty Diversity's Institute on Teaching and Mentoring, Boston.

Piore, M. 2001. Diversity and Capitalism. In *Who's Qualified?*, ed. L. Guinier and S. Sturm. Boston: Beacon Press.

Powell, C. 1995. *My American Journey.* New York: Random House.

Rains, F. 1998a. Is the Benign Really Harmless? In *White Reign: Deploying Whiteness in America*, ed. J. Kincheloe, S. Steinberg, N. Rodriguez, and R. Chennault. New York: St. Martin's Griffin Press.

———. 1998b. Is the Price Worth the Cost of Survival in Academic Apartheid? Women of Color in a [White] Research University. In *Keeping Our Faculties* conference papers. Minneapolis: University of Minnesota.

———. 1999. Dancing on the Sharp Edge of the Sword: Women Faculty of Color in White Academe. In *Everyday Knowledge and Uncommon Truths*, ed. L. Smith and K. Kellor. Boulder, CO: Westview Press.

Reiman, J. 1998. *The Rich Get Richer and the Poor Get Prison.* Boston: Allyn and Bacon.

Reis, R. 1998. Tomorrow's Professor Listserv. Message 4, March 16.

Reis, R. 2001. Tomorrow's Professor Listserv. Message 349, August 30. [To subscribe to this Listserv, send an e-mail message to majordomo@lists.stanford.edu.]

Reiss, S. 1997. Nell Painter: Making It as a Woman of Color in the Academy. In *Diversity Digest*, Fall, 6–7.

Rendon, L. 1992. From the Barrio to the Academy: Revelations of a Mexican American "Scholarship Girl." In *First-Generation Students: Confronting the Cultural Issues*, ed. S. Zwerling and H. London. San Francisco: Jossey-Bass.

———. 1999. Toward a New Vision of the Multicultural Community College for the Next Century. In *Community Colleges as Cultural Texts*, ed. K. Shaw, J. Valadez, and R. Rhoads. Albany: State University of New York Press.

Rendon, L., and R. Hope. 1996. *Educating a New Majority: Transforming America's Educational System for Diversity.* San Francisco: Jossey-Bass.

Reyes, M., and J. Halcon. 1991. Practices of the Academy: Barriers to Access for Chicano Academics. In *The Racial Crisis in American Higher Education*, ed. P. Altback and K. Lomotey. Albany: State University of New York Press.

Rodriguez, C. 2001. An Educated Move—Top School Systems Draw Asians to Wealthy Suburbs. *Boston Globe*, May 7, B1, B3.

Rodriguez, R. 2002. *Brown: The Last Discovery of America.* New York: Viking.

Rohlen, T. 1981. Education: Policies, and Prospects. In *Koreans in Japan*, ed. G. DeVos and C. Lee. Berkeley: University of California Press.

Rosenbaum, J. 1976. *Making Inequality: The Hidden Curriculum of High School Tracking.* New York: Wiley.

Roediger, D. 1994. *Toward the Abolition of Whiteness: Essays on Race, Politics, and Working-Class History.* London: Verso.

———. 1998. *Black Writers on What It Means to Be White.* New York: Schocken.

———. 1999. *The Wages of Whiteness: Race and the Making of the American Working Class.* London: Verso.

Rothblum, E. 1988. Leaving the Ivory Tower: Factors Contributing to Women's Voluntary Resignation from Academia. *Frontiers* 10: 14–17.

Rothenberg, P. 2000. *Invisible Privilege: A Memoir about Race, Class, and Gender.* Lawrence: University of Kansas Press.

Ryan, S. 2001. Freedom in His Blood, Frederick Douglass IV. *Boston Globe*, February 26, B7, B11.

Sacks, K. 1997. The G.I. Bill: Whites Only Need Apply. In *Critical White Studies*, ed. R. Delgado and J. Stefancic. Philadelphia: Temple University Press.

Sacks, P. 1999. *Standardized Mind: The High Price of America's Testing Culture and What We Can Do to Change It.* Cambridge, MA: Perseus.

Sagaria, M. 2002. An Exploratory Model of Filtering in Administrative Searches: Toward Counter-Hegemonic Discourses. *Journal of Higher Education* 73: 677–704.

Sanchez, G. 1993. *Becoming Mexican American: Ethnicity, Culture, and Identity in Chicano Los Angeles, 1900–1945.* New York: Oxford University Press.

Sanders, K., K. Ward, and E. Bensimon. 1996. The Department Chair's Role in Working with Junior Faculty. *Department Chair*, Winter, 7–8.

Sandler, B. 1992a. *The Campus Climate Revisited: Chilly for Women Faculty, Administrators and Graduate Students.* Washington, DC: Association of American Colleges.

———. 1992b. *Success and Survival Strategies for Women Faculty Members.* Washington, DC: Association of American Colleges.

Sanjek, R. 1994. Intermarriage and the Future of Races in the United States. In *Race*, ed. S. Gregory and R. Sanjek. New Brunswick, NJ: Rutgers University Press.

Schuster, J., and D. Wheeler. 1990. *Enhancing Faculty Strategies for Development and Renewal.* San Francisco: Jossey-Bass.

Scott, A. 1995. Why I Teach by Discussion. In *The Academic's Handbook*, ed. A. Deneff and D. Goodwin. Durham, NC: Duke University Press.

Seldin, P. 1987. *Coping with Faculty Stress.* San Francisco: Jossey-Bass.

Seymour, E. 1992. "The Problem Iceberg" in Science, Mathematics, and Engineering Education: Student Explanations for High Attrition Rates. *Journal of College Science Teaching* 21: 231–38.

Seymour, E., and N. Hewitt. 1997. *Talking about Leaving: Why Undergraduates Leave the Sciences.* Boulder, CO: Westview Press.

Shattering the Silences: The Case for Minority Faculty. 1997. Videotape. San Francisco: California Newsreel.

Shibutani, T., and M. Kwan. 1966. *Ethnic Stratification.* New York: Macmillan.

Shin, A. 1996. The Lily-White University Presses. *Journal of Blacks in Higher Education* (Summer): 78–82.

Shorris, E. 1992. *Latinos: A Biography of the People.* New York: Norton.

Smith, D. 1996. *Achieving Faculty Diversity: Debunking the Myths.* Washington, DC: Association of American Colleges and Universities.

———. 2000. How to Diversify the Faculty. *Academe*, September–October, 48–52.

Sorcinelli, M. 1992. New and Junior Faculty Stress: Research and Responses. In *Developing New and Junior Faculty*, ed. M. Sorcinelli and A. Austin. San Francisco: Jossey-Bass.

Sorcinelli, M., and J. Near. 1989. Relations between Work and Life Away from Work among University Faculty. *Journal of Higher Education* 60 (January–February): 59–81.

Stanton-Salazar, R. 1997. A Social Capital Framework for Understanding the Socialization of Racial Minority Children and Youths. *Harvard Educational Review* 67 (Spring): 1–40.

———. 2000. The Development of Coping Strategies among Urban Latino Youth. In *Making Invisible Latino Adolescents Visible: A Critical Approach to Latino Diversity*, ed. M. Montero-Sieburth and R. Villarruel. New York: Falmer Press.

———. 2001. *Manufacturing Hope and Despair: The School and Kin Support Networks of U.S. Mexican Youth.* New York: Teachers College Press.

Stanton-Salazar, R., and S. Spina. 2000. The Network Orientations of Highly Resilient Urban Minority Youth. *Urban Review* 32: 227–61.

Steele, C. 1992. Race and the Schooling of Black Americans. *Atlantic Monthly*, April, 68–75.

———. 2000. High-Stakes Testing. Presentation at Harvard University's Graduate School of Education, Cambridge, MA, October 25.

————. 2001a. Secrets of the SAT. *Frontline* interview. Public Broadcasting System. http://pbs.org/ wgbh/pages/frontline/shows/sats/interviews/steele.html.

————. 2001b. Understanding the Performance Gap. In *Who's Qualified?*, ed. L. Guinier and S. Sturm. Boston: Beacon Press.

Steele, C., and J. Aronson. 1995. Stereotype Threat and the Intellectual Test Performance of African Americans. *Journal of Personality and Social Psychology* 69: 797–811.

Stein, W. 1994. The Survival of American Indian Faculty. *Thought and Action* 10: 101–15.

Sternberg, R. 1998. *Thinking Styles.* New York: Cambridge University Press.

Sturm, S., and L. Guinier. 1996. The Future of Affirmative Action: Reclaiming the Innovative Ideal. *California Law Review* 84: 953–1036.

Suarez-Orozco, M. 1987. Becoming Somebody: Central American Immigrants in U.S. Inner City Schools. *Anthropology and Education Quarterly* 18: 287–99.

Suskind, R. 1998. *Hope in the Unseen.* New York: Broadway Books.

Takaki, R. 1987. To Count or Not to Count by Race and Gender? In *From Different Shores: Perspectives on Race and Ethnicity in America*, ed. R. Takaki. New York: Oxford University Press.

————. 1989. *Strangers from a Different Shore: A History of Asian Americans.* Boston: Little, Brown.

————. 1993. *A Different Mirror: A History of Multicultural America.* Boston: Little, Brown.

Tatum, B. 1992. Talking about Race, Learning about Racism: The Application of Racial Identity Development Theory in the Classroom. *Harvard Educational Review* 62: 1–24.

————. 1997a. Talking about Race, Learning about Racism. In *Whiteness: A Critical Reader*, ed. M. Hill. New York: New York University Press.

————. 1997b. *Why Are All the Black Kids Sitting Together in the Cafeteria? and Other Conversations about Race.* New York: Basic Books.

Teaching Science Collaboratively. 1992. Videotape. Cambridge, MA: Derek Bok Center for Teaching and Learning, Harvard University.

Thomas, L. 1992–93. Moral Deference. *Philosophical Forum* 24 (Fall–Spring): 233–50.

Tippeconnic, J. III. 2002. American Indians and Alaska Native Faculty in Academe: The Good, the Bad, and the Ugly. In *Keeping Our Faculties* conference papers. Minneapolis: University of Minnesota.

Thompson, B. 2001. *A Promise and a Way of Life: White Anti-Racism Activism.* Minneapolis: University of Minnesota Press.

Thompson, B., and T. Sangeeta. 1993. *Handbook for Anti-Racism Training.* Minneapolis: University of Minnesota Press.

Thurow, L. 1969. *Poverty and Discrimination.* Washington, DC: Brookings Institute.

Tien, C.-L. 1998. Challenges and Opportunities for People of Color. In *The Multicultural Campus: Strategies for Transforming Higher Education*, ed. L. Valverde and L. Castenell Jr. Walnut Creek, CA: Sage.

Tierney, W. 1992. *Official Encouragement, Institutional Discouragement: Minorities in Academe—The Native American Experience.* Norwood, NJ: Ablex.

Tierney, W., and E. Bensimon. 1996. *Promotion and Tenure: Community and Socialization in Academe.* Albany: State University of New York Press.

Tonn, J. 2003. *Mary P. Follett: Creating Democracy, Transforming Management.* New Haven, CT: Yale University Press.

Trix, F., and C. Psenka. 2003. Exploring the Color of Glass: Letters of Recommendation for Female and Male Medical Faculty. *Discourse and Society* 14: 191–220.

Trower, C. 1999. Alleviating the Torture of the Tenure Track: All It Takes Is a Little Show and Tell. *Department Chair*, Spring, 1999, 1, 16–17.

Trower, C., and R. Chait. 2002. Faculty Diversity: Too Little for Too Long. *Harvard Magazine*, March–April, 33–37. [At the Web site http://www.harvard-magazine.com are data tables that accompany Trower and Chait's article.]

Trujillo, A., and E. Dias. 1999. "Be a Name, Not a Number": The Role of Cultural and Social Capital in the Transfer Process. In *Community Colleges as Cultural Texts*, ed. K. Shaw, J. Valadez, and R. Rhoads. Albany: State University of New York Press.

Turner, C. 2000. Defining Success: Promotion and Tenure—Planning for Each Career Stage and Beyond. In *Succeeding in an Academic Career: A Guide for Faculty of Color*, ed. M. Garcia. Westport, CT: Greenwood Press.

————. 2002. *Diversifying the Faculty: A Guidebook for Search Committees*. Washington, DC: Association of American Colleges and Universities.

Turner, C., and S. Myers Jr. 2000. *Faculty of Color in Academe: Bittersweet Success*. Needham Heights, MA: Allyn and Bacon.

Turner, C., and J. Thompson. 1993. Socializing Women Doctoral Students: Minority and Majority Experiences. *Review of Higher Education* 16: 355–70.

Turner, C., M. Garcia, A. Nora, L. Rendon, eds. 1996. *Racial and Ethnic Diversity in Higher Education*. Needham Heights, MA: Simon and Schuster.

TuSmith, B. 2001. Out on a Limb: Race and the Evaluation of Frontline Teaching. *Amerasia Journal* 27: 1–17.

Twombly, S. 1992. The Process of Choosing a Dean. *Journal of Higher Education* 63: 653–93.

University of Michigan Faculty Work-Life Study Report. 1999. Ann Arbor: University of Michigan.

Valdez, J. 1993. Cultural Capital and Its Impact on the Aspirations of Nontraditional Community College Students. *Community College Review* 21: 30–43.

Valenzuela, A. 1999. *Subtractive Schooling: U.S.-Mexican Youth and the Politics of Caring*. Albany: State University of New York Press.

Valian, V. 1998a. Sex, Schemas, and Success—What's Keeping Women Back? *Academe*, September–October, 50–55.

————. 1998b. *Why So Slow? The Advancement of Women*. Cambridge, MA: MIT Press.

Valverde, L., and L. Castenell, eds. 1998. *The Multicultural Campus*. Walnut Creek, CA: Sage.

Vargas, L. 2002. Why Are We Still So Few and Why Has Our Progress Been So Slow? In *Women Faculty of Color in the White Classroom: Narratives on the Pedagogical Implications of Teacher Diversity*, ed. L. Vargas. New York: Peter Lang.

Vélez-Ibáñez, C. 1996. *Border Visions: Mexican Cultures of the Southwest United States*. Tucson: University of Arizona Press.

Wade, K., and A. Kinicki. 1995. Examining Objective and Subjective Applicant Qualifications within a Process Model of Interview Selection Decisions. *Academy of Management Journal* 38: 151–55.

Wanted: A Better Way to Boost Numbers of Minority PhDs. 1998. *Science* 281: 1268–70.

Washington, V., and W. Harvey. 1989. *Affirmative Rhetoric, Negative Action: African-American and Hispanic Faculty at Predominantly White Institutions*. ASHE-ERIC Higher Education Report. Washington, DC: George Washington University.

Waters, M. 1999. *Black Identities: West Indian Immigrant Dreams and American Realities*. Cambridge, MA: Harvard University Press.

Weinberg, M. 1977. *A Chance to Learn: The History of Race and Education in the United States*. Cambridge: Cambridge University Press.

Weis, L. 1985. *Between Two Worlds: Black Students in an Urban Community College*. Boston: Routledge.

Wenneras, C. and A. Wold. 1997. Nepotism and Sexism in Peer-Review. *Nature*. 387: 341–3.

Wenneras, C. and A. Wold. 2000. A Chair of One's Own: The Upper Reaches of Academe Remain Stubbornly Inaccessible to Women. *Nature*. 408: 647.

White, J., and J. Cones. 1999. *Black Man Emerging: Facing the Past and Seizing a Future in America*. New York: W. H. Freeman.

Wildman, S. 1996. *How Invisible Preference Undermines America*. New York: New York University Press.

Williams, C. 2001. *Technology and the Dream: Reflections on the Black Experience at MIT, 1941–1999.* Cambridge, MA: MIT Press.

Williams, P. 1991. *The Alchemy of Race and Rights.* Cambridge, MA: Harvard University Press.

———. 1997. *Seeing a Color-Blind Future: The Paradox of Race.* New York: Farrar, Straus and Giroux.

Willie, C. 1981. *The Ivory and Ebony Towers.* Lexington, MA: Heath.

———. 1990. *The Caste and Class Controversy on Race and Poverty.* Dix Hills, NY: General Hall.

Willie, C., A. Garibaldi, and W. Reed, eds. 1991. *The Education of African-Americans.* Boston: Trotter Institute, University of Massachusetts–Boston.

Willie, C., and A. McCord. 1972. *Black Students at White Colleges.* New York: Praeger.

Women of Color in the Academy Project at the University of Michigan. 1999. *Through My Lens.* Videotape. Ann Arbor: Center for the Education of Women, University of Michigan.

Woodward, C. 1966. *The Strange Career of Jim Crow.* New York: Oxford University Press.

Wu, F. 2002. *Yellow: Race in America beyond Black and White.* New York: Basic Books.

Wylie, N. 1990. A Consortial Approach: The Great Lakes Colleges Association. In J. *Enhancing Faculty Careers: Strategies for Development and Renewal,* ed. J. Schuster and D. Wheeler. San Francisco: Jossey-Bass.

Yetman, N., ed. 1999. *Majority and Minority: The Dynamics of Race and Ethnicity in American Life.* Needham Heights, MA: Allyn and Bacon.

APPENDIX

CHECKLIST OF CHAPTER CONTENTS

PART ONE: PROBLEMS

Chapter 1   Succeeding as a Professor on a Majority Campus: Disadvantages versus Advantages

1. Presumption of incompetence/presumption of competence
2. Outsider status often stressful/insider status often comfortable
3. Little mentoring and inside information/abundant mentoring and inside information
4. Representing whole tribe/representing only oneself
5. Super-visible, invisible, and overloaded with advising and committee assignments/psychological congruence and no overload
6. Constant proving that one is qualified and not an imposter/Entitled and accepted
7. Complex psychological dynamics/ordinary dynamics
8. Undervalued in evaluations because of stereotypes/Overvalued
9. Need formal affirmative action/already enjoy invisible affirmative action
10. Taboo against "brown-on-brown" scholarship/no taboo on scholarship
11. Hiring quota (one minority is enough)/no quota or limit
12. Raising the bar/no raising the bar.

Chapter 2   Succeeding Outside the Ivy Walls: Disadvantages versus Advantages

1. Devaluation of professional standing and exclusion from networks/steady valuation and inclusion
2. Accumulation of wealth slowed by federal, state, and labor union policies/wealth facilitated by the same policies
3. Stereotype threat brings underperformance on SAT, GRE, etc., with self-screening often resulting/no stereotype threat, better performance, greater self-confidence

4. Poor schools, chilled ambitions, social status immobility/ richer schools, higher ambitions, maintenance of higher status

Chapter 3 Extra Disadvantages for Colonized Minorities

1. Not all minority groups share the same status: Differences between colonized and immigrant minorities
2. Asian Americans: Immigrant minorities
3. Women as a colonized group?

PART TWO: SOLUTIONS

Chapter 4 Good Practices in Recruitment
Good Practices for Campus Presidents, Provosts, Deans, and Academic Departments

A-1. Avoid myths and easy excuses. (Also avoid sloppy, biased thinking and decision-making illustrated in A-27.)
A-2. Departmental specialist should do year-round recruiting.
A-3. Coach and monitor search committees.
A-4. Construct retention plan before recruitment begins.
A-5. Diversify within each search committee; add a diversity advocate within each committee.
A-6. Language in job ads should underscore the desire for diversity.
A-7. Ensure equitable salary and benefit packages are offered to new faculty hires.
A-8. Monitor recruiting processes and outcomes.
A-9. Have chair and dean do final choosing and hiring.
A-10. Hold deans and chairs accountable for faculty diversity.
A-11. Provide sufficient financial resources and staff for diversifying the faculty.
A-12. Assist with spousal job-hunting.
A-13. Pay attention to the lifestyle concerns of job candidates.
A-14. Provide housing assistance to new hires.
A-15. Promote cluster hiring.
A-16. Also hire senior faculty members.
A-17. Bring to campus non-majority visiting scholars.
A-18. Include non-majority speakers in every lecture and seminar series.
A-19. Start a visiting dissertation scholars-in-residence program.

Good Practices for Search Committees

A-20. Avoid easy excuses and self-fulfilling myths.
A-21. Recruit year-round.

A-22. Receive coaching from the provost.

A-23. Ensure diversity in the search committee's membership.

A-24. Use detailed language about faculty diversity in job ads.

A-25. Follow key pointers for campus visits and interviews of job candidates.

A-26. Send an *unranked* list of final candidates to the dean and chair.

A-27. Avoid sloppy, biased thinking and decision-making (e.g., avoid cloning; avoid snap judgments and seizing of pretexts; avoid elitist behavior; avoid wishful thinking; avoid disingenuous and willful innocence).

Chapter 5 Good Practices in Retention

Good Practices for Campus Presidents, Provosts, Deans, Trustees, and Mentoring Programs

B-1. Implement a formal campus-wide mentoring program.

B-2. Sponsor career-development workshops for faculty throughout the year.

B-3. Provide child-care facilities on campus.

B-4. Allow family leave.

B-5. Ensure leadership positions for non-majority faculty.

B-6. Hold critical-thinking workshops for chairs, senior faculty, and tenure-review committees.

B-7. Provide mentoring training for chairs, senior faculty, and new associate professors.

B-8. Reward senior faculty for their attentive mentoring of new faculty.

B-9. For faculty newcomers, arrange campus-wide orientation sessions and cordial visits with the dean.

B-10. Sponsor community-building events for new hires and pre-tenure faculty.

B-11. Bring in speakers chosen by junior faculty.

B-12. Develop a campus culture that is working to level the academic playing field, value multicultural diversity, and build community.

B-13. Encourage and develop senior faculty who serve as champions for diversity.

Good Practices for Departments

B-14. Prepare members of the department for the new hire's arrival.

B-15. Supply newcomers with essential information about departmental operations, months before their arrival.

B-16. Introduce and warmly promote newcomers to students and to other faculty colleagues.

B-17. Senior faculty must become persistently friendly and instrumentally helpful to newcomers.

B-18. The chair and senior faculty should protect junior faculty colleagues from excessive teaching, advising, and service assignments.

B-19. Actively work to help new faculty make scholarly connections within and outside the department.

B-20. The chair and senior faculty (as a review committee) should assess and monitor pre-tenure faculty and provide annual job-performance reviews.

B-21. Assign senior faculty the responsibility for actively mentoring newcomers.

Chapter 6   Good Practices in Mentoring
Good Practices for Senior Mentors

C-1. Recognize the hesitation of some mentees and try to move beyond it.

C-2. Disclose some of your own failures and confusions.

C-3. Address critical incidents experienced by mentees—and assist with damage control.

C-4. Understand the typical cumulative disadvantages for those viewed as "outsiders" and "tokens."

C-5. Understand the extra disadvantages for members of colonized minority groups.

C-6. Help mentees learn how to self-promote.

C-7. Undertake *instrumental, proactive* mentoring.

C-8. Observe some ground rules when *arguing* with mentees.

C-9. Rise above gender and racial/ethnic stereotypes.

C-10. Avoid the temptation to clone.

C-11. Realize you are providing invaluable guidance and collegial support.

Pointers and Strategies for Pre-tenure Faculty Mentees
Typical Stressors and What to do About Them

D-1. Lack of collegiality

D-2. Negativity

D-3. Unrealistic expectations

D-4. Not enough time

D-5. Lack of experience in teaching: Lessons from quick starters
D-6. Obstacles to writing and networking
D-7. Inadequate feedback
D-8. Balancing work and life outside work

Coping with the Special Stressors Faced by Non-majority Faculty

D-9. The extra taxes borne by faculty from *colonized* minority groups
D-10. Internalizing feelings of inadequacy
D-11. Being seen as an "affirmative action hire"
D-12. Finding a chilly climate within the department
D-13. Being given too little or too much attention
D-14. Having your scholarship undervalued
D-15. Experiencing the acute sting of negative incidents
D-16. Managing excessive committee assignments
D-17. Managing excessive student demands
D-18. Handling inappropriate behavior
D-19. Overcoming isolation
D-20. Not feeling entitled to be in academia

Chapter 7 Other Remedies: Macrocosmic and Microcosmic

A. Structural and institutional changes: Dismantle castelike elements; continue to act affirmatively; and pay reparations
B. Create more diverse student bodies and faculties
C. Educate students about unearned advantages and disadvantages
D. Create learning communities in colleges and universities
E. Create K–12 learning communities

PART THREE: ITEMS FOR DISCUSSION, ANALYSIS, AND PRACTICE

Chapter 8 Minority and Majority Faculty Speak

A. Why diversify the faculty? (quotations 1–5)
B. Stresses and vulnerabilities (quotations 6–16)
C. Different views of affirmative action in academia (quotations 17–21)
D. Bad practices that must be replaced (quotations 22–26)
E. New practices and new visions (quotations 27–34)

Chapter 9 Bad Practices: Scenarios for Discussion and Application (with Discussion Guides)

Scenario 1: Deliberations of an academic search committee
Scenario 2: An academic search committee narrows the field
Scenario 3: Second week as a new assistant professor of mechanical engineering
Scenario 4: Preparing for the tenure review
Scenario 5: Conversation between a mentor and mentee
Scenario 6: Deliberations of a tenure and promotion committee

INDEX

Abraham, A., 182
Abraham, N., 54
Abrams, C., 46
Academe, 20, 32
accumulating wealth, by majority and
    minority faculty, 44–50, 231–32
Adams, M., 119
Advanced Placement, 54
affirmative action
    programs of, 6, 32–34, 43, 231
    structural and institutional changes
        in, 162–63, 235
    views of an "affirmative action" hire,
        151, 178–79, 235
African American faculty
    as a colonized minority, 1, 3, 4, 70
    as *The Negro*, 13
    recruitment of, 95
Aguirre, A., 19
Alderete, J., 175
Alemán, A., 16, 25, 175
Algerians, 70
Alicea, I., 59
alienation, of minority faculty, 15–18, 231
Allen, T., 14
alumni, admission of offspring of, 33
Alvarez, R., 72, 73
American Academy of Science, 84
American Association for Higher
    Education, 141, 146

American Association for the
    Advancement of Science, 141
American Association of Colleges and
    Universities (AAC&U), 120
American Association of University
    Professors, 93
American Chemical Society, 93
American Educational Research
    Association, 93
American Historical Association, 147
American Indians. *See* Native American
    faculty
American Psychological Association, 93
André, N., 149
Anzaldúa, Gloria, 70
Appiah, A., 182, 183
Aronson, J., 58, 63
Asian American faculty
    as an immigrant minority, 1, 75–82,
        232
    as "honorary whites," 44
    as "model minority" group, 79–81
Association of American Colleges and
    Universities (AAC&U), 93
Astin, A., 17
Astin, H., 16–17, 22
Atkinson, R., 52, 53
"aversive racism," 20
Avilés, R., 180
Ayers, W., 60–61

bad practices
  by an academic search committee,
    186–94
  in communication between mentor
    and mentees, 204–8
  eliminating and replacing of, 179–81,
    236
  new assistant professor dealing with,
    194–99
  preparing for tenure review and
    coping with, 199–204
  recruitment cognitive fallacies in,
    107–10, 232–33
  scenarios, case studies and analysis of,
    185–214, 236
  by a tenure and promotion
    committee, 208–14
Banks, C., 119
Banks, J., 119
Barabino, G., 147–48
Bastrop Independent School District v.
  Delgado, 60
Bell, D., 36
Bell, E., 30, 85
Bell Curve, The (Murray), 28, 80
Benjamin, L., 13, 18–19
Bensimon, E., 19, 22, 24, 27, 119, 122, 145
Berliner, D., 56
Berreman, G., 75
Bibb, H., 148
*Big Test, The: The Secret History of the
  American Meritocracy* (Lemann), 56
Black Elite, The (Benjamin), 13
Black Physics Students Association, 93
Blackwell, J., 19–20
Blauner, R., 50, 73, 160
Blue-Eyed (1995), 161
Board of Education v. *Brown*, 60
*Boat People, The and Achievement in
  America* (Caplan, Whitmore, and
  Choy), 82
Boice, R., 15, 18, 114, 118, 126, 131,
  136–37, 138, 140, 141, 143, 144, 148,
  156
Boissevain, J., 43
Bok, D., 164
Bonilla, J., 23–24, 150

Borderlands (Anzaldúa), 70
Boston Globe, 46, 78
Bourdieu, P., 62
Bourque, S., 118
Bowen, W., 164
Brandenberger, R., 55
Breiger, R., 31, 43
Brender, A., 71
Bronstein, P., 23, 157, 174–75
Brotherhood of Locomotive Firemen, 48
Brotherhood of Railway Car-men, 48
Browne, S., 130, 137
"brown-on-brown" scholarship in, taboo
  against, 34–36, 231
Brown v. *Board of Education,* 60
Bruner, J., 74, 75
Burakumin caste, 70
Burgess, D., 180
Bush, George W., 68
Butler, J., 166

Cambodian population, 81
Caplan, N., 74, 82
Carter, T., 62, 69, 74, 160
case studies and scenarios, 6–7, 185–214,
  236
caste system in education, 74–75,
  161–62, 235
Castro, Fidel, 71
catching up, 51, 63
Catholic Irish, 70
Chait, R., 1, 18, 164
Chang, R., 80, 81
Chavez, J., 72
Chavez, R., 19
Choy, M., 74, 82
Christensen, C., 142
Civil War, 48, 80
Clance, P., 23
Clark, S., 12
Clerks, Mates, and Pilots Union, 48
cloning, in recruitment practices, 90,
  107–8, 134–35, 233
cluster hiring, 100, 102, 232
Cole, J., 12
Cole, S., 12
Coleman, A., 164

colonized minorities
 additional disadvantages of, 3, 65–86,
  232
 caste system treatment of, 74–75, 232
 special stressors during mentoring of,
  132–33, 149–56, 235
*Color-Blind: Seeing beyond Race in a
 Race-Obsessed World* (Cose), 110
Compact for Faculty Diversity, 2, 93,
 137, 182
competence versus incompetence, views
 of minority faculty, 12–15, 231
"concealed profits," of majority faculty,
 11–38, 231
Cones, J., 38, 48, 168
Conley, F., 84
Connor, K., 53
Cooper, J., 1, 13, 135
Corcoran, M., 12
Cordero, R., 29
Cose, E., 110
Couch, P., 32–33
*Crabgrass Frontier: The Suburbanization
 of the United States* (Jackson), 45
Creighton, Joanne, 54
Creswell, J., 144
cross-racial coalitions, 160
Cruz, D., 73, 177
cultural context of tests, 57–60, 231
cultural worker, minority faculty as, 25
Cummins, J., 69

Dahl, R., 34, 110, 121
"Dancing on the Sharp Edge of the
 Sword: Women Faculty of Color in
 White Academe" (Rains), 22
Darling-Hammond, L., 60, 61
Davis, P., 24
deep pockets, 146
Delgado, R., 17–18, 62, 179
*Delgado v. Bastrop Independent School
 District,* 60
Deloria, Vine, Jr., 72
*Demystifying the Profession: Helping Junior
 Faculty Succeed* (Moody), 6, 135
Denton, D., 94, 95
Denton, N., 44, 46, 47, 69

*Department Chair's Role in Developing
 New Faculty into Teachers and
 Scholars, The* (Bensimon, Ward, and
 Sanders), 122
DeVos, G., 69, 70, 73, 74
DiTomaso, N., 29
*Diversifying the Faculty: A Guidebook for
 Search Committees* (Turner), 93
Doane, A., 12
domains outside academia, advantages
 and disadvantages for minority
 faculty, 4
Douglass, Frederick, 49
Douglass, Frederick, IV, 160
Dovidio, J., 20
Dovidio, S., 110
Dresselhaus, M., 177
"driving while black," 40
DuBois, W. E. B., 49
Duster, T., 183

*Educational and Psychological
 Measurement,* 55
educational credentials, minority faculty
 acquisition of, 50–63, 231–32
Educational Testing Service (ETS), 52,
 53, 56
*Education for Judgment: The Artistry of
 Discussion Leadership* (Christensen,
 Garvin, and Sweet), 142
Elliott, J., 161
equal opportunity, Good Practices for, 6
Espy-Wilson, C., 148
European-American faculty, 1, 2
 See also majority faculty
evaluations, of minority faculty, 26–32,
 231
Excellence through Diversity, 2

*Facing Up to the American Dream: Race,
 Class, and the Soul of the Nation*
 (Hochschild), 43, 80
*Faculty of Color in Academe: Bittersweet
 Success* (Turner), 17
*Faculty Research Performance: Lessons
 from the Sciences and the Social
 Sciences* (Creswell), 144

Fair, B., 110
Farquhar, R., 93
Farris, G., 29
Feagin, J., 41–42, 161
Federal Glass Ceiling Commission, 31
Federal Housing Administration (FHA), 46, 50
Feshback, H., 176
FHA Underwriting Manual, 46
Fink, D., 124, 136, 138
Fischer, C., 31, 47, 56, 73, 221
Fisher, A., 181
Fitzgerald, T., 31
Follett, M., 169
Ford Fellowship Program, 93
Frank, F., 18, 32
Franklin, R., 74, 159
Fried, L., 84, 116, 121, 127
From Different Shores: Perspectives on Race and Ethnicity in America (Takaki), 110

Gaertner, S., 20, 110
Gainen, J., 18
Gallos, J., 33
Garcia, H., 27, 177–78
Gardner, H., 56
Garibaldi, A., 20
Garvey, J., 161
Garvin, D., 142
Garza, H., 35
Georas, C., 70, 71
Georgi, H., 54, 59
GI Bill, 50–51
Gibson, M., 69, 70, 74, 160, 164, 168
Ginorio, A., 151, 156
Giroux, H., 25, 62, 161
Gladwell, M., 57, 165
glass ceilings, 31, 36, 82–83
Glazer-Raymo, J., 27, 82–83
global and local changes in higher education, 159–69, 235
Good Practices
  for mentoring, 5–6, 18–19, 114–20, 231, 234–35
  in recruitment, 5, 89–111, 232–33
  for retention, 5, 113–28, 233–34

  See also bad practices
  See also scenarios, using Good Practices in
Gordon, M., 106
Graduate Record Examination (GRE), 39
  effects on minority students, 51–60, 231
  predictive value of, 54–55, 231
  structural and institutional changes in use of, 165
Graham, L., 33, 42, 162, 164, 176–77
Great Lakes College Association, The, 114
Greene, L., 102
Gregory, S., 18
Grillo, T., 176
Grosfoguel, R., 70, 71
Guinier, L., 55, 56, 110, 160, 163
Gustafson, M., 147
Gutmann, A., 182–83

Halcon, J., 36–37
Hammond, P., 42
Hardiman, R., 119
Harleston, B., 1, 91
Haro, R., 38
Harris, C., 47
Harvard Educational Review, 36
Harvard Law Review, 41
Harvey, W., 1
Hawaii. *See* Native Hawaiian faculty
Haynes, B., 45
Henkel, J., 144
Hewitt, N., 17
high-stakes testing, 39–64, 231
Hill, H., 34, 48, 49, 50
hiring practices
  by majority faculties, 31–32, 231
  See also recruitment, Good Practices of
Hispanic Outlook, 59
Hochschild, J., 4, 42, 43, 44, 80, 81, 160
hooks, bell, 175, 181
Hope in the Unseen (Suskind), 63
housing
  assistance in the recruitment process, 101–2, 232–33
  discrimination of minority faculty with, 43–44, 46–47, 231–32

Houston, Sam, 72
Howard, G., 34
Howard, R., 11
How Democratic Is the American Constitution? (Dahl), 110
How the Irish Became White (Ignatiev), 49
Hu-DeHart, E., 15–16, 78, 79, 120, 162, 181

Ibarra, R., 153
Ignatiev, N., 46, 49, 161
immigrant minority faculty
  voluntary and involuntary minorities in, 4, 66–75
  See also non-immigrant faculty
"imposter" of minority faculty members, 23–24
inappropriate behavior, dealing with during mentoring, 155–56, 235
income, accumulating wealth by majority and minority faculty of, 44–50, 231–32
Inequality by Design: Cracking the Bell Curve Myth (Fischer, Jankowski, Lucas, Swidler, and Vos), 25, 55
Initiative at the New England Board of Higher Education, 2
institutional and structural changes in higher education, 159–63, 235
intermarriage, 77–78
Internet, impact on Good Practices, 141
isolation
  of minority faculty, 16–17, 156, 231–32
  of outsiders, 16–17, 231–32
"Is the Benign Really Harmless?" (Rains), 110

Jackson, B., 119
Jackson, J. J., 179
Jackson, Jesse, 161
Jackson, K., 45
Jackson, S., 99
Jacobs, J., 30
Jacobson, M., 49
Jamaicans, in England, 95

Japanese Americans, WWII internment of, 75
Jarvis, D., 143–44
Jim Crow laws, 45, 72
Johnson, W., 35
Jones, C., 133, 181
Journal of the American Medical Association, 127

Kain, J., 74, 159
Kanter, R., 22, 163
Karabel, J., 61
"Keeping Our Faculty of Color," 18
Keeping Track: How Schools Structure Inequality (Oakes), 168
Kennedy, John F., 18
Kiang, P., 79, 80, 81, 167, 174
Kinicki, A., 107
Kitano, M., 119
Knowles, M., 1, 91
Koreans, Japanese treatment of, 70, 71, 73, 75, 95
Kozol, J., 61, 63, 167
Krebs, P., 101
Kushnick, L., 41

labor unions, impact on accumulating wealth by majority and minority faculty, 47–50, 231–32
Lambert, C., 162
Laotian population, 81
Lascell, T., 96
Latino/Latina, identity as professor and, 16
Latinos: A Biography of the People (Shorris), 70
Leaning Ivory Tower, The (Padilla and Chavez), 19
Lee, C., 70, 73
Lee, Y., 70, 71, 73, 75
Lemann, N., 52, 56
Light, I., 76
"Lily-white University Presses," 35
Lipsitz, G., 47
Littlefield, D., Jr., 46
Locke, Gary, 77
Lomotey, K., 125

Loo, C., 166
Losing the Race: Self-Sabotage in Black America (McWhorter), 80
Lost Land, The: The Chicano Image of the Southwest (Chavez), 72

MacQuarrie, B., 40
macrocosmic and microcosmic changes in higher education, 159–69, 235
Maher, J., 174
majority, defined, 8
Majority and Minority: The Dynamics of Race and Ethnicity in American Life (Yetman), 8, 76
majority faculty
　advantages outside academe, 39–64, 231–32
　"concealed profits" of, 11–38, 231
　speaking out and quotations from, 173–83, 235
　working on a majority campus, 11–38, 231
Malekzadeh, A., 30–31
Manifest Destiny, 72
Manufactured Crisis, The: Myths, Fraud and the Attack on America's Public Schools (Berliner and Normally), 56
Maoris, 70, 95
Marable, M., 44, 45, 47, 50
Martinez, O., 72, 80
Marty, K., 137–38
Massey, D., 44, 46, 47, 69
Matute-Bianchi, M., 70
Maya Indians, 70
Mazur, A., 143
McIntosh, P., 12, 17
McKay, N., 85, 174
McKinsey Management and Consulting Company, 52
McWhorter, J., 80, 81, 162
Meier, D., 58, 167
Mellon Fellowship Program, 93
Member of the Club: Reflection on Life in a Racially Polarized World (Graham), 42
Men and Women of the Corporation (Kanter), 22

Menchaca, M., 72
Mendez v. *Westminster School District,* 60
mentees, 5–6
mentoring, Good Practices for
　analysis of bad practices in, 204–8
　"elevator coaching" and "one-minute mentoring" in, 123
　function of mentoring committees in, 114–25, 129
　mentors outside school systems as, 168
　of minority faculty, 5–6, 18–19, 231
　for pre-tenure faculty mentees, 135–57, 234–35
　recognizing typical and special stressors with, 136–57, 235
　for senior mentors, 130–35, 234–35
　'underattention' versus 'overattention' in, 153
Mervis, J., 1
'*mestiza* consciousness,' 70
Mexican American faculty
　as colonized minority, 1, 3, 70, 71–73
　as non-immigrant group, 4
　recruitment of, 95
microaggressions toward minority faculty, 24–26, 231
Miner's Canary, The: Enlisting Race, Resisting Power, and Transforming Democracy (Guinier and Torres), 110
minority, defined, 8
minority faculty
　advantages and disadvantages advancement in academia, 3–4
　as advisors for all minority students, 22–23, 231
　confidence and entitlement of, 23–24, 231
　contextual reasons of success of, 86
　police harassment of, 40–43, 231–32
　as representative of entire tribe or group, 20–21, 231
　"smile work" of, 24
　speaking out and quotations from, 173–83, 235
　See also Good Practices

See also taxes and burdens of minority
    faculty
60 Minutes, 42
Mishra, U., 78
MIT Faculty Newsletter, 85, 98
Modern Language Association, 83, 143
Montoya, M., 152, 176
Moody, J., 24, 29, 135, 138, 156, 178
Moore, W., 13, 16, 18, 19, 66
Morey, A., 119
Morrison, Toni, 25–26, 49
Multicultural Course Transformation in
    Higher Education (Morey and
    Kitano, eds.), 119
Murray, C., 80
Myers, S., Jr., 16, 17, 18, 20, 22, 121
myths and biased thinking, in
    recruitment practices, 91, 94, 104,
    106–7, 232–33

Nahavandi, A., 30–31
National Academy of Sciences, 53
National Association for the
    Advancement of Colored People
    (NAACP), 69, 164
National Center for Individual Rights, 57
National Centers of Leadership in
    Academic Medicine, The, 117
National Latino Faculty Survey, 35
National Name Exchange, 93
National Science Foundation (NSF), 54,
    55, 83, 137, 141
Native Alaskan faculty, 70, 95
Native American faculty
    "brown-on-brown" scholarship of,
    34–36, 154
    as colonized minority, 1, 3, 4, 70
    mentoring and support of, 19, 231
    recruitment of, 95
Native Hawaiian faculty
    as colonized minority, 3, 4, 70
    recruitment of, 95
Nature, 33
Near, J., 136, 147
Needy, K., 143
Neimann, Y., 16
networks/networking

exclusion of minority faculty from,
    43–44, 231–32
    by mentees, 144
New Yorker, 57
New York Times, 66, 77, 175
Nieto, O., 62, 69
Nieto, S., 13
Nieves-Squires, S., 21, 153
Nkomo, S., 30, 85
non-immigrant faculty, voluntary and
    involuntary minorities of, 4, 66–75
Normally, B., 56
Northeast Consortium for Faculty
    Diversity, 2
Notes of a Racial Caste Baby: Color
    Blindness and the End of Affirmative
    Action (Fair), 110

Oakes, J., 168
O'Brien, E., 161
Office of Women's Health, 117
Ogbu, J., 69, 70, 74, 159
Ogletree, C., 40
Olivas, M., 178–79
Oliver, M., 44, 45, 46, 47
"100 Black Men of America," 70
Oquendo, A., 57–58, 70
Our Separate Ways: Black and White
    Women and the Struggle for
    Professional Identity (Bell and
    Nkomo), 30, 85
outside academe, disadvantages of
    minority faculty in, 39–64, 231–32
"outsiders" versus "insiders," 15–18, 132,
    231

Padilla, R., 19, 150
Painter, N., 13, 14, 29, 150
Paterson, W., 176
Patterson, O., 33, 43, 78, 162–63
"Peer Mentoring among Graduate
    Students of Color" (Bonilla,
    Pickeron, and Tatum), 150
Pepion, K., 177
Peterson-Hickey, M., 35
Pew Charitable Trusts, 141
Pickeron, C., 150

Pigford, A., 152–53, 155
Piore, M., 95, 162
political power, defined, 8
poll taxes, 55
poverty, faculty accumulation of, 44–50, 231–32
Powell, Colin, 33, 68, 95
practicum, scenarios and using Good Practices, 6–7, 185–214, 236
"probation" of minority faculty, 13
procrastination, 143
professional achievement, minority faculty disadvantages for, 18–19, 231
professional standing, majority advantages and minority disadvantages outside academe, 39–64, 231–32
Promotion and Tenure: Community and Socialization in Academe (Tierney and Bensimon), 19, 119
Psenka, C., 28
psychological isolation, of minority faculty, 16–17, 231
publishing by faculty, 144–45
Puerto Rican American faculty, 1, 3, 4, 70, 95
put-downs of minority faculty, 24–26, 231

"quick starters," 139, 140–43
quota system in faculty hiring, 36–37

race-to-ethnicity conversion, 78
racism
    "aversive racism" in, 20
    in education systems, 2–3
    structural and institutional changes of, 159–63
    Un-raced and, 12
Rains, F., 11, 21–22, 29, 110
"raising the bar" syndrome, 37–38, 231
Ramsey, J., 33
"real ceiling," 36
recruitment, Good Practices of, 5, 89–111
    cognitive fallacies and bad practices of, 107–10, 232–33

guidelines for search committees in, 104–7, 232–33
    for presidents, provosts, deans, and academic department, 90–104, 232–33
Red Lines, Black Spaces (Haynes), 45
Reed, W., 20
Reiman, J., 41
Reis, R., 143
Reiss, S., 13
Rendon, L., 23, 60, 61, 182
retention, Good Practices for, 5, 113–28
    for academic departments, 120–27, 233–34
    for key campus leaders and mentoring programs, 114–20, 233–34
Reyes, M., 36–37
Rholen, T., 73
Rice, Norm, 77
Rodriguez, C., 78
Rodriguez, E., 28
Rodriguez, K., 156
Rodriguez, R., 183
Roediger, D., 46, 49
Rolison, G., 166
Rothblum, E., 23, 157, 174–75
Rothenberg, P., 176
Rowe, M., 24
Ruderman, J., 95
Ryan, S., 161

Sacks, P., 52, 55, 56
Sagaria, M., 107
Sanchez, G., 179
Sanders, K., 122
Sandler, B., 146
Sangeeta, T., 161
Sanjek, R., 78
Savage Inequalities: Children in America's School (Kozol), 61
scenarios, using Good Practices in, 6–7, 185–214, 236
Scholastic Aptitude Test (SAT), 39
    predictive value of, 52–54, 231
    stereotypical expectations of, 52–54, 231
    structural and institutional changes in use of, 165

schools/education, access to poor schools and resource-rich schools, 60–63, 232

Schuldberg, D., 138

Scott, A., 142

Seeing a Color-Blind Future: The Paradox of Race (Williams), 110

Segura, R., 62, 69, 74, 160

self-talk, recognizing during mentoring, 150–51, 235

sexism
in "concealed profits" of majority males, 11
in education systems, 2–3
See also women faculty

Seymour, E., 16–17

Shapiro, T., 44, 45, 46, 47

Shattering Myths: Women in Academe (Glazer-Raymo), 82–83

Shattering the Silences: The Case for Minority Faculty (1997), 15

Shin, A., 35, 43, 154

Shorris, E., 70

Sikes, M., 41–42

Simmons, R., 42

Simons, H., 70

Sloan Foundation, 141

"slow starters," 143

"smile work," 24

Smith, D., 1, 15, 16, 27, 32, 34, 91

social capital, 43

Society for the Advancement of Chicanos and Native Americans in Science (SACNAS), 175, 180

Solomon, S., 23, 157, 174–75

Sorcinelli, M., 136, 138, 147

Southeast Asian population, 79, 81–82

spousal job hunting, 100–101

Standardized Aptitude Test (SAT), effects on minority students, 51–60, 231

Standardized Minds: The High Price of American's Testing Culture and What We Can Do to Change It (Sacks), 56

Stanton-Salazar, R., 62, 70

Steele, C., 52, 57, 58, 59, 63, 69, 74, 165, 168

Stein, W., 19, 35, 154, 178

Steitz, J., 27

stereotyping
stereotypical expectations of, 51–60, 231–32
of token minority persons, 22, 231

Sternberg, R., 145

Stevens, D., 1, 13, 135

stressors and vulnerabilities, identifying and coping with, 136–57, 175–78, 235

structural and institutional changes in higher education, 159–63, 235

students/student body
creating diversity in, 164–65, 174–75, 235
creating learning communities within K-12, 167–69, 235
educating about advantages and disadvantages with diversity, 165–66, 235
learning communities within campus community of, 166–67, 235

Sturm, S., 55, 56

Suarez-Orozco, M., 69

Subtractive Schooling: U.S.-Mexican Youth and the Politics of Caring (Valenzuela), 59

super-visible versus invisible minority faculty, 21–23, 231

Suskind, R., 63, 69

Swedish Medical Research Council, 33

Sweet, A., 142

Takaki, R., 33, 34, 48, 49, 76, 77, 78, 80, 81, 110

Tapia, R., 53, 63

Tatum, B., 25–26

Tatum, T., 150

taxes and burdens of minority faculty
affirmative action programs and, 32–34, 231
competence versus incompetence, 12–15, 231
hidden profits and, 4, 12–26, 231
mentoring and academic sponsorship of, 18–20, 231
"outsiders" versus "insiders" in, 15–18, 132, 231

taxes and burdens of minority faculty
(*Continued*)
"raising the bar" syndrome in, 37–38,
231
special stressors as mentees, 149–57,
235
as super-visible or invisible faculty
members, 21–23, 231
token number of minority faculty in,
36–37, 231
unfair/overly generous evaluations in,
26–32, 231
view of minority as entire tribe or
group in, 20–21, 231
views of "brown-on-brown"
scholarship in, 34–36, 231
Teaching Science Collaboratively (1992),
143
*Technology and the Dream: Reflections of
the Black Experience at MIT*
(Williams), 28
*Tenure in the Sacred Grove: Issues and
Strategies for Women and Minority
Faculty* (Cooper and Stevens, eds.),
135
"terminators," 137
"testocracy," 55
tests/testing
cultural context of tests in, 57–60, 231
self-screening by minority students
about, 50–60, 231–32
stereotypical expectations and
predictive values of, 39–60, 231–32
Thomas, L., 14, 15
Thompson, B., 161
Thompson, J., 20
Through My Lens (Women of Color in
the Academy Project at the
University of Michigan), 15
Thurow, L., 45, 48
Tien, Chang-Lin, 77
Tierney, W., 19, 22, 24, 27, 62, 119, 145,
166
Tippeconnic, J., III, 21
token diversity, 36–37, 231
Tonn, J., 139, 169
Torres, G., 110, 160

Trix, F., 28
Trower, C., 1, 18, 145, 164
Trower, K., 101
Turner, C., 16, 17, 18, 20, 22, 25, 29, 32,
37, 93, 97, 121
TuSmith, B., 132
Twombly, S., 107

Underhill, L., 46
unions, historic impact on accumulating
wealth, 47–50, 231–32
United States Constitution, 34
United States Department of Health and
Human Services, 117
United States National Cancer Institute, 33
*University of Michigan Faculty Work-Life
Study Report,* 14
Unlocking the Clubhouse Door (Fisher),
181
Urban League, 69, 164

Valenzuela, A., 59, 168
Valian, V., 33, 83, 97, 163
Vargas, L., 16
Vargyas, E., 53
Vélez-Ibáñez, C., 73
Vera, H., 41, 161
Veterans Administration, 46, 50
Vietnamese population, 81
voluntary immigrant minorities in the
U.S., 67–68, 232
"Volvo principle," 54

Wade, K., 107
Wagstaff, L., 13, 16, 18, 19, 66
Wakimoto, R., 123
Ward, K., 122
Waters, M., 69
wealth, majority and minority faculty
accumulation of, 44–50, 231–32
Weinberg, M., 62
Wenneras, C., 33, 83, 116
Westminster School District v. *Mendez,* 60
White, J., 38, 48, 168
white-supremacist systems, effects on
minority professional standings,
40–43, 231–32

Whitmore, J., 74, 82
"Why I Teach by Discussion" (Scott), 142
*Why So Slow? The Advancement of
    Women* (Valian), 83
Wildman, S., 176
Williams, C., 14, 17, 28, 35, 42, 66, 120,
    176, 177
Williams, P., 25, 26, 34, 47, 110
Williams, Patricia, 12
Willie, C., 20, 44, 139, 163
Wilson, W., 44
Wingard, D., 134
Wold, A., 33, 83, 116
*Women and Minority Faculty in the
    Academic Workplace* (Aguirre), 19
women faculty
    as a colonized group, 2, 82–85, 232
    effects of isolation as outsiders, 16–17,
    231

job evaluations of, 26–32, 231
level of sponsorship for, 18–19, 231
self-doubt experienced during
    mentoring, 150–51, 235
self-screening of tests and testing,
    58–59, 231–32
"smile work" of, 24
"super-duper" women in, 27
views of competence and
    incompetence of, 13, 231
Woodward, C., 46
Working Mother, 113
Wu, F., 76, 78, 81–82
Wylie, N., 114

*Yellow: Race in America beyond Black and
    White* (Wu), 76
Yetman, N., 8, 76, 77–78

JoAnn Moody, Ph.D., J.D., consults nationally with a variety of colleges and universities. Specifically, she works with academic departments, deans, mentoring programs, department chairs, search committees, provosts, trustees, and professional-development programs for pre-tenure faculty and graduate students. Dr. Moody has had extensive experience in higher education, as a former professor and administrator. Her highly acclaimed monographs, *Demystifying the Profession: Helping Junior Faculty Succeed* and *Vital Info for Graduate Students of Color*, are used widely in orientation and mentoring sessions. The national Compact for Faculty Diversity recently recognized her for outstanding service to the profession. More details about Dr. Moody's consulting practice and publications are available at the website: www.diversityoncampus.com.